Recovering the U.S. Hispanic Literary Heritage

Volume VI

Recovering the U.S. Hispanic Literary Heritage

Board of Editorial Advisors

Recovering the U.S. Hispanic Literary Heritage

Volume VI

Edited by
Antonia I. Castañeda and
A. Gabriel Meléndez

Recovering the U.S. Hispanic Literary Heritage

Arte Público Press
Houston, Texas

This volume is made possible through grants from the City of Houston through The Cultural Arts Council of Houston, Harris County and by the Exemplar Program, a program of Americans for the Arts in collaboration with the LarsonAllen Public Services Group, funded by the Ford Foundation.

Recovering the past, creating the future

Arte Público Press
University of Houston
452 Cullen Performance Hall
Houston, Texas 77204-2004

Jacket design by Pilar Betancourt

The Library of Congress has catalogued Volume I of
Recovering the U.S. Hispanic Literary Heritage as follows:

Recovering the U.S. Hispanic literary heritage / edited by Ramón Gutiérrez and Genaro Padilla
p. cm.
ISBN-10: 1-55885-063-5: $34.95 / ISBN-13: 978-1-55885-063-7
ISBN-10: 1-55885-058-9 (trade pbk.) : $17.95 / ISBN-13: 978-1-55885-058-3

1.
PS153.H56R43 1993

92-45114
CIP

ISBN-10: 1-55885-139-9 (Volume II) / ISBN-13: 978-1-55885-139-9
ISBN-10: 1-55885-251-4 (Volume III) / ISBN-13: 978-1-55885-251-8
ISBN-10: 1-55885-361-8 (Volume IV) / ISBN-13: 978-1-55885-361-4
ISBN-10: 1-55885-371-5 (Volume V) / ISBN-13: 978-1-55885-371-3
ISBN-10: 1-55885-478-9 (Volume VI) / ISBN-13: 978-1-55885-478-9

∞ The paper used in this publication meets the requirements of the American National Standard for Information Sciences—Permanence of Paper for Printed Library Materials, ANSI Z39.48-1984.

6 7 8 9 0 1 2 3 4 5 10 9 8 7 6 5 4 3 2 1

Contents

Part III
Translating Latinidad, Hispanismo in the World

Part IV
From Canton to the Nation-state and Beyond, Transnational Authors and Activists

Introduction
Antonia Castañeda and A. Gabriel Meléndez

The eighth conference of the *Recovering the U.S. Hispanic Literary Heritage Project* held in Albuquerque in November 2004 was realized in partnership with the 15th Annual Spanish and Portuguese Department Conference on Hispanic American Culture and Society at the University of New Mexico. The meeting represented a departure from what had come to be the established practice over some years of hosting the conference at the University of Houston, the Recovery Project's home institution. In this way, the joint-conference, the first to be held away from strong conceptual and archival moorings that Houston represents for Recovery scholars may have moved the conference organizers to commit scholars and researchers to the conference theme, "The Critical Importance of Region." New Mexico, in matters of U.S. Hispanic culture and society, is commonly regarded as a region that both deeply configures and contains the vestiges of those earlier moments of scholarship known as Southwest regionalism. And these vestiges come with the perceived limitations of writings filled with nostalgia, parochialism, and sentimentality. Despite apprehensions that the very idea of regionalism might irreversibly and forever place Recovery scholars in some backwater camp of dim-witted, uncritical parochialists, the site committee boldly moved forward its call for scholarly engagement in "critical regionalism," thus challenging Recovery scholars to aim for a region studies model, that specifically not be construed as criticism from a circumspect inquiry, but that would emerge as critical engagement to re-theorize and re-conceptualize how region, place, and nation operate along the fluid continuum of the local and the global. Place, indeed had become a relevant consideration for the conference in as much as an earlier call for participation included the caveat, "In this regard, New Mexico seems like the perfect conference site to consider the implicit and explicit perimeters of regional markers that make up what we consider the U.S. Hispanic Recovery Project." Responding to this provocation the conference was immensely fruitful as can be deduced from perusing a sampling of session titles:

- The Hemispheric Dimensions of Recovery Literature
- Religion, Mythology, and Representations of Colonialism
- Corridos. Patria Chica, patrimonio grande: la universalidad del corrido regional
- Translating Latinidad for the Anglo-American Audience
- Women Bridging the Gaps Between Space, Gender, and Nation
- (Re)Imagining Regional, Literary, and Historical Values
- Constructions of Gender, Nation, and Literary Culture in Early Hispanic Periodicals

In all, some sixty-plus scholars grappled over the two days of the conference with a set of critical questions such as: How do recovered authors consider region as opposed to nation? When does region become nation? How might we re-theorize or re-historicize the importance of "place" in the colonial period or after 1848 or 1898? In the 21st century, is the Recovery Project aiding and abetting the "browning" of America—a code word that might mean spatializing/racializing Anglo America?

It is from the powerful exchange and interaction of these scholars that the twelve essays comprising this sixth in a series of volumes document the decade and half of interdisciplinary work fostered by the Recovery Project. Each of these essays, and, indeed nearly all the scholarship that the Recovery Project has fostered has never been reducible to circumspect matters of local color or local context and, even when the staring point of recovery work is nearly always a locale, a site, be it canton [*mi cantón* as pachucos came to understand it] or province or region. We would do well to remind ourselves that all locales, by virtue of having been engulfed in global human affairs, in colonialism and postcolonialism, are always situated in ever widening frames of political and social meaning resulting from the processual associations of *plaza, pueblo, comarca, cantón, estado, nación, hemisferio, reino, imperio* and *diáspora*.

Thus, the most apt methodological description of what critical regionalism has meant to the present volume comes from the procedure digital imagery affords contemporary scholars. Here we speak in terms of the technological means that contemporary researchers have at their disposal with which to digitally enhance, enlarge, augment, reduce, sharpen, shade, shave, filter, center, and de-center at will any image in any given data bank. It should, therefore, not surprise us that the simultaneous and coterminous "zoom," so ubiquitous a feature of photo software can help us conceptualize the methodological approach that we see operating in scholarship given to recovered texts. This is most especially true, when this engagement demands that we reframe knowledge and concern ourselves critically with place, site, and region. It is therefore most recommendable that scholars "zoom in" and "zoom out" out of the text in an endless and continual sweep of vision, that sizes the local against the global, inverts background (past) and foreground (present), moves from accession to recession point, measures longitude to latitude, fits the past to the present and so forth. Critical regionalism therefore makes every point of convergence on a given text, a potential doorway for critical examination, just as Jorge Luis Borges imagined Pascal's sphere and thought of it as "a fearful sphere whose center is everywhere and whose circumference is nowhere." The marvel for us today, of course, is that we not only can speak of such an imaginary, but that we can see it demonstrated before our eyes with technology. It is, of course, this newfound ability to calibrate for scale, with the virtual simultaneity and precision that digitalization allows that can be a most useful parallel to the new critical regionalism that emerged from the Recovery Project's eighth conference. Therefore, much of the work included here reflects a simultaneous and precisely displayed consideration of the local to global, of region to hemisphere, and of past to present. It is precisely by adjusting for scale, by resizing and re-imagining the local in the global, the canton in the hemispheric, as it were, and the past in the present and, by alternatively and repeatedly reversing these operations, that we are made aware that things do not stand monolithically as the stasis of imposed representative moments, locked as they might once have been in parochialism, sentimentality, and nostalgia. Technology, in the service of the phenomenology of critical regionalism, permits us to consider all moments at once as it were, and to reconsider how seemingly isolated places in "our Américas" have always been fused to historical processes (how could it be otherwise?) and that locales have and continue to be in relation to all other parts of the planet. Technology, as we have been discussing here, redeems our paradoxes, resolving as it were the apparent contradictions we see boldly writ and unfettered in the language of our conference program: "The Hemispheric Dimensions of Recovery Literature"; "Patria Chica, patrimonio grande: la universalidad del corrido regional"; and "Translating Latinidad for the Anglo-American Audience." Thus, as editors of Volume VI we seek to embrace the virtual simulteanity and precision imparted by virtual displays of texts, what we now know to be inherent to the contemporary ways by which we assign meaning to region. To this end we have sought to group the essays in this volume into the four thematic areas, which we see as evocative of the method we have been describing:

I. Recalibrating the Local and Global: History as Region and Region as History
II. Voicing Dissent, Staging Identity, Speaking into Time
III. Translating Latinidad, Hispanismo in the World
IV. From Canton to the Nation-state and Beyond, Transnational Authors and Activists

In Part I, "Recalibrating the Local and Global: History as Region and Region as History," we group essays by Juan José Alonso, Erlinda Gonzales-Berry, Manuel M. Martín-Rodríguez, and Melina Vizcaíno-Alemán. Alonso's article, "Representing the Tejano on Screen: Américo Paredes and *The Ballad of Gregorio Cortez,"* is a well-written piece that brings into play competing notions, often at odds, stemming from the screen representation of the story of Gregorio Cortez as Alonso asks readers to consider what weight should be given to the views expressed by Américo Paredes in unpublished items in his archives? The premise that Paredes's views should be given special regard and consideration in assessing the film is an interesting one and is well realized in this essay. Including a film study in the work of the Recovery Project adds a fresh new perspective to the recovery work.

Nuevo Mexicanos' struggle for historical veracity and interpretive authority, evinced in the historical writings of Benjamin Read and the literary imaginary of Fray Angélico Chávez focuses the long-lived critique of U.S. historiography that unmoors New Mexico and the Southwest from the global, hemispheric, and national anchors of its Spanish colonial and Mexican Republic past, and thus from its Hispano legacies. Gonzales-Berry's "Benjamin Read: New Mexico's Bernal Díaz del Castillo," spatializes time and historicizes space and links two pivotal eyewitness accounts of invasion, of Spain in Mexico and the U.S. in New Mexico, that del Castillo and Read respectively write to tell *la verdadera historia*, and to contest "official" hegemonic history. In Read's published and unpublished histories, in his struggle with the *New Mexico Historical Review* and the politics of historical erasure, Gonzales-Berry underscores critical issues and tensions in the larger historiographic design of U.S. History—the construction of Euro-American centered national history and national identity—within which the local arbiters of the nationalist project marginalized Read and misconstrued New Mexico history.

In "'Las Almas y Las Letras:' Recovering Fray Angélico Chávez's Poetry," Manuel M. Martín-Rodríguez interprets Chávez's literary and cultural production, here centered on his poetic works, as the scholarly priest's own recovery project—his intervention in the growing Anglo American displacement of New Mexico's Hispanic history, culture, and identity. In Chávez's poetry (1939-1969), Martín-Rodríguez reads not only the most successful distillation of his religious thought but a bicultural fusion, a cultural syncretism and synthesis of English- and Spanish-language lyric poetry traditions designed to provide spiritual and cultural nourishment to Nuevo Mexicanos, and to reinstate Hispano cultural agency.

Chávez's complex historical vision is the subject of Melina Vizcaíno-Alemán's "New Mexican Triptycs: Anglo Southwesternism, Chicano Nationalism, and the Tri-Partite Cultural Critique of Fray Angélico Chávez's Fiction." In her examination of the learned friar's historical novel, Vizcaíno-Alemán deftly crosses temporalities (17th to 20th centuries), genres (poetry, painting, and novel) and historiographies to develop a sophisticated and convincing argument that this New Mexican author-priest's triptych work moves beyond dualism to a more complex hybridity in which the myth of tri-cultural harmony among Native Americans, Spanish-Mexicans, and Anglos becomes a mode of triptych cultural critique. The triptych critique, Vizcaíno-Alemán further argues, is a useful methodology for recovering U.S. Hispanic literature precisely because "it points to the Southwest's triple-voiced literary history, its hybrid colonial histories, and contested cultural icons and foreshadows Chicana feminist's third space, while simultaneously showing up the limitations of oppositional ideologies" (22).

In Part II, "Voicing Dissent, Staging Identity, Speaking into History," Patricia Gubitosi's work on 19th century Hispanic journalism provides a qualitative analysis of nine instances of language/linguistic practices that help chart the social discourse of the New Mexico historical newspaper *La Voz del Pueblo.* In describing these linguistic practices, Gubitosi shows how a set of cultural, ideological, and political assumptions operated and were shared by the readership of *La Voz del Pueblo*. While also examining the role of Hispanic journalists, Edwin Karli Padilla Aponte draws our attention to the advocacy of the Spanish in New York in support of Puerto Rican nationhood at the end of World War II. The theme of nation status for Puerto Rico, here, is critically important for assessing notions of community and nation and for righting about the short-shrift literary scholars have given to the press as an important institution of community.

In "Josephina Niggli as a Regional Voice: A Rexamination of *Mexican Village* and *Step Down Elder Brother,*" Donna M. Kabalen de Bichara uses concepts of cultural space, Lotman's theory of the semiosphere, and Bakhtin's notion of the folkloric chronotope to analyze Niggli's two works, written in the mid 1940s, as an expression of coming to terms with the ideological conflicts resulting from dual Mexican and Euro North American identities. In Niggli, who affirms the mestizaje of Hidalgo and Monterrey in the Mexican north as the transformative agent of modern Mexico, Kabalen de Bichara finds an early and powerful, if not prophetic, regional voice. The future, proclaims the Mexican-American Niggli, is mestizo.

Part III, "Translating Latinidad, Hispanismo in the World," speaks most directly to the continual sweep of vision evident in the serious critical assessment of region. In particular, Melissa Marie González's piece entitled, "Resisting the 'Fatal Allurement' of Local Color: María Cristina Mena's Mexico in *American Magazine* and *The Century Magazine*" is especially centered on the act of sizing the local against the global. The paper rests on the premise that Mena is aware and conscious of her role as cultural translator and mediator and that her submissions to *The Century Magazine* reveal an author who is writing with and against the grain of the misimpressions widely held about Mexico and Mexican culture by her American readership. Key to González's assertions is her use of Mena's letters as co-relational texts that support her argument. From these letters readers can now better consider translational tensions and questions of Mena's translatability and non-fictional sentiment.

Charting new recovery ground, Guillermo de los Reyes Heredia's "Translating, Smuggling, and Recovering Books in Nineteenth Century Mexico: Thomas Smith Webb's *El Monitor de los Masones Libres: ó, Ilustraciones sobre la Masonería*, reveals the world of Freemasonry books translated from English to Spanish, published in Philadelphia and New York, and smuggled into Mexico and Latin America during the political upheavals and independence movements of the 1820s. Among different nationalist movements, de los Reyes Heredia reminds us, translation was important to the process of building a national culture. Recovery of translated Freemasonry texts is central to a more complete understanding of complex intellectual, political, and ideological developments in Mexico, among Hispanics in the United States, and indeed, in the Américas.

In Part IV, Sergio Reyna's article, "La resistencia cultural en la novela de inmigración mexicana a los Estados Unidos," examines five shared attributes in early novels of Mexican immigration to the United States The author has chosen well among possible texts upon which to rest the premise that there is a shared and common experience registered in El *sol de Texas* (Espinosa, 1926); La *patria pérdida* (Torres, 1935); *La aventuras de don Chipote* (Venegas, 1928), and *Aventuras de un bracero* (Topete, 1948). One finds a clear synthesis and a well-estimated unfolding of ideas, that allows amply discussion in the paper of "a) la resistencia cultural del inmigrante, b) nacionalismo cultural de la comunidad inmigrante, c) El "México de fuera" d) el papel de la prensa en la formación del nacionalismo cultural," and "e) lo carnavalesco como una filosofía de vida in the four works being studied."

While revolution impelled Mexican immigration to the United States, Mexicana journalists, intellectuals and activists writing and publishing in San Antonio, Texas, challenged masculinist gendered constructs of revolution and nation. In "Sara Estela Ramírez and Andrea Villarreal Gonzalez: Revolutionary Voices?," Pilar Melero recalibrates the cultural space of motherhood to analyze the contestatory discourse on the emancipation of women of two pivotal Mexicana writers, regarded as transnational precursors of Chicana/Latina feminisms. Ramírez and Villarreal González, Melero convincingly argues, utilized motherhood, an integral element in Mexican woman's construction of self, as a heteretopian site of resistance—one that both reproduced and challenged hegemonic propositions of orthodox Mexicana femininity. Finally, in this section, Melissa L. Garland, offers "Deism and the Authorship of *Jicoténcal*," a cleanly written article that evaluates deism and Enlightenment ideas in *Jicoténcal* as a means to further authenticate the authorship of the novel as the work of Félix Varela.

The twelve essays that compose the sixth volume of the series zoom in and out of recovery material as they respond to considerations of the local to global, of region to hemisphere, and of past to present.

Part I

Recalibrating the Local and Global: History as Region and Region as History

Representing the Tejano on Screen: Américo Paredes and *The Ballad of Gregorio Cortez*

Juan José Alonzo
Texas A&M University

The 1982 PBS-television debut of *The Ballad of Gregorio Cortez*, a film adapted from Américo Paredes's *"With His Pistol in His Hand": A Border Ballad and its Hero* (1958), was anything but auspicious. Chicano/a critics rejected the film for what was perceived to be its Anglo-centric perspective. The critics claimed that neither Cortez nor the Mexican community are given a voice as *The Ballad of Gregorio Cortez* explores the legal injustices visited upon Tejanos at the turn of the twentieth century. In the most sustained critique of the film, Rosa Linda Fregoso praises Robert Young for his "antiracism politics," but she critiques the film for its "subordination of Cortez within the narrative discourse" (70). Still, not all the criticism of the movie has been completely unfavorable. Chon Noriega, for instance, argues that the film effects "an intertextual dialogue with previous Hollywood representation," while it "deconstructs both the classical western and the silent 'greaser' genre of the period depicted" (153). While numerous Chicano/a scholars have taken a position on the movie, Paredes's own sentiments over the cinematic adaptation of his most celebrated work remain unclear.[1] Paredes never wrote formally on *Ballad*, but numerous anecdotes prevail that he had strong negative feelings about the movie. Recent archival findings at the University of Texas at Austin's Nettie Lee Benson Latin American Collection, where the Américo Paredes Papers are housed, indicate that Paredes's critical response may be tied to his conceptualization of a proper Mexican masculinity as expressed in folkloric forms such as the *corrido*. His personal papers and correspondence, when examined in conjunction with his scholarly writings on the *corrido* and machismo, reveal that Paredes was troubled less by the silencing of Cortez and the Mexican community than by the film's lack of a strong and proper heroic element, most tellingly lacking in the acting choices made by the lead actor in the film. I argue that despite the conspicuous absence of film analysis and criticism in Paredes's body of scholarship—he was, after all, a folklorist with a keen interest in all popular cultural forms—students of Paredes can learn a great deal by reading several of his significant works on the *corrido* and machismo alongside his class notes, working papers, and the letters written at the time of the cinematic adaptation of *With His Pistol in His Hand*. Paredes's cultural analysis may then be applied to our understanding of ethnic representation, particularly Mexican representation, in American film.

Although Paredes never published on the subject of ethnic representation in film, this is not to say that he was unaware of the growing importance of the film medium as a mode of not only popular culture and entertainment, but also as a disseminator of stereotypical images and ideology about the ethnic subject. In *With His Pistol in His Hand* for instance, Paredes discusses idealizations and stereotypes about Texas lawmen at the turn of the twentieth century, and he comments that the "'shoot first and ask questions later' method of the rangers has been romanticized into something dashing and daring, in technicolor, on a wide screen, and with Gary Cooper in the title role"(28). This statement reveals an understanding of film's iconic power to render certain subjects—the cowboy, the Ranger, the Anglo hero—as mythically heroic. Paredes's novel, *George Washington Gómez* (1990), provides a telling instance of film's ambivalent attraction in Don Pancho, a Mexican worker who goes to

> the picture show, and for fifteen cents you went in and watched the cowboys. They had sound now. These Gringos! They could do anything. Yes, they had sound now, and you could hear the shots and the smacks when the cowboy hit the badman. It was nice going to the picture show. And when you came out you walked the aisle to the door with a cowboyish swagger you couldn't control, though you felt ashamed and tried to break your step. (181)

Don Pancho is a Mexican, yet he derives pleasure from watching the Anglo-American hero defeat the "badman," a film character who was often a Mexican. In this passage, Paredes draws our attention to the powerful process of interpellation: the movie-watching experience hails Don Pancho to root for the Anglo cowboy against his better judgment, and he feels torn between acceptance and rejection. The passage also shows Paredes's cognizance of the cinema's successful transfer of literary and historical stereotypes—the 'good' Anglo cowboy, the Mexican badman—into an image medium, and its ability to make these stereotypes seem like accepted reality.

Paredes had much to say about the creation of stereotypic images about Mexicans, but not in the language of the film critic. *With His Pistol* contains a well-developed and oft-cited analysis of the "Anglo-Texan legend," a set of beliefs about the Mexican used to justify his wanton mistreatment.[2] The Texas legend states that the Mexican is cruel, cowardly, prone to thievery, and that his degeneracy is due to racial miscegenation (16). Against these characteristics, the legend places the Anglo Texan as the Mexican's superior. In noting the oppositionality between the "good" Texan and the "bad" Mexican, Paredes is establishing a relation that applies to the working of stereotypes, cinematic or otherwise, for stereotypical construction often relies on the simple binary relation of good/bad. Unlike in the cinema, however, the Texas Legend was initially employed with real rather than symbolic effects, in "the war propaganda works of the 1830's and 1840's about Mexican 'atrocities' in Texas, a principal aim of which was to overcome Northern antipathy toward the approaching war with Mexico"(16). To create the antinomial relationships necessary to lead a people to war, the Mexican must occupy the category of evil. And as Paredes notes, long after the U.S.-Mexico War, into "the 1870's, when the Indian danger was past, it was possible to idealize the Plains savage. But the 'Mexican problem' remained. A distinction was drawn between the noble Plains Indian and the degenerate ancestor of the Mexican"(21). As evidenced in dime novels of the late 1800s and subsequently in early American film, the Mexican continued to be a favorite subject of negative stereotyping in Anglo-American cultural production.[3]

In terms of the cinematic adaptation of *With His Pistol in His Hand*, stories told by his colleagues at the University of Texas, where he spent most of his career, have always indicated that Paredes did not look favorably upon *The Ballad of Gregorio Cortez*.[4] Chicano/a film scholars have generally commended Robert Young's sincere but failed attempt to portray the Mexican character positively. In spite of the participation of Moctezuma Esparza as producer and Victor Villaseñor as screenwriter (the screenplay was subsequently adapted by Young), Chicano/a critics have followed a "stereotypes and distortions" model of criticism "devoted to demonstrating that certain films, in some respect or other, 'got something wrong' on historical, biographical, or other grounds of accuracy" (Shohat and Stam 178). While critics have acknowledged Young's even-handedness in portraying the "true" story of Gregorio Cortez, most have faulted the film for silencing Cortez and the Mexican American community as active protagonists in the story. Rosa Linda Fregoso, for instance, notes that Cortez's "character hardly speaks on screen. . . . Cortez's silence is moreover significant because the film privileges Anglo-Texans as the subjects of verbal discourse, thus relegating Cortez to the status of a mute-silent Other. . . . Cortez's marginality from the verbal part of cinematic discourse directly corresponds to the elision of the Chicano point of view in the film" (70). At the time of the film's release, the most prominent review of the film appeared in an essay written by Tatcho Mindiola, in *La Red/The Net*, a Chicano/a education newsletter. Mindiola's review is paradigmatic of the contemporaneous Chicano/a response: the film "does not develop a perspective which puts the viewer within the Mexican community looking out. The audience is not given a sense of how Mexicans lived and how they were involved with Gregorio Cortez individually or collectively, nor of his importance as a symbol"(14). Mindiola's critique agrees with Fregoso's in calling attention to the Anglo-centric perspective of the film, despite its good intentions.

Not all responses to the film have been negative, as I have noted in Chon Noriega's assessment of the film's revisionary stance vis-à-vis the traditional Western. At the time of *Ballad*'s release, Tomás Rivera, one of the leading Chicano/a public intellectuals of his generation, wrote a glowing review of the film in San Diego's *Voz Fronteriza*. Rivera was particularly impressed with Edward James Olmos's interpretation of Gregorio Cortez, unlike Paredes. Recognizing that Cortez speaks but a few words throughout the film, Rivera states, "Olmos excellently portrays the accumulation of his cultural background by his actions, by his facial and body language." Rivera also cautions,

> the film is not a replica of the book on which it is based. It shouldn't be. The excellent study by Paredes *creates* the myth and adds to the legend. The film . . . recreates a spiritual history and allows Gregorio Cortez to converse silently throughout history. The film is not a study nor a true interpretation but a different metaphor, as human as the one wrought by the book. The film is clear and true poetry. Endless. With the stuff of humans. (7)

In his effusive review, Rivera disagrees with Fregoso on the issue of a "silent" Cortez, and he suggests that the film's importance is precisely in its ability to render Cortez's actions, and the power of those actions to open a historical dialogue.

While not entirely consistent, then, the Chicano/a response to *The Ballad of Gregorio Cortez* has been generally critical, especially in scholarly works. Yet almost twenty-five years after its release, one still wonders what Paredes himself thought about the movie. The collected papers, which include unpublished articles, class notes, and correspondence, reveal that Paredes perceived in the film a limited understanding of Mexican character—evidenced by a recapitulation of Mexican stereotypes—but not on the part of the Anglo-American director, as much of the criticism implies. Instead, Paredes looked disapprovingly upon Olmos's inability to portray Cortez with appropriate heroism and dignity.

The archives contain, for instance, a copy of *La Red/The Net*, the education journal in which Tatcho Mindiola's essay appeared. In a short, handwritten note attached to the article, Paredes commented that this was "the only critique of the film that is worth a damn." He elaborates no further here, but we get a fuller sense of Paredes's dissatisfaction in letters written to colleagues at the time of the film's premiere on PBS in June 1982.[5] In a response to a congratulatory letter from Carlos E. Cortés, who was at the time chair of History at UC Riverside, Paredes expresses a strong sense that the characterization of Cortez by Olmos reproduced harmful stereotypes about Mexicans. In his letter, Paredes acknowledges that "[a]rtistically, it was a superior piece of work; Robert Young deserves a great deal of credit for that." He laments, however, that it "is too bad that the actor playing Cortez chose to portray his character as a cross between Chaplin and the racist stereotype of the Mexican as a timid little peon. Is Olmos a Chicano, really?" And in a letter written to Carolyn Osborn during the same period, Paredes remarks that the movie "is a good job, with most of the credit going to Robert Young, the director, who rewrote a trite script by Villaseñor. The woman translator was Young's idea, and a good idea it was. I was not as happy with the 'teatro' scene, which was added by one of the Chicanos. It was strictly 1960s-1970s stuff, and the hobby horse was just a little too much for me." Paredes then concludes that the "thing that bothered me most . . . was Eddie Olmos' interpretation of Cortez. He took a character noted for his coolness, dignity, and courage and turned him into a scared little peon, a kind of Tex-Mex Charlie Chaplin." Paredes's displeasure with the movie, moreover, only seems to grow into genuine antipathy as the years pass. In a 1990 handwritten note to a student requesting information on the film, Paredes writes: "I do not own a video of '*The Ballad of Gregorio Cortez*' [sic] nor would I want to own one. Nor do I know who ultimately retained the rights to this travesty made out of a book of mine, *With His Pistol in His Hand*."

Paredes's negative response to the film centers on his vision of what the real Cortez must have been like, in comparison with what he judged to be Olmos's overly passive and submissive portrayal of Cortez. Paredes also deems Villaseñor's original script to have been weak, and he implies that the insertion of contemporary Chicano/a politics—the *teatro* scene he references—is anachronistic and over the top. Paredes, therefore, stands ironically at odds with critics who concentrate their analyses upon the Anglo director's failings rather than on any of the Chicano/a participants' choices over acting or storytelling techniques.

In none of his letters does Paredes specify the cinematic moment that led him to call Olmos's Cortez a "scared little peon," and, at least initially, it is difficult to find one because the movie begins at mid-chase, with Cortez on the run from a well-armed posse of Rangers. The film narrative then elliptically returns—again and again—to the moment of misunderstanding between Cortez and Sheriff Morris that leads to the sheriff's death. Because the encounter between Cortez and the sheriff is retold from multiple perspectives, and because this is one of the rare scenes in which Cortez speaks, we may speculate that it is upon this instance that Paredes based his critique of Olmos's acting miscalculation.

Let us look, then, at the encounter between Cortez and Sheriff Morris. The scene is presented in flashback, from the perspective of Boone Choate, the interpreter who was at least partially responsible for the misunderstanding and mistranslation between Cortez and the sheriff. It is crucial to note that although the flashback begins from the subjective viewpoint of Choate, in cinematic practice a flashback constitutes a form of objective narration (Bordwell and Thompson 106); the narrative viewpoint, therefore, agrees with the omniscient narrative voice of the film, which is sympathetic with Cortez. The scene opens with Cortez, his brother Romaldo, and the rest of the family at their small farm. As Sheriff Morris and Boone Choate approach, Gregorio sends his family inside the house while Romaldo stands at the gate. Gregorio also hides a revolver behind his back. Morris and Choate step off their buggy and ask to speak with Gregorio Cortez. Cortez steps forward and speaks to the sheriff in Spanish, as he does throughout the film. We begin to see in this scene Paredes's objections to the character as developed by Olmos. Through the translator, the sheriff speaks first to Romaldo, and Romaldo relates to Cortez that the sheriff is looking for him. Cortez responds, "Gregorio Cortez, a sus ordenes [at your service]." This salutation is not unusual, but its manner of delivery is overly obsequious, and the rhythm of the words is delivered in the sing-song of the Mexican Indian stereotype—seen most famously in the Mexican movies starring Mario Moreno "Cantinflas." This mischaracterization, by a Mexican American actor hailed for his powerful role as "El Pachuco" in *Zoot Suit* (1981), is likely what caused Paredes to reject the film. According to the chapter entitled "The Legend" in *With His Pistol in His Hand*, Gregorio Cortez was a respectful, quite man, but one who always stood with dignity and self-control (34-36). The obsequiousness of the Mexican peon that Paredes complains about is out of character here.

As the scene unfolds, Olmos's portrayal of Cortez is plagued by further inconsistencies and contradictions. In the moment when Cortez thinks he is about to be unjustly arrested, he speaks with some urgency, "No nos puede arrestar [you cannot arrest us]." The tone in this instance is pleading. In the next moment, when his brother is shot in the face, Cortez responds with a fury of bullets, shooting the sheriff in the chest, and as the sheriff goes down, Cortez seems terror stricken and out of control as he shoots at the fallen sheriff several more times. The scene ends with Cortez sobbing as he holds Romaldo in his arms. The characterization, thus, shifts radically: in one moment Cortez acts submissively, in the next he is pleading, and finally he is violently out of control. We can see, then, that for Paredes this portrayal lacked the "coolness, dignity, and courage" for which the real and legendary Cortez was apparently known. The inconsistencies in Olmos's acting notwithstanding, the physical and psychological responses to the shock of witnessing one's brother shot are not in and of themselves unusual, and Olmos's performance appears realistic and against the conventions of a typical Western with its unassailable hero. Commenting on the movie's interrogation of the "limitations of the epic hero figure," Fregoso comments that a "departure from the male-hero concept of a previous era of Chicano cultural politics weighed heavily in Edward James Olmos's motives for portraying Cortez. . . . Olmos stated that in his characterization he 'intended to portray Gregorio Cortez as a 'human being' rather than a 'macho''" (80-81). As I discuss below, however, for Paredes being "macho" was not a question of machismo.

A second instance that depicts a peon-like Cortez occurs in his meeting with an Anglo-American cowboy when Cortez is nearing the end of his journey. In the scene, Cortez comes upon the lone cowboy sitting by his campfire, eating his dinner. Desperate, hungry and exhausted, Cortez approaches the cowboy, and the cowboy offers him food. Cortez devours the food, in the animalistic fashion of a man who has not eaten in days. The two men talk a while, although it is the cowboy who is doing most of the talking. Cortez listens, seeming to understand, but showing no evidence that he can speak English. As a show of gratitude, Cortez offers the cowboy what appears to be his only belonging, his knife. Cortez utters the words, "Señor, gracias. Gracias por todo," and his tone is subservient and he is almost in tears.

The Gregorio Cortez of the *corrido* and legend, as is well known, would not have been so obsequious. Paredes would have seen the distinction between a proper display of gratitude and the stereotypic groveling of the peon. The revised script that Robert Young delivered to Paredes contains this scene, but it contains none of the obsequiousness characteristic in the quality of the acting itself. Instead, the script emphasizes the camaraderie the two men achieve despite their language barrier. "The cowboy begins to eat and talk. It is apparent that he is lonely for companionship. He quickly learns that Gregorio speaks but little English, although it seems he understands some of what the cowboy is saying, for he nods his head as he listens" (Young18). The cowboy tells Cortez a funny story, and the scene ends in laughter. "He begins to laugh and laugh at his story. Cortez begins to laugh too. Soon they are both laughing heartily, caught up infectiously in their laughter and in the absurdity of the situation. The cowboy then shakes his head. 'Damn, but it's real good to have someone to talk to.' (Cortez has not said a word.)"(19). While the scene with Cortez and the cowboy ends with a sense of equality and camaraderie in the screenplay, the same scene ends with Cortez in a more compromising position. If Olmos was truly attempting to avoid a 'macho' stance, this scene not only eviscerates the masculine heroics of the *corrido*, but Cortez's humanity as well.

The question of an appropriate male response is central to Paredes's perception of *The Ballad of Gregorio Cortez*, and this same question appears to have been on Olmos's mind in his portrayal, but with a wholly different response. Was Paredes expecting Cortez to be a boastful *macho* who would respond to the sheriff, "I am Gregorio Cortez," as in the many versions of the ballad? While the *corrido* contains such language as, "Ah, so many mounted Rangers / Just to take one Mexican!" Paredes makes clear in the second chapter of *With His Pistol in His Hand*, "The Legend," that Cortez was "[n]ot a gunman, no, not a bravo. . . . He was a peaceful man." Still, Paredes emphasizes that Cortez "was a man, very much of a man"(34), and by this Paredes means that Cortez was a man who would stand up for his rights. For Paredes, Cortez represents what Renato Rosaldo calls the "Chicano warrior hero," a symbol of "an updated version of the ancient ideal of manhood"(154). While Rosaldo acknowledges that the warrior hero "should be understood more poetically than literally," he argues that in the contemporary moment "changing Chicano narratives have dismantled these masculine heroics"(155). The question remains, then, if Paredes nostalgically clung to a "primordial pastoral patriarchy" (155), and if such a stance influenced his view that Olmos had completely misplayed his role as Gregorio Cortez. Put another way, did Paredes reject one stereotype—that of the submissive Mexican peon—in favor of another one—that of the Mexican *macho*? I have argued elsewhere that Paredes cannot so simply be reduced to the position of an essentialist Chicano patriarchy, that his conception of Chicano/a cultural identity is based on the understanding that cultural formations are characterized not by static traditions, but by the constant renovation of those traditions.[6]

Paredes's anthropological work[7] suggests that his expectations of Olmos were less about an idealized masculine hero than about cinematic accuracy vis-à-vis the film's cultural and historical setting. Among his unpublished work, the Paredes archive contains a working paper entitled "Some Stereotypes About the Mexican-American," which sheds light on his understanding of stereotypes, both negative and positive.[8] This working paper critiques the production of stereotypes about Mexicans and argues that some of these are based on psychological projections, on a lack of factual evidence, and on a mistaking of universal human traits for cultural specificity. The paper lists several stereotypes of the Mexican, such as his supposed fatalism, his inability to think for himself, his laziness, and his excessive machismo. Significantly, these stereotypes are usually gender-specific, applying mostly to men. When the Mexican woman appears, she is an object of erotic attraction, while the male consistently remains an object of derision.

The distinction in the depiction of Mexican men and women appears most prominently in "visual stereotypes":

> The Mexican woman in the majority of cases is portrayed in Spanish dress. . . . The Mexican man . . . is most often portrayed as an Indian peon sleeping against an adobe wall; a ragged, unshaven bandit. . . . Needless to say, the man is portrayed in a decidedly negative (or 'Mexican') stereotype that reflects attitudes developed by Anglos during generations of conflict. . . . On the other hand, the 'Spanish' stereotype in which the woman is portrayed is romantic and idealized. (3)

Paredes concludes that the "señorita, then, not only is desirable but acceptable as a prospective mate, since in terms of Anglo prejudices she can be considered 'white.' The Mexican man—who is a potential competitor for the señorita's attentions—is shown to have nothing but negative traits"(3). This last statement speaks to his understanding of the processes of domination and desire, as well as the malleability of stereotypes.

Analyzing the provenance of the stereotype of the Mexican American's fatalism, Paredes notes that this has been transferred from liberal social scientists' preconceived notions of the "village Indian." Ethnographers, too, are liable to produce beliefs about the Mexican's character based on assumptions rather than facts.

> It may be that the 'village Indian' himself is a projection of the American social scientist's own political and social views. Most often liberal in his outlook . . . the Anglo-American social scientist has sought new ideals of peace and cooperation among men, and he has projected them into the objects of his research. Thus the humble Mexican is seen as idyllically happy and integrated into his environment because the Mexican has defeated no one in the world wars or taken away anybody's national territory. The stereotype, in effect, has been turned inside out. But it still limits the observer's vision in many ways. (5)

Rather than the negative stereotype of the violent Mexican, some ethnographers produce a different, and no less negative stereotype of the happy Mexican peon. Of course, neither figuration adequately describes the "village Indian," much less a contemporary U.S. Chicano/a.

Let us return to *The Ballad of Gregorio Cortez* and Paredes's vision of the appropriate representation of Mexican masculinity. It is not so well known that before the 1982 adaptation of *With His Pistol in His Hand*, at least one other film treatment was proposed to Paredes by Charles W. Smith in 1976. Smith sent Paredes a copy of the film treatment, and Paredes read and commented upon it extensively. Paredes's response reveals a sense of nuance for verisimilitude, and an aversion for stereotypes or exaggerations of Mexican masculinity and heroics that simply reverse good/evil polarities. In the opening scene of the proposed movie, the main antagonist, Ranger Captain John Scully, is "snake-eyed . . . a coward without his two large goon-sidekicks"(Smith 1). Paredes writes to Smith that he is "bothered by the rendering of Scully; believe it or not, because he is made a bit too villainous and too cowardly. . . . Border Mexican folklore shows the Ranger as a coward when the shooting starts; otherwise he is overbearing" (Comments 1). Paredes also criticizes the representation of Captain Scully as a sexual degenerate, specifically in the rape of Cortez's wife, named Leonor in Smith's screenplay: "It adds a bit of sensationalism that, in my opinion, does more harm than good. . . . Too much attention is focused on Scully . . . rather than on Cortez being pursued like a hunted animal because he stood up for very elemental rights as a citizen. The rape scene will get very negative reactions. . . . The apologists of the Texas Rangers could make a case that the whole film was an exaggerated libel on the Rangers, since raping Mexican women was not really their forte" (Comments 2). Paredes's comment on the characterization of Scully evidences his sense that to make the story believable and palatable, neither the Anglo-American nor the Mexican characters could be wildly stereotyped.

In one of the final sequences, which narrates Cortez's lynching and its prevention by a newspaper reporter, Paredes demonstrates his sense that the depiction of Mexican heroism, while unavoidably linked with the depiction of Anglos, should not be idealized. With regards to this particular scene, Paredes felt it lacked realism, for why would a reporter hold sway over a mob? Paredes suggested "this might be a good place to give some credit to Sheriff F.M. Fly of Gonzales, who did save Cortez from lynching at the Gonzales jail." And he adds: "There is no reason to show all Anglos as blood-thirsty monsters; some of them were quite decent in the Cortez affair, and even the most partisan Chicanos admit that" (Comments 3). In a final observation to the screenwriter, Paredes states: "I think even Chicanos would not find an extremely exaggerated Ranger villain plausible. I would guard against making Cortez too much like an Anglo cowboy hero, on the other hand. Again, I believe that the sympathies of Anglo audiences, which will be in the majority, will be reached by showing that some Anglos were sympathetic toward Cortez in his situation, as they actually were" (3). These passages clearly suggest that Paredes had no patience of stereotypes or idealizations of any kind. As a good ethnographer, he sought to represent his subjects with verisimilitude, even within a fictional framework. In the previous statement, Paredes pointedly cautions against reversing the discourses of domination: Cortez should not follow the idealized heroism of the Anglo cowboy, and the Anglo cowboy should not follow the stereotyped cowardice of the Mexican peon.

The comments Paredes provided to Smith bear directly on the pivotal encounter between Cortez and Sheriff Morris in *The Ballad of Gregorio Cortez*. The scene, as I have alluded, shows the actor's performance veering between extreme submissiveness—Cortez meekly saying "a sus ordenes [at your service]"—and exaggerated heroics—Cortez standing over the fallen sheriff, emptying his revolver into the sheriff's inert body. Paredes could not have approved of either aspect of the performance, although he objected most vociferously to the portrayal of Cortez as cowardly peon. As we can see, the unpublished essays, working papers, and correspondence strongly suggest that Paredes thought deeply about the cinema's influence on culture and society, even if he never wrote formally on the subject. His collected papers should prove a valuable resource for understanding and reading of ethnic representation in film, and the particular representation of the Mexican American male in *The Ballad of Gregorio Cortez*.

Notes

[1]For significant discussions of *The Ballad of Gregorio Cortez*, see Tatcho Mindiola, "*The Ballad of Gregorio Cortez*," Guillermo Hernández, "*The Ballad of Gregorio Cortez*," Carl Gutierrez-Jones, "Legislating Languages: *The Ballad of Gregorio Cortez* and the English Language Amendment," and Rosalinda Fregoso, *The Bronze Screen: Chicana and Chicano Film Culture.*

[2]For a discussion of "Anglo-Texan legend" and Paredes's revisionary and critical poetics, see Renato Rosaldo, *Culture and Truth*, Ramón Saldívar, *Chicano Narrative: The Dialectics of Difference*, and José E. Limón, *Mexican Ballads, Chicano Poems: History and Influence in Mexican-American Social Poetry,* and *Dancing With the Devil: Society and Cultural Poetics in Mexican-American South Texas.*

[3]For a discussion on the representation of Mexicans in late nineteenth-century American literature and in the early American Westerns, see Juan Alonzo, "From Derision to Desire: The Greaser in Stephen Crane's Mexican Stories and D. W. Griffith's Early Westerns."

[4]This information is based on informal conversations with José E. Limón, who was a student and colleague of Paredes.

[5]Interestingly, Paredes received many positive letters immediately after the television premiere of the film. Friends and colleagues were for the most part happy that Paredes was receiving broader public recognition for his accomplishments, and they felt the film accurately portrayed the plight of Gregorio Cortez.

[6]See Juan Alonzo, "Américo Paredes's *The Shadow*: Social and Subjective Transformation in Greater Mexico."

[7]The film's historical setting would have required a heroe cognizant of the futility of a hyper-masculine stance, yet aware of the need for cultural preservation and dignity in the wake of Anglo domination.

[8]On the top right-hand corner of this working paper, the words "Not for Publication" demonstrate that Paredes saw this as a work-in-progress. Notwithstanding this possibility, multiple copies of "Some Stereotypes About the Mexican" are found in different folders within the collection, indicating that Paredes's thoughts on the subject on the stereotype were well developed. Some of the ideas in this working paper are encapsulated and amplified in "On Ethnographic Fieldwork Among Minorities," and "The United States, Mexico and Machismo."

Works Cited

Alonzo, Juan J. "Américo Paredes's *The Shadow*: Social and Subjective Transformation in Greater Mexico." *Aztlán: A Journal of Chicano Studies* 27.1 (2002): 27-57.

_____. "From Derision to Desire: The Greaser in Stephen Crane's Mexican Stories and D. W. Griffith's Early Westerns." *Western American Literature* 38 (Winter 2004): 374-401.

Bordwell, David, and Kristin Thompson. *Film Art: An Introduction.* Fifth Ed. New York: McGraw-Hill, 1997.

Fregoso, Rosa Linda. *The Bronze Screen: Chicana and Chicano Film Culture.* Minneapolis: University of Minnesota Press, 1993.

Gutiérrez-Jones, Carl. "Legislating Languages: *The Ballad of Gregorio Cortez* and the English Language Amendment." Noriega, Chicanos and Film 168-82.

Hernández, Guillermo. "*The Ballad of Gregorio Cortez.*" *Crítica* 1.3 (Spring 1985): 122-31.

Limón, José E. *Dancing with the Devil: Society and Cultural Poetics in Mexican-American South Texas.* Madison: University of Wisconsin Press, 1994.

_____. *Mexican Ballads, Chicano Poems: History and Influence in Mexican-American Social Poetry*. Berkeley: University of California Press, 1992.

Mindiola, Tatcho. "*The Ballad of Gregorio Cortez*." *La Red/The Net*: *Newsletter of the National Chicano Council on Higher Education* 80 (May 1984): 11-17.

Noriega, Chon. "Between a Weapon and a Formula: Chicano Cinema and its Contexts." Noriega, *Chicanos and Film* 141-67.

_____. ed. *Chicanos and Film: Representation and Resistance.* Minneapolis: University of Minnesota Press, 1992.

Paredes, Américo. "Comments on '*The Ballad of Gregorio Cortez*.'" Américo Paredes Papers. The Nettie Lee Benson Latin American Collection. U of Texas at Austin. n.d.

_____. *George Washington Gómez*: *A Mexicotexan Novel.* Houston: Arte Público Press, 1990.

_____. Letter to Carolyn Osborn. 15 July 1982. Américo Paredes Papers. The Nettie Lee Benson Latin American Collection. University of Texas at Austin.

_____. Letter Carlos E. Cortés. 27 July 1982. Américo Paredes Papers. The Nettie Lee Benson Latin American Collection. University of Texas at Austin.

_____. Letter to Mary Lou Hornbuckle. 13 May 1990. Américo Paredes Papers. The Nettie Lee Benson Latin American Collection. University of Texas at Austin.

_____. "On Ethnographic Fieldwork Among Minorities." *Folklore and Culure on the Texas-Mexican Border.* Ed. Richard Bauman. Austin: CMAS Books-University of Texas at Austin, 1993. 73-110.

_____. *The Shadow.* Houston: Arte Público Press, 1998.

_____. "Some Stereotypes About the Mexican-American." Working Paper. Américo Paredes Papers. The Nettie Lee Benson Latin American Collection. University of Texas at Austin. n.d.

_____. "The United States, Mexico, and Machismo." *Folklore and Culure on the Texas-Mexican Border.* Ed. Richard Bauman. Austin: CMAS Books-University of Texas at Austin, 1993. 215-34.

_____. *"With His Pistol in His Hand": A Border Ballad and its Hero*. 1958. Austin: University of Texas Press, 1986.

Rivera, Tomás. "*The Ballad of Gregorio Cortez*." *Voz Fronteriza* 9.1 (September/October): 5-7.

Rosaldo, Renato. *Culture and Truth: The Remaking of Social Analysis.* Boston: Beacon Press, 1993 [1989].

Saldívar, Ramón. *Chicano Narrative: The Dialectics of Difference.* Madison: The University of Wisconsin Press, 1990.

Shohat, Ella, and Robert Stam. *Unthinking Eurocentrism: Multiculturalism and the Media.* London: Routledge, 1994.

Smith, C. W. "'*The Ballad of Gregorio Cortez*': A Treatment for an Adaptation." Américo Paredes Papers. The Nettie Lee Benson Latin American Collection. University of Texas at Austin. n.d.

Valdez, Luis, dir. *Zoot Suit*. Universal Pictures, 1981.

Young, Robert. "*The Ballad of Gregorio Cortez*." Screenplay. Américo Paredes Papers. The Nettie Lee Benson Latin American Collection. University of Texas at Austin. n.d.

Young, Robert M., dir. *The Ballad of Gregorio Cortez*. Embassy Pictures, 1982.

Benjamin Read: New Mexico's Bernal Díaz del Castillo

Erlinda Gonzales-Berry
Oregon State University

But mine are still forgotten people.
George I. Sánchez

George I. Sánchez, in his seminal study *Forgotten People: A Study of New Mexicans,"* wrote regarding the Treaty of Guadalupe Hidalgo that "in setting for the boundaries of the territory acquired and in making casual provision for the citizenship of individuals, [the treaty] failed to recognize the major issues involved in the incorporation of people into a new culture. In the march of imperialism a people were forgotten, cast aside as the by-product of territorial aggrandizement" (12). In this chapter, I will explore how one specific Nuevomexicano*,* historian Benjamin Read, was cast aside by "the march of imperialism," in this case, intellectual and academic imperialism.

Spanish Borderlands/Wester Frontier: A Contested Geographic and Intellectual Terrain

The historiography of the colonial Spanish borderlands did much to plant the idea of the Southwest as part of a distinct cultural region for purpose of academic study. This same territory, reframed through the lens of an Anglo-American, capitalist, colonizing enterprise, was designated by Frederick Jackson Turner in 1893, as part of the Western Frontier. Both conceptual frameworks have co-existed but served the needs of scholars trained in distinct traditions. One of these categories was to become quite charged in the late twentieth century, leading one historian to characterize the debate over the definition and meaning of the western frontier as "a scholarly tug of war over the f-word." (Limerick 72). In their comparative work, historians Howard Lamar and Leonard Thompson joined this tug of war. Accordingly, these historians state that a frontier "is not a boundary or line, but a territory or zone of interpretation between two previous distinct societies." They add that a frontier "'closes' when a single political authority has established hegemony over the zone" (cited in Limerick 76). I find their definition of frontier persuasive for addressing conditions in New Mexico at the turn of the twentieth century. New Mexico indeed was a frontier where distinct cultures vied not only for land and resources but for the historiography of the region as well. A lively chapter in the contestation over New Mexico's historiography involved Benjamin M. Read, author of spirited polemics in which he accused the state's leading historians of producing erroneous histories of the region. I sustain that while his arguments were ostensibly over the veracity of the facts, they really were about a broader issue; namely, *who* had the *authority* to write that history. So long as New Mexico was an open frontier, it stands to reason that its history would be contested. However, once Anglo-American hegemony laid exclusionary claim to the frontier, the question Read raises was rendered moot, his contestatory treatises buried in the archival dustbin, virtually erased from the *nuevomexicano* collective memory.

Benjamin Read: His Life and Work

Ralph Twitchell, L. Bradford Prince, Hubert Bolton, all are recognized and respected names in the annals of New Mexico historiography. With the exception of material included in Meléndez' book *So All Is Not Lost* (1997), and in Doris Meyer's *Speaking for Themselves* (1996), a peer and critic of the former, Benjamin—or perhaps I should say Benjamín—Read, remains excluded from those annals despite the fact that he wrote a significant number of New Mexico histories. This exclusion is owed, I argue, to a deliberate act of erasure once Anglo hegemony was achieved in the cultural institutions of the State.

Benjamin Maurice Read saw himself as the "Bernal Díaz del Castillo" of New Mexico historiography. He minced no words in accusing many fellow historians of misinterpreting or misrepresenting the facts and, in some cases, of engaging in outright columniation. In one of his more vitriolic attacks he exclaims, "Pero eso todo es un mito y solo un mentecato puede creer tales burradas" (*Historia Ilustrada de Nuevo México,* 1911, 28). Examination of his published works and of the materials in the Benjamin Read Collection in the New Mexico Records and Archives Center (NMRAC) reveals that Read spent a good part of his life in contestatory struggle to shed light on what he saw as *la verdadera historia de Nuevo México.*

The earliest information on Read's life comes from a sketch in *Illustrated History of New Mexico* published in 1895.[1] Read was the son of an Anglo who arrived in New Mexico with General Kearny's battalion in 1846 and of Nuevomexicana Ignacia Cano. His father, George Read died in 1857, leaving Ignacia Cano Read with three young sons. Cano remarried and brought up her mestizo sons with their half brothers and half-sister in a Spanish-speaking home where they were raised with a strong Nuevomexicano identity and sensibility. Benjamín would show his predilection for his maternal language over English by writing all of his books first in Spanish and subsequently translating or having them translated to English. Read's involvement in the civic life of New Mexico, as a lawyer, public servant, and historian gained him the admiration and respect of the Hispano community and, according to Meléndez, made him a figure that "galvanized the sentiments of his generation in its pursuit of a *Nuevomexicano* presence in public life during the territorial period" (1997, 124).

Read, a proflific writer, published several major books in his lifetime, but his most important publications were: *La Guerra México-Americana,* printed in Santa Fe in 1910, and *Historia Ilustrada de Nuevo México,* which appeared in 1911. A five hundred volume run of the latter, corrected, augmented and translated into English by Eleuterio Baca, was issued by the New Mexican Printing Company in 1912. Read published a third history, *Popular Elementary History of New* Mexico, designed for classroom use in 1914. Additional publications by Read include *A History of Education in New Mexico;* two short pamphlets titled *A Treatise on the Disputed Points of the History of New Mexico* (1919), and *A Short History of Slavery in America* (1919); and *Chronological Digest of the Documentos Inéditos del Archivo las Indias.* The latter represents an inestimable contribution to the historiographic endeavor in that it made accessible to American historians an extensive annotated bibliography of documents found in Spanish archives pertinent to the history of Spanish America. He also left several manuscripts that were never published. A manuscript entitled *Sidelights of New Mexico History* and an account of the participation of New Mexicans in the various wars of the United States (*Nuevo México en las guerras de la unión americana, 1885-1919)* are in the archives. The latter included personal narratives collected from soldiers who participated in WWI. In a letter Read wrote to F.M.Chacón he suggests that this manuscript was in an advanced stage of preparation, as he charges Chacón with delivering the manuscript immediately to the Valiant printing company for a cost analysis.[2] There are several references to a third manuscript, *Hernán Cortés and his Conquest of Mexico.* Meléndez states that this manuscript was accepted for publication in 1923 by a press in Boston. I found neither an extant copy of the manuscript nor evidence of its publication, though I did find a two-page introduction penned by Paul A. F. Walter, editor of the *New Mexican* and member of the School of American Archeology.

The record shows that the publication of these texts was extremely costly to Read, as in addition to printing costs, there were expenses for the purchase of original documents. Read underwrote these costs was by selling subscriptions. A subscription entitled an individual to inclusion of a photograph and biographical sketch, provided by the subscriber, in the appendix of *Historia Ilustrada*. The Spanish subscription cost $2.50 plus the price of the book. The Spanish text contains 107 entries, mostly of influential Nuevomexicanos such as Casimiro Barela, Octaviano Larazolo, General Armijo, and Padre Jose Antonio Martínez. Nineteen Anglos are also included. Among the latter we find such illustrious—and infamous—figures as Thomas Catron, Albert Fall, Max Frost, and fellow historians Ralph Twitchell and Bradford Prince. Twenty nine of the sketches included in the Spanish version (mostly of Hispanos) appear in the English text and thirty new sketches, fourteen of them of Hispanos not included in the Spanish text, represent new entries in the English edition. These numbers suggest that Nuevomexicanos of means were indeed eager to have their memory preserved in the annals of history. More important, according to Melendez, is the fact that "These 'snapshots . . . suggest a communitarian will to historical and cultural presence . . . [and they]become essential to sociobiographical credentialing along the lines of communitarian values of individual agency within *Neo-Mexicano* communities after 1848" (1997, 115). I would add that these sketches or *bocetos,* as they were called in Spanish (Melendez), further confirm, contrary to what defamatory writings of the period would have us believe, that a class of educated and literate Hispanos indeed existed in territorial New Mexico. We can be certain that without these sketches, recovery work of this region would be severely limited for they often represent the only biographical record of nineteenth-century Nuevomexicano literati.

Subscriptions for the English version appear to have been $5 plus the price of the book. I say 'appear' because an unflattering entry in Governor Otero's autobiography, *My Nine Years as Governor of New Mexico,* suggests that the price was variable. Fulminating against Read as someone "whom we could have gotten along without very well" (in the legislative assembly), Otero relates that Read demanded $300 from his father and another $300 from himself for publication of their biographical sketches. Because they refused to pay this amount both were left out of the book. Furthermore, Otero decries the fact that "he left out any mention of my administration as governor of the territory, although I served for nine years as such. He also questioned the record of the old bell brought to this country by Francisco Vasquez de Coronado—simply because it belonged to me, and I had refused to donate $600 to his *supposed* history of

New Mexico" (1940, 76). Indeed there seems to have been bad blood between Governor Otero and Benjamin Read, which perhaps was owed to Read's close association with Otero's avowed enemy, Thomas Catron. The latter, who allegedly made an attempt on Governor Otero's life, in fact, wrote the introduction to Read's history of Hernán Cortés.

Read took advantage of the English edition of *Historia Ilustrada* to correct omissions or errors in the bocetos of the Spanish edition. In a letter to Rafael Chacón, the author apologizes for not being able to lengthen the entry in the Spanish edition, as Chacón requested, because of cost. He does however augment the entry considerably in the English edition. In a tactic that seems less than subtle, he also seizes the moment to call Don Rafael's attention to the fact that several individuals—among them Casimiro Barela, José Montaner, and the Don's own son, Eusebio—generously supported his work with contributions of $50.00 each. Lest we make Mr. Read out to be a bit of a money grubbing fellow, it is worth noting that in this same letter he assures Don Rafael that "para beneficio de la gente pobre haré una segunda edición (sin los bosquejos) menos costosa" (BMR Collection, NMRCA, Series II, Folder 108). Unfortunately, there is no evidence that such an edition ever came to fruition.

In Pursuit of the 'True History of New Mexico'

Correspondence with Don Rafael Chacón, an eminent Nuevomexicano of the nineteenth century whose life and work Genaro Padilla included in *My History not Yours* (1993), figures prominently in the Read Collection. Though Don Rafael Chacón's letters are not in the Read collection, we can infer a good deal from Read's extant responses. Apparently Chacón had much to say about *Historia Ilustrada* and was not shy about correcting what he perceived as errors in the work. Read, who given his self-expressed passion for writing *la verdadera historia* of New Mexico, responds by putting into question Don Rafael's historical source, which is none other than the disputed work of López de Gómara. Going into great detail regarding Bernal Diaz del Castillo's debunking of Gómara's erroneous history, Read writes:

> En lo referente a Gómara la autoridad que usted leyó está absolutamente errada. Gómara no solo fue sacerdote sino que por el año de 1540 entró al servicio de Hernán Cortés en España y fue él/Gómara, quien escribió la primera Historia de la Conquista de la Nueva España. De lo que (se presume) le dijera Cortés. Esa historia salió tan llena de errores que unos años después de su publicación cayó un ejemplar a manos de Bernal Díaz del Castillo, a la sazón miembro del municipio de Guatemala, quien fue uno de los conquistadores de Hernán Cortes. Bernal Díaz notó desde luego las

> innumerables mentiras de Gómara y, en seguida, escribió su "Historia Verdadera de la Conquista de la Nueva España." La historia de Bernal Díaz tuvo el efecto de hacer condenar la obra de Gómara, la cual no volvió a reimprimirse . . . hasta siglos después. (BMR Collection, NMRCA, Series II, Fólder 33)

At a time when the future of New Mexico was very much at stake, and as Doris Meyer perceptively points out (1996), the issue of how its past would be represented for future generations was especially at stake, Bernal Díaz del Castillo's history had a tremendous impact on Benjamin Read; so great, in fact, that Read very self-consciously emulated Bernal Díaz laying out for himself the task of setting the historical record straight. He pursued this task with passion and gusto engaging in lively polemics with Anglo historians at every turn of the page.

There are a number of New Mexico histories that Read finds acceptable, among them those written by Bancroft, Prescott, Juan Bautista Salpointe, and Bradford Prince, though with regard to the latter he does engage in a bit of "back biting" in a letter to Father Zephyrin, author of the *Spanish Missions of California*. After requesting information for an article on New Mexico Penitentes, Read informs the priest:

> You have a rival here in New Mexico in our friend L. Bradford Prince. He is now writing a book on "The Missions in New Mexico". As soon as the book is published I shall see that you get a copy. I hope you will find time after you read it to dissect the plagiarisms, for I know the book will be full of them. Plagiarism is now the order of the day here in New Mexico.
>
> (BMR Collection, NMRAC Series II, Folder 36)[3]

He finds Archbishop Salpointe's sacred and profane histories, including his problematic thesis postulating that New Mexico's indigenous populations descended from Noah, accurate and especially laudatory. But others he found quite remiss. Regarding Hubert Bolton's work, Read issues a tactful challenge in *Disputed Points of the History of New Mexico:* "In conclusion, the reader is earnestly requested to compare Dr. Bolton's statements and his authorities with what I say and with the authorities citied by me in my *Illustrated History of New Mexico* on the points and propositions discussed and alluded to in this treatise" (1919, 17). Attempting to establish scholarly interchange with this eminent historian, Read sends him a copy of his *Treatise on the Disputed Points of the History of New Mexico* and in a follow-up letter requests "thorough criticism from you on the merits of the same." (BMR Collection, NMRAC, Series II, Folder 108). Bolton's dismissive response suggests that he was not too thrilled about Read's work: "I have glanced over it, but I cannot profess to have exhausted its contents. The points which you discuss are all matters of interest, and some of them of importance . . . I note your complementary remarks with regard to my writings, but I have not had time to read them closely enough to ascertain whether you quoted them with agreement or disagreement" (BMR Collection, NMRAC, Series II, Folder 108).

Read excoriates Josiah Gregg, whose work he finds abundant in "asinities [sic] and calumnies"; and W.W.H. Davis, whose work was inspired by the "obscene nonsense written by Gregg" (*Illustrated History*, 52). Regarding Helen Haines, who according to Read wrote that Indians in New Mexico were forced by the Spaniards to live in Pueblos, he opines: ". . . it may well be that, from a strange rumor, or through a stretch of her own imagination she may have made such a fabrication, as no author of respectable standing has ever uttered such nonsense" (*Illustrated History,* 53). Though the evidence is circumspect regarding Read's feelings toward his colleague, Ralph Twitchell, we can surmise that much of the latter's work, especially *A History of the Military Ocupation of the Territory of New Mexico 1846-1851,* did not settle well with Read, a point I shall return to presently. Among the Spanish and Mexican historians, he praises the work of Sahagún, Solis, Bruno Babi, Torres Quintero and, of course, Bernal Díaz del Castillo, and he finds Villagrá's poem a most useful tool to the historian. He finds the work of Clavijero, Mendieta, and Torquemada deficient particularly when "put against the original reports" (*Illustrated History,* 13).

In his *Illustrated History,* Read observes that many of the histories written by monolingual English speakers regarding the discovery of America by Columbus, the Christianization of Mexico by Cortés, and the conquest of Peru are rife with contradictions when compared with original documents penned by participants in the events. He owes these discrepancies to the fact that historians have depended on translations by individuals who, "by reason of their never having seen the said originals and also because of their not being Spanish scholars, have not . . . rendered into correct English the spirit of the original texts. . ." (np). He observes that the same can be said about New Mexican histories written "by other writers without knowing enough Spanish to ascertain the truth of the translations they copy from. . . ." In order to right these wrongs Read stresses that he "dedicate[d] many years to the study of the original writings, with the end in view of writing, as correctly as possible a *true history*, for which purpose [I] spared neither means nor expenses . . ." (my emphasis, 6). Read incurred these expenses by retaining literary agents in Madrid who obtained for him copies of valuable documents pertinent to the history of Spanish America. Read also had an agent collect materials for him in Mexico. In addition, he acquired a valuable collection of the local materials and had occasion to comment on the merits of personal narratives of Nuevomexicanos. In his introduction to the published reminiscences of Don Doroteo Pérez, he wrote: "The above reflections appeared to me opportune and indispensable as a preface or introduction to the narrative of Don Demetrio; in order that the reader may understand and appreciate the historical value of the reminiscences" (*New Mexico Historical Review* 1927, 91). For someone as concerned with the "truth tests" of linear histories as was Read, these words bear surprising testimony to his faith in counter-memory. George Lipsitz, however, reminds us that counter-memory "subjects itself to an even more rigorous test—the standard of collective memory and desire" (1990, 228) and it succeeds precisely because it "must address the part of audience memory in touch with real historical oppressions and memories" (228). Obviously, Read was in a position to not only understand but also to feel deeply the conditions of oppression from which these memories emerged. In that sense he was, in Lipsitz words, "[brought] closer to the truth" (Lipsitz 228) he so desperately sought to command.

Throughout his correspondence and in the body of the published texts, Read boasts repeatedly of having exclusive access to original documents. In order to give his work the imprimatur of authority and authenticity, Read repeatedly included long passages from said documents, and in many cases entire manuscripts. As this practice runs contrary to the tradition among historians of producing well-crafted narrative, fellow-historians were quick to find fault with his writing, finding it cumbersome and lacking in elegance. However, at least on one occasion, L. Bradford Prince, in a letter to Read, lauds his inclusion of Fray Benavides' report on the province and Pedro Bautista Pino's speech to the Spanish Congress in 1812. (*Illustrated History* 806).[4] In a letter to a John Griffith from Socorro, New Mexico, Read thanks him for his interest in the forthcoming English edition of his *Historia Ilustrada,* informing him that it "is the result of nearly 25 years work without regard to expense and labor in order to procure the original authority from the very fountains, as I did by the employments for months and months of a literary agent in Madrid, Spain, by which means I was able to secure data so as to make my History the standard authority and I think I have succeeded" (Benjamin Read Collection, NMRAC, Series II, Folder 112). In another letter, this one to the elder Chacón, Read boldly states: "Me siento, no obstante todo eso, muy feliz con ver el fruto de tantos años de constante estudio realizado en forma que mi obra NECESARIAMENTE vendrá a ser AUTORIDAD en lo referente a *nuestra* (my emphasis) historia . . ." (BMR Collection, NMRAC, Series II, Folder 108). The fact that Read emphasizes the words 'necesaraimente' and 'autoridad' by writing them in upper case, attests to his profound desire to produce a history that would eclipse all other histories, the lot of them, in his judgment, deficient if not distorted.

Staking a Claim on 'Nuestra Historia'

While Read was deeply concerned regarding historical veracity, a more fundamental issue underpins his contestatory struggle. And that issue was: Who had the authority or the right to write this history or, as he says to Rafael Chacón in the letter cited above, *nuestra historia*? Benjamin Read, like so many other Nuevomexicanos, was disheartened by the unjust beating that the Nuevomexicano character had taken in works like those of Josiah Gregg, W.W. Davis, in the Beveridge statehood hearings, and in the defamatory articles produced during the statehood debates. From Read's perspective, Anglo-Americans had, in addition to mistranslating the historical record, misrepresented it as well, thereby engaging not only in faulty *traducción* but in egregious *traición* as well. Given this betrayal, Read believed that Anglo historians had not earned the right to represent *nuevomexicano* history. He, on the other hand, by virtue of being a native son, boldly lays claim to the right to write the true and just history of his people. In the preface to *Guerra Mexico-Americana* he affirms:

> Siendo esta la primera obra de historia escrita por un hijo nativo de Nuevo México, descendiente de ambas dos razas, la anglo-sajona y la latina, siente su autor gran satisfacción en presentarla al público como la precursora de otra, la "Historia Ilustrada de Nuevo México," que desde años ha, tiene en estudio, queriendo coronar con ellas el fin de sus esfuerzos y luchas que en pro de la muy injustamente tratada raza latina—la raza de mi madre—ha venido por muchos años haciendo y sosteniendo. No busco la gloria, sino, sí, la consolación que mi alma siente al creer que, aunque muy humildemente, en algo he contribuido en aclarar la verdad en pro de la justicia histórica que hayan sido privados los descendientes de los bizarros conquistadores. Si con mis insignificantes escritos se realiza mi ideal, redundando ellos en honor de la verdad y honra de los hijos de Nuevo México, quedarán mis deseos ampliamente recompensados. (6)

He reiterates this sentiment in the letter cited above to Rafael Chacón to whom Read discloses: ". . . y lo que más me agrada, por haberle dado a la raza de mi madre una obra que los hará sentirse orgullosos de sus antepasados y de sus proezas" (BMR Collection, NMRAC Series II, Fólder 108).

Community Authenticates Read's Claim

I find it puzzling that Read is silent on this facet of his mission in *Historia Ilustrada*, (both the English and the Spanish version). It is tempting to conclude, as does Meyer (1996),[5] that perhaps Read was concerned that an expression of things too close to the heart would lead readers, particularly fellow historians, to dismiss his work as sentimental rather than scientifically rigorous. Speculation aside, what I believe is important here is that such a statement was not necessary for Nuevomexicanos. They deemed the mere act of taking pen in hand an act of subaltern agency and of contestation; and Benjamin Read, an organic intellectual, respected and esteemed by his community, indeed had earned the right to represent the history that was their legacy. Even before publication of *Historia Ilustrada*, poet Luis Tafolla writes a poem on this proposed work in which he clearly sanctions Read's right to tell this history. He charges him with the responsibility of being true to the facts and of defending his homeland and his people. This poem, the very form of which is a favored expressive vehicle for popular oral verse— the *copla*— becomes, in effect a public endorsement of Read's historical project issued on behalf of *el pueblo:*

Arriesgada empresa es esa
Que Vd. Intenta afrontar,
Con esperanza y promesa
De honor y fama ganar.

No es el primer aspirante
A dar cima a nuestra historia,
Otros ya han ido adelante
Deseosos de adquirir gloria.

Y aunque sin disputa fueron
Notables por su instrucción
Para Historiar no tuvieron
Suficiente información.

Resultando a consecuencia
Sus historias sin sustancia
Por mostrar clara evidencia,
De errores y disonancia

Pues a todo historiador
Se le exige al principiar,
Que antes de ser escritor
Sepa lo que va a tratar

Porque si escribe a ciegas
Siguiendo modelos crudos
Dará errores a fanegas
En informes sesudos

Y que [no] sea historiador
De los hechos solamente
Con verdad defensor
De sus país y de sus gente
(*El Independiente,* May 5, 1910))

Obviously, Tafolla was well informed regarding Read's agenda to write a true history based on original documents (Myer tells us that the two were close friends who collaborated in the same newspaper.) Thus, we can also read this poem as an *ars poética* for Read's work, one written not by the author, but by a fellow Nuevomexicano who understood well the contested terrain of New Mexican historiography.

Documentation in the Read collection demonstrates clearly that the Nuevomexicano community indeed endorsed this subaltern's right not only to speak, but to do so in a way that restored communal honor. Fifteen letters from Nuevomexicanos acknowledge receipt of one or another of Read's book, and all but one enthusiastically express appreciation for his work.[6] Eminent acholar at Stanford University, Aurelio Espinosa penned one such letter in which he proclaims: "El capítulo que trata de los acontecimientos históricos de Nuevo Méjico desde 1846 hasta ahora, o sea, todo el libro cuarto es donde ha expuesto verdades y hechos (y bien documentados y probados) que deben ruborizar a los enemigos de nuestra raza y de nuestro pueblo" (BMR Collection, NMRAC Series II, Fólder 110). Eusebio Chacón, in a review of *Guerra Mexico-Americana,* praises Read for his treatment of Padre José Antonio Martínez and for having "steered away from the cheap anti declamatory diatribe with which historians, more or less respectable, have heaped insults on General Armijo for having retired without a battle" (BMR Collection, Series II, Folder 105).[7] This statement no doubt refers to Ralph Twitchell whose history, published one year prior to Read's, does not spare harsh words in its reference to Father Martínez, General Armijo, and other Nuevomexicanos. (In fact, it would not be wrong to infer that Read's history *Guerra México-Americana* was written in direct contestation to Twitchell's text.) Chacón adds, "Another feature of the work is the fact that it comes from the first native New Mexican, who has taken the trouble and time to delve into that most unpleasant subject, the period of disaster when our forefathers received such terrible chastisement from American arms." Chacón, who himself on many occasions assumed the obligation to speak the subaltern's version of Nuevomexicano history, enthusiastically acknowledged Read's right to the same.

While Benjamin Read certainly was a man of integrity and lofty ideals, he was also a pragmatic individual. Having spent a small fortune on the publication of his books, he undoubtedly was concerned with recouping some of his investment. After statehood, the School Board was about to select a text of New Mexico History for use in the public schools. The author of the chosen textbook would be guaranteed a substantial income, and Read was eager to have his text selected. Thus it was crucial that his work be deemed "the authentic" history of the State. To that end Read engaged in a lively promotional campaign. His carefully choreographed plan included numerous laudatory and legitimating articles in the New Mexican, with which Read was closely associated and also of letters of legitimizing praise addressed to Read, which were reprinted in the New Mexican and in several of his published texts. By 1912, his efforts appear to have paid off. In a letter to Archbishop J.B. Pitival, Read informs him that *Illustrated History* had been adopted for use in the public high schools and libraries. There were, however, three texts vying for the elementary school slot: Read's soon to be published *Elementary History of New Mexico*, and texts by L. Bradford Prince and Dr. Frank Roberts. Read believed at the time that all three would be adopted, a strategy he found disconcerting because "there is a very serious variance between my book and the other two" (BMR Collection, NMRAC Series II, Folder 122). In other words, according to Read's reckoning, Prince and Roberts' texts did not qualify as *verdadera historia.* However, the work of at least one of these gentlemen subsequently would become part of the official history of New Mexico, while Read's work eventually would be subjected to an astonishing, deliberately orchestrated act of erasure.

Erasure and the Triumph of Hegemonic Historiography

At the heart of this erasure was a necrology appearing The *New Mexico Historical Review* upon Read's death in 1927. Lansing Bloom was editor of the journal and secretary of the New Mexico Historical Society, and it is quite likely that it was he who penned the piece. As such a note on this individual's background and his relation to Read is in order. Bloom first came to New Mexico as a Presbyterian missionary, but in 1917 he began to study history as a protégé of Ralph Twitchell. He played an important role in the New Mexico Historical Society, of which Twitchell was one of the founders, and in time he became a tenured professor in the History Department at the University of New Mexico. In 1913 Bloom wrote an article in which he accused the Catholic Church of denying church members access to the bible and of keeping Nuevomexicanos in the dark ages. Among his more blustering statements was the following: ". . . Jesus Christ as only savior and supreme master was unheard of in New Mexico throughout the Roman Catholic administration" (*Old Santa Fe,* I:2, October 1913, 138). California historian, Father Zephyrin Engelhardt, with whom Read maintained a close collegial relationship, issued a scathing rebuttal in the *San Francisco Monitor*, in which he chastises both Bloom and Bradford Prince: "It is to be regretted that ex-governor L. Bradford Prince permits his name to appear in the octave as Associate editor, among whom the Rev. L.B. Bloom sounds the dominant note. The editor-in-chief's prattle is not a surprise. His own history of New Mexico has been proved to be wholesale plagiarism" (Dec. 6, 1913).[8] In a letter to Read, Englehardt offers the following opinion: ". . . and I suspect he [Prince] belongs to the Bloom-Twitchell crowd, the book will afford me another picnic like that with Bloom . . . Old Santa Fe [written by Twitchell] was gotten up to lift Presbyterianism on its shaky feet" (March 20, 195, BRC, NMARC, Series II, Folder 35). Engelhardt continues to rail against Twitchell blasting his recently published book, *Old Santa Fe.* Statements of the following nature found in that book, no doubt account for the priest's animosity: "The practically complete catholicity of the people was a barrier to innovations and social customs to them unwelcome because they were neither understood nor appreciated" (1925, 455). What is apparent from these bits of information is that, in addition to the native/interloper polarity, at the heart of New Mexico's contested historiography there was also a clash in perspective between Catholic and Protestant writers, and Read definitely belonged to the former. The staunch defenses of the Catholic Church present throughout his writings and his life-long friendship with various New Mexican prelates confirm the depth of Read's loyalty to the Church. His correspondence with Englehardt likewise reveals a strong desire to paint the role of the Catholic Church in the development of the Southwest in the most positive light possible. And while Read worked avidly to create what he considered the most authoritative writings on New Mexican history, focusing always through a Catholic optic, it was the Protestant historians Twitchell, Prince and Bloom—depicted by Englehardt as an unholy triumvirate—who controlled the New Mexico Historical Society and its prestigious literary mouthpiece, the *New Mexico Historical Review.* Hence they were in a position to define and delimit the parameters of official New Mexican historiography; that is, of selecting the histories that subsequently would be canonized in the institutions of higher learning which they also controlled—Bloom was eventually to join the Department of History at the University of New Mexico—and of excluding those they so desired. Given that Benjamin Read had repeatedly rebuked these gentlemen's "false histories," it is no wonder that upon his death they would seize the opportunity to destroy his credibility, despite the fact that he had been elected as a fellow of the Historical Society. They did so most effectively in three brief sentences: "Mr. Read's writing hardly struck a popular chord. At the same time, his lack of scientific training barred him from the recognition which his zeal and persistent endeavor should have brought him.

The fact that he thought and wrote in Spanish and insisted upon a literal translation, robbed his English work of much of the spirit and smoothness of his Spanish diction" (*New Mexico Historical Review*, 11:4, October, 1927). That Read, as a fellow of the New Mexico Historical Society was in essence one of their own, makes this act particularly astonishing. Meléndez (1997) accurately notes that Twitchell was not a trained historian [and neither was Prince for that matter]. The speciousness of this argument notwithstanding, it was to stand as the predominant characteristic associated with Read's work. In the introduction to a reprint of the 1926 volume of the *New Mexico Historical Review,* University of New Mexico historian Donald Cutter assessed the contributions of various historians to the journal. Reviving the dismissive language of Read's necrology, he wrote: "Benjamin Read was a distinguished senior lawyer with an *untrained* but vigorous interest in history" (n.p., my emphasis). It is noteworthy that of Read's peer, Frances T. Cheetam, Cutter uttered not one word regarding his status as an untrained historian: "He was a politician and a lawyer, and officer of the State Historical Society." Moreover, in confining the notion of popularity exclusively to an English reading audience, the author of the necrology rendered inconsequential Read's overwhelming popularity among Nuevomexicanos. To deny merit to his English writing was to leave future readers, as Melendez aptly observes "with little or no compulsion to seriously entertain Read's work further" (1997, 130). True, the author acknowledges the positive aspect of Read's Spanish writing style; however, this praise rings hollow in light of the fact that by 1927 diglossia was the order of the day in New Mexico, with Spanish having been relegated to unofficial, unthreatening, and subsequently declining status.

Thus, is the erasure of Nuevomexicano historian, Benjamín Read achieved. The ultimate irony of this case is that ten years later, Lansing Bloom purchased Read's private collection of documents for the NM Historical Society for $350, assuring himself and his colleagues propriety control of materials that were so dear to Read's heart as he struggled in his endeavor to write *la verdadera historia de Nuevo Mexico.*[9]

Consequences of This Non-isolated Phenomenon

I would indeed be remiss if I treated Read's demise as a singular case. George I. Sánchez, whose words open this essay, is, ironically, another chapter in the history of relegation perpetrated against Nuevomexicano scholars by the purveyors of hegemonic agendas. With funding from the Carnegie Corporation Sánchez published in 1940 a study of the social, political and economic conditions affecting the lives of Nuevomexicanos in Taos Country. Despite broad acclaim and the significant contribution of this study to a deeper understanding of the region and its people, Sánchez was denied a promised tenured position at the University of New Mexico. Instead the University appointed him as a non-tenured research associate, thus minimizing the value of his work as a scholar and civil rights advocate. In order to save face, Sánchez had to leave his homeland and take a position at the University of Texas at Austin. His book, *Forgotten People,* would remain in the shadows until it was reissued in the wake of civil rights political movements that made visible America's forgotten racialized populations. And it was Chicano scholars, intent on challenging the reigning academic orthodoxy and the powers that sustained it, who rescued George I. Sánchez from oblivion and reinserted him into the annals of American history.

The acts if erasure discussed in this essay had severe consequences in that they severed several generations of Nuevomexicanos from the legacy of *another* historical perspective, one produced self-assuredly and authoritatively from the bottom up. Meanwhile, the self-fashioned, 'legitimate' historians of the power bloc ensured that their histories would reign supreme in the institutions responsible for educating future generations of Nuevomexicanos from the top down.

Notes

[1]Meléndez and Myer synthesize and elaborate on this biographical information; hence I include only the highlights of Read's biography.

[2]While this work was never published, it certainly struck a chord with fellow historians who issued a serialized version of the topic in the first issues of the *New Mexico Historical Review* making no mention of Read's previous work.

[3]Aside from this quip, it appears that relations between Read and Prince were on the whole friendly and courteous. Prince, in fact, was always respectful and admiring in his assessment of Read's work, and Read likewise found occasion to complement Prince's work.

[4]"I consider the acquisition of the speech made by Don Pedro Bautista Pino, while representing New Mexico in the Congreso de las Españas, November 20, 1812, as a specially brilliant achievement" (p. 806).

[5]Meyer rightly observes that Read knew his work "would not be taken seriously by Anglo scholar-historians who were, at the time, very preoccupied with professionalization in their ranks and dedicated to a 'posture of objectivity.' . . . Read knew that written documents would be persuasive in scholarly historical circles in a way that the traditional New Mexican oral folklore, the vehicle of much popular history, would not" (1996, 195). One might conclude, however, that her treatment of his contestatory work so heavily in terms of linguistic

injustice results in downplaying Read's preoccupation with the issue of narrative authority based on ethnic considerations.

[6]On May 21, 1911, Read responds to one Hon. Acacio Gallegos , who it seems complained to a gentleman who delivered his copy of the book about errors in his biographical sketch. Apparently Read did not take kindly to criticism; his curt response was as follows: "Sea eso como fuere me permito sugerir a ud. que me haga el favor de retornarme el libro si es que no esté ud. completamente satisfecho con él, pues no quiero que haya una sola persona que al comprar la obra venga a creer que lo hace meramente por hacerme favor a mi. Si la obra no tiene mérito para ser apreciada por el que la compra no seré yo quien me esmere en empujar la venta y mendigar la aprobación de la mismo siendo que el libro de por se recomiendo o se condena." (BMR Collection, NMRAC Series II, Folder 108)

[7]This particular point merits further discussion for it once again privileges counter-memory, using it as the basis to undermine the truth test of linear texts. In a footnote in chapter 17 of *Historia Ilustrada* Read confesses that new information received from the elder Aniceto Abeytia, a contemporary of Armijo, led him to alter the chapter. As previously written he had merely repeated the accusations of cowardice propagated by other historians, among them Bancroft. According to Abeytia, Armijo realized that he had insufficient arms with which to supply his men and his decision to not face Kearney was made in the interest of avoiding "innecesario derramamiento de sangre" (*Guerra* 1910, 229).

[8]A rebuttal by Bloom to Father Zephyrin Englehardt and other critics of his work can be found in the journal, *Old Santa Fe*, I:4, April 1914, pp. 437-442.

[9]Bloom writes the following to one Hester, who seems to be the secretary for the New Mexico Historical Review: "My first offer was $300 for the lot, including my first estimate of about 50 books from the shelves. But when I made my selection, we found I had about 100 volumes, and they asked if I wouldn't make it $350—the same amount I told them we had paid the Twitchell estate for MSS and books. I felt it was wise to leave them satisfied, and they said they were with that amount. $200 for that portfolio of MSS may seem high, but I believe they are well worth it; and$100 is certainly reasonable for the books and pamphlets which we got" (BMR Collection, NMRAC, Series II, Folder 58).

Works Cited

An Illustrated History of New Mexico. Chicago: The Lewis Publishing Co., 1985. (No author listed)

Bloom, Lansing. "New Mexico in 1822." *Old Santa Fe: A Magazine of History, Archeology, Genealogy, and Biography* I:2 (October 1913): 132-209.

Limerick Nelson, Patricia. "The Adventures of the Frontier in The Twentieth Century." In Grossman James, R. editor, *The Frontier in American Culture*. Chicago: The Newberry Library, 1994.

Lipsitz, George. *Time Passages: Collective Memory and American Popular Culture.* Minneapolis: University of Minnesota Press, 1990.

Meléndez, A. Gabriel. *So All Is Not Lost: The Poetics of Print in Nuevomexicano Communities, 1834-1958*. Albuquerque: University of New Mexico Press, 1997.

Myer, Doris. *Speaking for Themselves: Neomexicano Cultural Identity and the Spanish-language Press, 1880-1920.* Albuquerque: University of New Mexico Press, 1996.

Padilla, Genaro. *My History, Not Tours: The Formation of Mexican American Autobiography.* Madison: University of Wisconsin Press, 1993.

Read, Benjamin M. *Guerra México-Americana.* Santa Fe: Compañía Impresora del Nuevo Mexicano, 1910

_____. *Historia Ilustrada de Nuevo México.* Santa Fe: Compañía Impresora del Nuevo Mexicano, 1911.

_____. *Illustrated History of New Mexico.* Santa Fe: New Mexico Printing Co., 1912.

_____. *Popular Elementary History of New Mexico.* Santa Fe: B.M. Read. 1914.

_____. *Chronological Digest of the "Documentos inéditos del Archivo de las Indias."* Albuquerque: Albright A. Anderson Printers-Binders, 1914.

_____. *A Short History of Slavery in America*. St. Louis: Amerika, 1919.

_____. *A Treatise on the Disputed Points of the History of New Mexico.* Santa Fe: B.M. Read, 1919.

Sánchez, George I. *Forgotten People: A Study of New Mexicans.* Albuquerque: Calvin Horn Publisher, 1967.

Otero, Miguel Antonio. *My Nine Years as Governor of the Territory of New Mexico, 1897-1906.* Albuquerque: University of New Mexico Press, 1940..

Twitchell, Ralph Emerson. *The History of the Military Occupation of the Territory of New Mexico from 1846 to 1851 by the Government of the United States.* Denver: The Smith-Brooks Company, 1909.

_____. *Old Santa Fe: The Story of New Mexico's Ancient Capital.* Santa Fe: Santa Fe New Mexican Pub. Corp. 1925.

Archival Collections:

Benjamin Read Collection, New Mexico Records and Archives.

Bruce T. Ellis Collection, Fray Angelico Chavez Library.

L. Bradford Prince Collection, New Mexico Records and Archives

Journals and Newspapers:

El Independiente, May 5, 1910.

The New Mexico Historical Review, Rpnt. Vol. 1:1 1926; II:4, 1927.

Old Santa Fe: A Magazine of History, Archeology, Genealogy, and Biography. Santa Fe: Old Santa Fe Press, I:2, October 1913.

"Las Almas y Las Letras:" Recovering Fray Angélico Chávez's Poetry

Manuel M. Martín-Rodríguez
University of California, Merced

Religion and Poetry: The Cervantine Background

Biographers and critics often describe Fray Angélico Chávez as a Renaissance man, given his multifaceted activity as a priest, a humanist, a historian, a poet, a narrator, a painter, an architect, and a soldier.[1] Testimonies of those activities are found in his years as a missionary in several Indian pueblos of New Mexico, his documentary reconstruction of the Nuevomexicano past, numerous books of poetry and short stories, his frescoes at and overall restoration of the Peña Blanca church, and his participation as an army chaplain in World War II.

Consequently, focusing on any one of those activities to the detriment of the others might be perceived as a somewhat reductionist approach to this monumental figure of Hispanic New Mexico and, indeed, the case has been made for a more encompassing discussion of Chávez's intellectual and artistic contributions. Ellen McCracken, for instance, suggests that

> [f]or Fray Angélico the verbal and the visual are elements of a continuum in which 'strong' forms of one or the other predominate at either end, and numerous intermediary, composite works fill in the center positions. ("Iconicity" 53)

In the same vein, and in the same volume in which McCracken's article appeared, I analyzed the intricate web of literary and visual discourses that combined to produce Fray Angélico's poetic masterpiece *The Virgin of Port Lligat* ("Painting the Word" passim).

And yet, even the most integrated or integrationist analysis of Chávez's artistic and scholarly activities must reveal that, much in the Tomistic tradition, his entire creative production is ancilla theologiae, that is, subordinate to religious thought and doctrine.[2] Such is indeed the case for his stories and poems, as well as for his paintings, exceptions notwithstanding. Moreover, that is also the case for most of Chávez's historical production. As Mario T. García suggests, Fray Angélico approached the discipline of history with the same missionary zeal he had shown in his pastoral endeavors. García concludes that for Chávez "[h]istory, especially the role of the Hispano Church, would bring new spiritual and cultural nourishment to his people" ("Fray Angélico" 27). Accordingly, García continues, "Chávez's focus on religion was a way of asserting ethnic identity and opposing a growing Anglo-American historical presence that was pushing Chávez's subjects to the margins" (26-27), something that should be apparent to anyone who has read Chávez's *My Penitente Land*, the rather personalistic history of Hispanic New Mexico that is both the sum of and the best introduction to Chávez's intellectual and artistic world.

Given this tension between the integrated, Renaissance-inspired portrayal of Fray Angélico, on the one hand, and the necessary gradation of his activities, on the other, I frame this essay on Chávez around a formula that summarizes the somewhat similar and much better known debate on the superiority of either las armas or las letras (i.e. the military or the literary career). The debate can be traced to ancient Greek literature and, as far as the Hispanic world is concerned, it culminates in Don Quijote's famous speech on the subject in the first part of Cervantes' novel (1605):[3] at the threshold of the Baroque, the ideal of the Renaissance caballero who (like Garcilaso de la Vega) represented the harmonious combination of both disciplines was no longer viable; Cervantes (a war veteran himself, much like Fray Angélico), thus has his Don Quijote assert that military activity is doubtless superior to letters. Leaving aside the ironic nuances of such a proclamation (coming, as it does, from a literary character whose sanity is compromised by avid reading), what interests me is the exception that Don Quijote immediately acknowledges. According to the hidalgo, divine letters, whose intention is "llevar y encaminar las almas al cielo" (I, 465), are superior to both military discipline and humanistic letters.

With such a subtle switch from "armas" to "almas," Cervantes—true to the spirit of his times—acknowledges the primacy of religion and religious thought over any other human activity; and he does so in a novel first published in 1605, only seven years after Juan de Oñate's expedition to New Mexican lands, and well before the second colonization by De Vargas that followed the Pueblo revolt of 1680 (at a time when Cervantes' novel had circulated widely throughout the Americas, including New Mexico).[4]

Fray Angélico, a descendant of Dulcinea,[5] experienced a Lepanto of his own three centuries later in the Pacific Ocean and, after a taste of both armas y letras, did not hesitate to concur with Don Quijote and to reaffirm the superiority of divine letters, in what Father Jack C. Robinson has called "an entire life spent bringing art and history to the service of faith" (115).

In a sense, therefore, and precisely because of the emphasis that Fray Angélico places on history, genealogy, and the foundational moments that Cervantes, Oñate, and De Vargas represent for Hispanic New Mexico, Chávez's work is first and foremost a documentation of how the late-Renaissance/early-Baroque view that Cervantes represented in his novel extended into the Southwest colonial enclave of New Mexico and shaped its cultural and spiritual life for centuries to come. In *My Penitente Land*, Chávez makes the task quite explicit, when he compares Oñate's expedition and the first Spanish settlements with Sancho Panza's promised reward of an ínsula to govern: "At last Don Quijote had led Sancho Panza to his very own dukedom around the time that their fictional history was being written" (173). But, much as Sancho was to discover the intricacies and difficulties of a just government during his short stay at the headship of the Ínsula Barataria, the victory of the Spanish armas in New Mexico (that Oñate epitomized) also presented the problem of what to do with the almas of the newly subjected peoples as well as those of the colonists. The ensuing tensions between the military commanders and the Franciscan friars in New Mexico are well documented,[6] and they appear as a topic in many of Fray Angélico's works. That he normally sides with his Franciscan brethren should come as no surprise, but the strategy he employs to do so is most relevant for this analysis, as I will explore in the next section.

Fray Angélico's "Recovery Project"

Throughout his works, Fray Angélico (re)constructs a chain of religious texts from or about New Mexico that provides spiritual continuity while serving as an alternative history of the Spanish colony. In *My Penitente Land*, for instance, he follows the above quote on Sancho Panza with a discussion of Fray Alonso de Benavides' 1630 *Memorial*, the first long colonial text authored by a fellow Franciscan in New Mexico.[7] This, in turn, is accompanied by a similar reclamation of other religious leaders of Hispanic New Mexico, including Fray Francisco Atanasio Domínguez (in the eighteenth century), and Padre Antonio José Martínez (in the nineteenth century). Chávez's documentation and discussion of the intellectual and religious history of New Mexico could be described, therefore, as a recovery project of sorts, that attempted to retrace and preserve a cultural and historical experience marked by the continuous habitation of a certain geographical space by the descendants of a group of settlers from the Spain of Cervantes, and by the spiritual and intellectual guidance of the Franciscan friars first, and of native religious leaders later.[8] It would not be farfetched to think that Chávez must have considered himself and his works as part (if not as the culmination) of that continuum, and that his writings must be read, therefore, not only against the synchronic background of his visual arts endeavors—as McCracken pertinently suggests—but also as the diachronic continuation and climax of colonial and nineteenth-century religious thought in New Mexico, that is, as a history of how las letras have served las almas over time in New Mexico.

In this sense, Chávez's own contribution to religious thinking permeates all aspects of his works. This includes paintings (the frescoes in Peña Blanca, 1938), explicitly spiritual works (*Seraphic Days*, a 327 pp. tome published anonymously in 1940),[9] historical treatises on the Church in New Mexico (*The Old Faith and Old Glory: Story of the Church in New Mexico since the American Occupation*, 1946), novels (*La Conquistadora*, 1954), short stories (*From an Altar Screen*, 1957), history (*Coronado's Friars*, 1968), biography (*But Time and Chance: The Story of Padre Martínez de Taos*, 1981), and—-of course—-an abundant corpus of (predominantly) religious poetry, on which this essay concentrates.

Fray Angélico Chávez's Poetry

Fray Angélico published five books of poetry during his lifetime. They appeared over a period of thirty years, from 1939 (*Clothed with the Sun*), to 1969 (*Selected Poems with an Apologia*). In addition, Chávez published numerous poems in religious and lay periodicals since 1925. With few exceptions, Chávez's poetic activity is almost entirely restricted to the second quarter of the twentieth century, since only a few of his poems appeared after 1950.[10] The latter part of Chávez's literary and scholarly life was devoted to creative prose and historical works and editions.

In *Selected Poems*, the "apologetic" Chávez explains this switch, noting that "the pure English lyric poetry which I so much loved and strove after in the first half of this century suddenly became outmoded—-and I myself with it" (n.p.). Expressing well-earned pride in some of his accomplishments, Chávez closes out his poetic days with *Selected Poems*, confessing that having been "noticed briefly by the [literary] gods of his day" (n.p.) was satisfaction enough for him.

I would like to propose a different reading of Fray Angélico's poetry; one that is not dependent upon the interests of the "gods of his day," but that considers how his poems continue to be relevant for readers in our own times, and particularly for those readers who share with the friar his intense love and respect for their U.S. Hispanic origin. Moreover, I propose to consider Chávez's poetry as the most successful distillation of his religious thoughts, and to read it as one of the latest links in that chain of religious texts that Fray Angélico himself so carefully reconstructed. Consequently, I believe that his poems acquire an added dimension of historical depth and cultural agency that goes well beyond what the artistic rigors of the pure English lyric poetry might have demanded from their author.

In addition, in re-reading Chávez's poetry against the grain of his literary testament (the "Apologia" just quoted), I also intend to restore the balance that Fray Angélico disrupted there. In that poetical swan song, Chávez alluded only to his enjoyment and appreciation of Anglo-Saxon letters (including Burns, Tennyson, Stevenson, and Poe, among others), and he portrayed himself as a continuation of that venerable line; but he neglected to remind his readers of how deeply he also felt the presence of the Spanish mystic poets and of the Mexican romantic and post-romantic bards.

By restoring those de-emphasized presences in his poems, I claim that Fray Angélico's verses can also be read as a literary response to the predominant bent that the "gods of his day" had given to lyric poetry and, to paraphrase Mario García, as a way of asserting ethnic identity and opposing a growing Anglo-American historical presence that was pushing Chávez's subjects to the margins. Like his beloved Santa Fe, therefore, Chávez's poetry stands at a crossroad between the Hispanic and the Anglo-American worlds, and it seems important to explore those other avenues he left unmentioned in his "Apologia" as a way to initiate a full recovery of his poetical work.

Major Works

Chávez's first published book of poems, *Clothed with the Sun*, is a collection of thirty-one pieces, twenty-nine of which had already appeared in print in periodicals. The book is divided in three sections, "Morning . . . ," "Noon . . . ," "and Night . . . ," within which several thematic clusters develop. The larger of these is, not surprisingly, composed of poems inspired by biblical events or characters. But, in many of them, Chávez gives biblical solemnity a down-to-earth twist that becomes characteristic of much of his poetry.[11] In "Trees," for example, the good thief compares his crucifixion (which allows him to "steal" Jesus' heart) with the joy of climbing trees to enter people's houses.

Throughout the book, this emphasis on the human side of the religious experience is aided by several compositions in which a Franciscan spirit combines with the deeply-ingrained New Mexican veneration for nature to result in a sustained canticle to the Southwest, its landscape, and its people. "Peña Blanca," "A Dance in Cochití," "Singing Cowboy" and other similarly inspired compositions are representative of this trend. This is, of course, no impediment to other more theologically profound poems, such as the much celebrated "Stigmata of Saint Francis" or "Ecce Ancilla."

Stylistically, *Clothed with the Sun* is also significant for several conceptual short poems, each of them devoted to the development of a central metaphor, such as "Communion" and "Prisoner." These poems are important in themselves for the craftsmanship they demonstrate, but also because they allow us to begin reconstructing that other side of Fray Angélico's literary genealogy to which I alluded above: Spanish (religious) poetry. While the conceptual poems in *Clothed with the Sun* are not as hermetic as those of Spanish conceptismo, it is clear nonetheless that Chávez was well acquainted with Calderón de la Barca and other Baroque poets from Golden Age Spain, and that his conceptual poems are to be understood as a twentieth century offspring of that tradition.[12]

The importance of the cult of the Virgin Mary, announced in the title of Fray Angélico's first book (and central to Hispanic Catholicism worldwide), is made all the more explicit in the next volume he published, *Eleven Lady-Lyrics* (1945). With Mary as an overwhelming presence, Chávez combines in *Eleven Lady-Lyrics* three kinds of poems. The first, of particular significance for Chicano/a and Mexican American literature, is composed of those pieces inspired by his experiences in World War II. Anticipating by several decades the Korean War poems of Rolando Hinojosa, as well as later compositions inspired by the Vietnam war, Fray Angélico is here at his elegiac best, particularly for his ability to bring the brutal experience of combat into a human dimension that includes poems to fallen comrades as well as Franciscan-inspired, tongue-in-cheek compositions about dealing with bugs and other less than likable animals while in the trenches.

In addition, in *Eleven Lady-Lyrics* Fray Angélico continues with his conceptual poetry (as in the superb "Candidate" and "Vestments," in which he fuses natural cycles with liturgical rituals), as well as with his humoristic takes on everyday life, as in "To a Bishop Unfrocked" (on the transformations that render St. Nicholas into Santa Claus) or the much reprinted "To a Fly (on an Old Friar's Head)."

Occasionally, the poems in this book engage in a kind of subtle social criticism that can also be found elsewhere in Fray Angélico's works.[13] In "Brother Francis to Brother Sun," for instance, the poet goes a bit out of his poetic ways to criticize those matrons who prefer caring for a pet over maternity, thus commenting on modern social transformations in New Mexico. Likewise, in "A

Caballero Recalls Lamy," the poetic I expresses distrust for "those few foreigners/ Coming from the States of late" (83), while excepting Lamy from that distrust because of his "southern blood like ours" (83).

It is worth noting that Fray Angélico's intertextual web is extended at its fullest in this second book of his, in which explicit references to Homer, Dante, Enrique González Martínez, and Stevenson, among others, combine with other implicit presences (from the Spanish mystical writers mainly) to situate Chávez's poetry at the cultural and artistic crossroad that early twentieth century New Mexico represented. This synthesis of traditions, already noticed by Major and Pearce (147), allows Fray Angélico to embark on a rather ambitious poetical road in parts of *Eleven Lady-Lyrics* and, most noticeably, in his following volume, *The Single Rose: Poems of Divine Love* (1948). In fact, the third group of poems included in *Eleven Lady-Lyrics* is already written in the mystic vein that will characterize Chávez's next book of poetry, and since they reappear in *The Single Rose* with little or no variation (though incorporated into a more cohesive unit), I will discuss them in that context.

The Single Rose is, in fact, a single poem in seventeen cantos (plus a prologue and an epilogue), and it is written in the tradition of San Juan de la Cruz and Santa Teresa de Jesús.[14] As such, *The Single Rose* may be read as a New Mexican cántico espiritual or camino de perfección, in which every image is at the service of the sustained allegory that Fray Angélico constructs.xv True to mystical convention, however, in the commentary that accompanies the poems Chávez confesses the impossibility of his task, since he has to work with words, and he readily avows that "human language" cannot explain the religious simple fact that a rose is a Rose (38). But, read from a U.S. Hispanic context, one senses that Chávez's linguistic conundrum is also a metacommentary on his attempt at bicultural fusion, since he often resorts to introducing (and explaining) terms in Spanish into his English-language text whenever he finds the latter insufficiently expressive, as in the following passage:

> Our Spanish tongue has a word for this rare combination of white and red, namely, color de rosa, a hue in which the purity of whiteness and the ardor of redness have not entirely lost their identity. (38, original emphasis)

In so doing, Fray Angélico clearly separates what is truly ineffable (in a mystical sense) from what purely belongs to linguistic differences among human languages. At the same time, by engaging in this kind of bilingual commentary the poet succeeds in delineating his ideal (though not exclusive—-nor necessarily largest) audience: a New Mexican/Hispanic readership. This may also explain why, in such a complex and profound poetic work as *The Single Rose*, the populist Chávez keeps showing up here and there with the heartiness of a New Mexican Sancho Panza, as evidenced in the numerous sayings interspersed in the commentary in prose that accompanies the poem.[16]

After that sustained allegorical effort in *The Single Rose*, Chávez must have felt at the height of his poetic powers, for he then realized the pinnacle of his metaphoric and synthetic ability in the long poem *The Virgin of Port Lligat*, which appeared first in *Spirit* in 1956 and, three years later, was published as Fray Angélico's fourth book of poetry. *The Virgin* is an even more ambitious project than *The Single Rose*, for in it Chávez departs from what in the previous book could still be perceived as somewhat derivative, to engage in a truly original attempt at cultural syncretism. *The Virgin*, as I have suggested elsewhere,[17] is the poetic equivalent of St. Anselm's Monologium and Proslogium, where the deductive "proof" of God's existence was formulated. With the rhetorical discipline of his scholastic predecessor, and yet with the flair of the great poet he had become by then, Chávez combined in *The Virgin* classical mythology, nuclear science, surrealistic painting, and religious doctrine to explain the dogma of the Trinity. The result was a rather compelling poem full of surprising and well-crafted images that earned the praise of T. S. Eliot, and that never should have gone out of print.

For *The Virgin*, Fray Angélico tapped on well established literary precedents, from the English Metaphysical poets to Sor Juana Inés de la Cruz (as Paul Horgan has observed)[18] and many other Hispanic baroque poets, including Lope de Vega, Calderón de la Barca, and Góngora. Like to the latter, who often utilized the glosa to transform a lay stanza into an extended religious allegory, Fray Angélico used Salvador Dalí's painting "The Madonna of Port Lligat" as a catalyst for constructing a complex allegory of the Holy Trinity and of the life of Christ. The poem begins with an enigmatic interpretation of the painting (where Gala, the Spanish painter's wife and muse, appears as the Madonna, floating over an ethereal throne):

> The Sphinx of this our age is gentle-formed and sweet
> Not only in her woman's face and breast, for she
> Is all Eve's daughter to her feet.
> Whatever there may be of lioness
> Is energy;
> Whatever wings, a hovering loveliness
> Heedless of need for leaning hard on pedestal of stone,
> Untouched and touching nothing, free (1-3).[19]

Toward the end of the poem, in lines 76-81, the mystery is confronted directly, with a rhetorical question that explains it in a religious and scientific context, by way of an analogy to the atom's structure:

And days before, when earth and heaven were begun
With but a Word on which the Spirit swept in flight,
He spoke and breathed as *Elohim*;
Might not the tiniest indivisibles demand
That even the infinitely opposite Extreme
Have Proton, mutual Pneum, and still be One?
(23-25, original emphasis)

By invoking the galaxies next, the Franciscan Chávez manages to further connect science with religion, always highlighting the primacy of the latter:

Praised be the Lord for Brother Sun
And Sister Moon, for all great things above . . .
But most of all for that one Sister Star
That pointed to a stall
Where ox and ass one night
Saw in a wailing Nova how the Word that fashioned all,
By fusing with a maiden's molecules, geared infinite
To nuclear (25-27),

and thus the birth of Jesus is explained as a process of the nuclear fusion of "a maiden's molecules" and God as "the Word that fashioned all." With this reference, the poem brings the reader back to the beginning of the text (or even further back, to the painting as pre-text), rendering understandable what in Dalí was somewhat enigmatic: an egg that Dalí painted suspended over the Madonna, according to Chávez's poetical interpretation, emblematically contains the Holy Trinity, since it is an image of the fertilizing Word (God the father), the unborn baby (God the son), and the power of the Holy Spirit to "fus[e] with a maiden's molecules" (God the Holy Spirit, also implicit in the word "pneum" on page 25).

In *The Virgin*, Fray Angélico brings together many of his own previous interests (painting, religion, poetry), while adding science and others to the mixture that enrich his poetry with both artistic and social connotations. For a New Mexican context, in particular, the poetic inclusion of atomic energy becomes rather significant in light of the Trinity site nuclear test near Alamogordo in 1945, to which Chávez refers in his own commentary to the poem as an "uncanny coincidence" (61).

In fact, the connection between literature and the atomic test in New Mexico begs some analysis beyond the simple coincidence Fray Angélico claims. According to Richard Rhodes, nuclear laboratory head J. Robert Oppenheimer selected the Trinity name inspired by some of John Donne's metaphysical poems, most notably the sonnet "Batter my heart" (571). Oppenheimer is also said to have alluded to the Hindu sacred text *Bhagavad Gita* just after the test, in particular a verse that reads "I am become Death, the shatterer of worlds" (Hijiya 123). In contrast to Oppenheimer, Chávez invokes the nuclear, in his own metaphysical way, as a "visual symbol for the Trinity" (59), in the tradition of the Church Fathers and, in doing so, he emphasizes Incarnation as the origin and symbol of life, not death:

> the real Core and Purpose of all things made is the Incarnate Word, the Infinite One Whose act of Creation was, and is, child's play. As He sustains Creation in being through the continual re-birth of things in energy and matter, He causes further and lovelier transubstantiations in the Eucharist . . . (71, original capitals)

A World War II veteran, Chávez was no stranger to war and death, and he must have been acutely aware of the devastating effects of the nuclear bombs dropped on Japanese soil shortly after the New Mexican test. That he chose to emphasize life and redemption in *The Virgin*, however, is yet another sign of his deep religiosity at the time, and of his belief in the subordination of all human activities (nuclear science and literature included) to theological doctrine. His poem, therefore, is not only a masterful example of literary craft, but a New Mexican canticle to life and rebirth in the wake of destruction. As such, and in the context of the widespread Cold War nuclear fears, *The Virgin* reads as an utmost instance of Chávez's desire to provide spiritual and cultural nourishment to his people, and to do so in a way that reinstated a degree of cultural agency by bringing together the English- and Spanish-language lyric poetry traditions, classical mythology, and the art of Salvador Dalí, and by fusing them in a text that is proudly New Mexican and Hispano. Significantly, the book is dedicated "To John Duns [Scotus] fraternally, and to my dear parents on their Golden Wedding," thus emphasizing theology, history, family, and genealogy.

Conclusion

Chávez's decision to stop writing poetry shortly afterward, leaving as his testament and legacy the *Selected Poems*, is clearly his readers' loss, for it is likely that he would have been able to produce many more of what he called "inspired" poems in the latter part of his life. Furthermore, had he been active as a poet during his latter years, perhaps his poetry books would have been reprinted and made available to younger readers. But they were not, and Fray Angélico, the poet, remained better known among the "gods of his days" than among the mortals of our own.

To compound the problem, many of those poems that Fray Angélico began publishing in periodicals in 1925 were not included in his five poetry volumes. Out of a corpus of over three hundred and twenty original poems identified so far, fewer than thirty-five percent were printed in book form during his lifetime. That percentage changed dramatically with the recent and most welcome publication of *Cantares*, where almost one hundred and sixty poems that had never appeared in book form before were compiled. Yet, *Cantares* introduces another problem for the study of Fray Angélico's poetry, namely that it uses a manuscript dated 1925-1932. As such, *Cantares* makes available to our contemporary readers the original versions of poems that, in some cases, Chávez rewrote for subsequent publication in one of the more than forty periodicals and anthologies where his poetry appeared.

Additionally, even after the publication of *Cantares*, more than fifty of Fray Angélico's known poems remain unavailable in book form, buried in journals not easily accessible to the average reader. Recovering and reprinting Fray Angélico's complete poetry is thus a most urgent task that would result in a number of advantages for the scholar and for the reader in general, including better accessibility, the possibility to document Fray Angélico's evolution as a poet (through revisions and changes), and the facilitation of critical studies in the future. The Chicano/a Movement of the 1960s and 1970s, pressed as it was with a more urgent literary and social agenda, largely failed to notice the oppositional nuances and the artistic achievements of Fray Angélico's poetry and, in doing so, allowed the friar's poetic works to fade away from the public arena. I believe it is time to redress that unfortunate turn of events, and to embark on a serious recovery of Chávez's lyrical works. If that recuperation is done with attention to intellectual, social, and artistic events of the times in which his poetry books were published, and if the poetry is read alongside Chávez's historical works and his creative works in prose, it would become apparent that recovering Fray Angélico's verses would also serve to bring to light the work of those other religious writers whom he considered his precursors in producing an alternative cultural history of New Mexico.

Notes

[1]Cf. Tomley: "In Santa Fe, on March 18, 1996, Father Angélico Chávez passed from the scene late in his eighty-fifth year. This Renaissance man, who in addition to being a Franciscan priest was a poet, a dramatist, a novelist, a translator, a historian, an archivist, an architect, a literary reviewer, a soldier, and an artist, was to many the essence of a true New Mexican" (n.p.).

[2]While traditionally associated with Thomas Aquinas, the idea of the subordination of philosophy to theology is older than St. Thomas (St. Peter Damian, for

instance, was already suggesting this in the eleventh century), and it continues beyond St. Thomas to permeate—among others—Franciscan thinkers such as Aquinas's contemporary Raymond Lull (see Copleston 456ff).

[3]For a summary of this debate, see Avalle Arce's footnote 10 on his edition of *Don Quijote de La Mancha* (vol. 1, 470). As I will discuss below, Fray Angélico considered *Don Quijote* a most revealing text for what he terms the "soul history" of New Mexico, and thus my selection of this text to frame my research is all the more appropriate. "The Soul History of Spanish New Mexico" is the subtitle of *My Penitente Land.*

[4]For America in general, see Leonard, chapter 7. In the case of New Mexico, Adams and Scholes identify *Don Quijote* as one of the books in Governor López de Mendizábal's library (262). Other relevant books Adams and Scholes mention include works by St. Teresa de Jesús (among the books found by De Vargas at Zuñi in 1692), as well as works by the Spanish conceptistas Quevedo and Gracián (260-65).

[5]Chávez applies this term several times to characterize New Mexicans: "Fully aware that he is no longer a 'Spaniard' properly so called—-un gachupín—-the Spanish New Mexican still feels that he is somehow a true español, somehow a long-lost scion of *Don Quijote*'s Dulcinea del Toboso even when a Vivaldo from Spain might raise an eyebrow" (*My Penitente Land*, 267; original italics). See also pp. 173, 179, and 202 of the same work.

[6]The escalation of tensions culminates in 1661-1664, when Governor Diego de Peñalosa arrests the head of the Inquisition in New Mexico, and when he is, in turn, tried by that ecclesiastical body. For a useful chronology of these and other events in the evangelization of New Mexico, see Lachaga, 38-46.

[7]Fray Angélico was also well acquainted with an even earlier New Mexican text, Gaspar Pérez de Villagrá's *Historia de la Nueva México* (1610), which he discusses in *My Penitente Land* repeatedly.

[8]See, for instance, his *But Time and Chance.*

[9]The book is a series of meditations on different saints' days and other religious festivities (chronologically arranged according to the liturgical calendar), interspersed with personal, devotional fragments.

[10]One of those poems, "*The Virgin of Port Lligat*" appeared in 1956 in *Spirit*, later becoming a book on its own, upon the recommendation of T.S. Eliot.

[11]Major and Pearce have also commented on this trait of Fray Angélico's style. For them, Chávez "is reminiscent of William Blake with Biblical images employed unexpectedly, often whimsically" (147).

[12]On the presence of books by Spanish conceptistas in New Mexican libraries, see note 4. In addition, Chávez's early manuscript (later published as *Cantares*) includes a "Sonnet from the Spanish of Calderón."

[13]For examples, see *From an Altar Screen*, pp. 79-80, where Chávez treats one of his favorite subjects (the lack of appreciation by French priests of New Mexican santos), or the story "My Ancestor Don Pedro" (in *The Short Stories*, 125-219), where he pokes fun at the Easterners who appropriate New Mexican lore. For a critical assessment, see Padilla's "Introduction" to *The Short Stories*, especially pp. xvi-xvii.

[14]The influence is made explicit in the commentary that follows the poem, where the commentator states with appropriate modesty: "I doubt if our land will be blessed with another Juan de la Cruz or another Sor Teresa, at least not in our time" (37). The commentary included with *The Single Rose* is attributed to Fray Manuel de Santa Clara, an allusion to the poet's real first name and to his place of birth (see Morales, 15).

[15]Moreover, Fray Angélico anticipates a subsequent interest in the Spanish mystics by Chicano/a authors such as Gloria Anzaldúa and Cherríe Moraga, some of whose compositions resonate with the amorous oxymorons that permeate the stanzas of San Juan and Santa Teresa. For more on this connection, see my *Life in Search of Readers*, ch. 3.

[16]"It may also be said in all truth . . . that the love of an imperfect lover can be just as ardent as that of the perfect one; but while the latter falls into the Beloved's arms, the former meets with a closed door, as we say in Spanish. (Le dan con la puerta en las narices)" (42, original parenthesis and emphasis). In this, of course, Chávez is not entirely unlike Santa Teresa or San Juan de la Cruz, who likewise resorted to colloquialisms in their mystic poems.

[17]"Painting the Word," 93.

[18]Horgan's ideas are quoted on the jacket copy of *The Virgin*'s first edition. For his part, Chávez himself had commented on his fascination with Blake's poetry on his *Selected Poems, With an Apologia*.

[19]The text of the poem is printed on the odd pages only in the first edition. The even pages contain a drawing representing an atom.

Works Cited

Adams, Eleanor B., and France V. Scholes. "Books in New Mexico, 1598-1680." *New Mexico Historical Review* XVII (1942): 226-270.

Cervantes Saavedra, Miguel de. *Don Quijote de la Mancha*. Ed. Juan B. Avalle-Arce. Madrid: Alhambra, 1983. 2 vols.

Chávez, Fray Angélico. *But Time and Chance: The Story of Padre Martínez of Taos, 1793-1867*. Santa Fe: Sunstone Press, 1981.

_____. *Cantares: Canticles and Poems of Youth*. Houston: Arte Público Press, 2000.

_____. *Clothed with the Sun*. Santa Fe: Writers' Editions, 1939.

_____. *La Conquistadora: The Autobiography of an Ancient Statue*. Patterson: St. Anthony Guild, 1954.

_____. *Coronado's Friars*. Washington, D.C.: Academy of American Franciscan History, 1968.

_____. *Eleven Lady-Lyrics and Other Poems*. Patterson: St. Anthony Guild, 1945.

_____. *From An Altar Screen/El Retablo: Tales from New Mexico*. New York: Farrar, Straus & Cudary, 1957.

_____. *The Old Faith and Old Glory: Story of the Church in New Mexico since the American Occupation, 1846-1946*. Santa Fe: The Santa Fe Press, 1946.

_____. *My Penitente Land: The Soul Story of Spanish New Mexico*. 1974. Santa Fe: William Gannon, 1979.

_____. *Selected Poems With an Apologia*. Santa Fe: The Press of the Territorian, 1969.

_____. *Seraphic Days: Franciscan Thoughts and Affections on the Principal Feasts of Our Lord and Our Lady and All the Saints of the Three Orders of the Seraph of Assissi*. Ed. Sebastian Erbacher, O.F.M. Detroit: Duns Scotus College, 1940.

_____. *The Short Stories of Fray Angélico Chávez*. Ed. Genaro M. Padilla. Albuquerque: University of New Mexico Press, 1987.

_____. *The Single Rose: Poems of Divine Love*. Santa Fe: Los Santos Bookshop, 1948.

_____. *The Virgin of Port Lligat*. Fresno: Academy Library Guild, 1959.

Copleston, Frederick, S.J. *A History of Philosophy, vol. 2: Medieval Philosophy*. 1962. New York: Doubleday, 1993.

García, Mario T. "Fray Angélico Chávez, Religiosity, and New Mexican Oppositional Historical Narrative." McCracken 25-36.

Hijiya, James A. "The Gita of Robert Oppenheimer." *Proceedings of the American Philosophical Society* 144.2 (June 2000): 123-67.

Lachaga, José M. de. *El pueblo hispano en USA: Minorías étnicas y la Iglesia católica*. Bilbao: Desclée de Brouwer, 1982.

Leonard, Irving A. *Books of the Brave: Being an Account of Books and of Men in the Spanish Conquest and Settlement of the Sixteenth-Century New World*. 1949. Berkeley: University of California Press, 1992.

Major, Mabel, and T.M. Pearce. *Southwest Heritage: A Literary History with Bibliographies*. Albuquerque: University of New Mexico Press, 1972.

Martín-Rodríguez, Manuel M. *Life in Search of Readers: Reading (in) Chicano/a Literature*. Albuquerque: University of New Mexico Press, 2003.

_____. "Painting the Word/Wording the Painting: Allegory and Intertextuality in *The Virgin of Port Lligat* by Fray Angélico Chávez." McCracken 91-100.

McCracken, Ellen. "Iconicity and Narrative in the Work of Fray Angélico Chávez." McCracken 53-90.

_____. ed. *Fray Angélico Chávez: Poet, priest, and artist*. Albuquerque: University of New Mexico Press, 2000.

Morales, Phyllis S. *Fray Angélico Chávez: A Bibliography of His Published Writings (1925-1978)*. Santa Fe: The Lightning Tree, 1980.

Rhodes, Richard. *The Making of the Atomic Bomb*. New York: Simon and Schuster, 1986.

Robinson, Jack C., O.F.M. "Fray Angélico Chávez: The Roots of Franciscan Priesthood." McCracken 111-25.

Tomley, Don. "Homage to an Extraordinary Man: Fray Angélico Chávez, O.F.M. (1910-1996)." <http://nmsantos.com/cgi-local/shop.pl/SID=1068469781.11938/page=FrayAngelico14.htm>.

New Mexican Triptychs: Anglo Southwesternism, Chicano Nationalism, and the Tri-Partite Cultural Critique of Fray Angélico Chávez's Fiction

Melina Vizcaíno-Alemán
University of New Mexico

Introduction: Triculturalism, Triptych, and Chávez's Cultural Critique

Fray Angélico Chávez published his first book of poetry, *Clothed With the Sun*, in 1939, one year before the Coronado Cuatro Centennial celebration. The book and the fiesta were products of the Santa Fe writer's colony, its vision, and its funding—all three of which facilitated the emergence, development, and dissemination of what Chris Wilson calls the state's "tri-culturalism," an ideology that fancies the (mostly) harmonious historical relations between Native, Hispanic, and Anglo Americans in the Southwest.[1] *Clothed With the Sun*, for instance, "was spearheaded by Witter Bynner, John Gould Fletcher, Haniel Long, and Alice Corbin [Henderson], the latter a co-founder of *Poetry* magazine" (García xxvii). The book participated in the inauguration of the state's tri-cultural Indian-Anglo-Hispanic paradigm, as Chávez's poem, "Adventurers in Cibola," demonstrates. While the poem's history and form maintains New Mexico's tri-cultural apparatus, it simultaneously maintains and blurs time and space, producing in the process a cultural critique that works through three panels of imagery, history, and ideology. Chávez's literary work thus provides a foundation on which to negotiate the history of Chicano/a cultural production and Anglo American "Southwesternism" because he participated in both the counter-hegemonic and orientalist modes of Southwestern narration.

As Marta Weigle explains, Anglo "Southwesternism," the appropriation of New Mexico's native cultures, is a "'discourse' that can be examined in the development of Santa Fe Style and other aspects of tourism and Southwestern lures" (Weigle 1990 535). Weigle posits the notion of orientalism to describe New Mexico's post-World War I tourist industry, and Ramón Gutierrez applies the term specifically to Charles Lummis' writings about the Southwest. White men like Charles Lummis, Gutierrez argues, used the Southwest to resolve the U.S.'s anxiety over masculinity during the nineteenth century's urban industrialization, and Pueblo Indians "were the true America that had to be preserved for citizens of the Eastern United States" (Gutierrez 21). In 1892, Charles Lummis, a Harvard graduate and friend of Theodore Roosevelt, made his fabled journey across America in which he walked from Ohio to Los Angeles seeking refuge in the Southwest's arid climate and a job with the *Los Angeles Times*. Lummis participated in what Gutierrez calls "an ideology of primitive masculinity" that redeemed Anglo-American men during the Progressive era (Gutierrez 15). Thus, as Frederick Jackson Turner was literally closing the Western frontier, Lummis and a cadre of Anglo American refugees were literarily re-opening the Southwest and re-imagining New Mexico as the U.S. Orient. Anglo-American art and literature, alongside the emergence of anthropology and the ethnographic moment, generated New Mexico's romance and in the process reconfigured the mytho-poetic landscape to insert an Anglo American historical presence alongside the Southwest's Native and Hispanic histories.

Chávez's published writings reverse dominant Anglo narratives and histories about the Southwest in much the same way that Chávez reversed Lummis' path: when Lummis was telling the nation to "see America first," Chávez trekked to Ohio in 1924 to study in a Franciscan seminary. As Chávez studied in the Midwest, members of the Santa Fe art colony, led by Mary Austin, initiated the Spanish Colonial Arts Revival Movement in 1926, seven years after the School of American Research revived the Santa Fe fiesta. Anglo American authors and New Mexican art colonies during the 1930s fueled the tourist industry and reconfigured the Progressive era's orientalist narratives about the Southwest through the myth of tri-cultural harmony (Weigle and Fiore 1982 vii). The interest in New Mexico's Spanish identity inaugurated the state's Mexican American population into its tourist economy and art colonies. When Chávez returned to New Mexico to receive the Franciscan habit in 1937, he was a prolific Catholic poet who quickly became an affiliate of the Santa Fe artist's colony.

Chávez was an artist who participated in New Mexico's tri-culturalism, but he was also a priest whose religious devotion—and later, disillusionment—shaped his work as well. The tri-cultural model that identifies New Mexico as a state compliments the Trinitarian structure of Chávez's religious ideology, and his repetition of the number three in both the form and content of his work recalls the medieval notion of trinal triplicity, a Christian fascination with the numeral three (Cosman 249). Chávez's triadic narratives are products of both the secular and religious discourses that shape New Mexico history, and the trinal base of his work is both a mythic and historic trope that collapses binaries and the categories that define Anglo Southwesternism and Chicano nationalism. In particular, the notion of a triptych, a medieval art form that consists of a "series of three hinged panels, arranged and attached so that the outer wing panels can fold together to cover the central panel" (Cosman 250), is a useful paradigm of analysis to understand the cultural, political, and religious layers of New Mexico history in Chávez's writing. Chávez's Franciscan namesake, the Dominican Florentine painter, Fra Angelico, produced a series of paintings in the form of a triptych, and Chávez adapted the triptych form to his regional stories about New Mexico.[2] New Mexico's tri-culturalism accounts for one facet—the surface—of Chávez's work, while the politics of resistance are somewhere beneath the surface, but the triptych narrative mode adds a third category to challenge both the surface and subtextual narrative layers to view Chávez's work as a hyprid corpus complicit with and oppositional to Anglo and emergent Chicano/a discourses in the Southwest.

Chávez develops this literary triptych in his 1940 book of short stories, *New Mexico Triptych*, through the incorporation of Chávez's black-and-white drawings arranged in three panels to represent visually his three short stories. The overall affect of the book's front cover recalls a black-and white picture of an eighteenth-century New Mexican *retablo* (tableaux). "The Penitente Thief" is the second of three stories in *New Mexico Triptych*, and it re-tells the biblical narrative of the good thief against the backdrop of the Penitente brotherhood's demise in Northern New Mexico with the rise of Anglo American enterprise and a commercial economy. By 1940, the year of Coronado's Cuatro Centennial Celebration and official inauguration of the state's Spanish American population into its tri-cultural paradigm, the Spanish Colonial Arts revival movement was in full swing with the support of Anglo artists, philanthropists, and writers. Chávez's story is as much about the displacement of Hispano autonomy and the Penitente power structure in the nineteenth century as it is about the modern, Anglo-authored narratives about New Mexico's Spanish folk heritage. The story pushes the boundary between real and imagined events, and the literal and symbolic practices of New Mexico's folk cultures, and while the story's theme of theft literally refers to its two Hispano protagonists, Lucero and Maldonado, it also points to the theft-like displacement of Hispanos from the Anglo-authored discourses about New Mexico's Hispanidad.

Chávez structures the story in three sections to maintain his triptych metaphor, and "The Penitente Thief" takes place over the course of three years, following the odd events that recur in Lucero and Maldonado's lives during Holy Week and Good Friday, ostensibly the day of the Penitente's re-enactment of Christ's crucifixion. Lucero and Maldonado, two drunken old friends, are thieves of opposable natures, for while Lucero robs for a quick fix of *aguardiente*, Maldonado is an educated (Anglicized) thief, an attorney, who preys on widows and orphans. Maldonado advises Lucero to "cheat the widow and the orphan, even kill—but never rob the bank or steal a horse. The government and the vigilantes will surely get you!" (Chávez [1940] 1976 37). Each year, while in drunken states of stupor, Lucero and Maldonado proceed up Mt. Calvario and earnestly crucify a Christ-like figure in the absence of their Penitente brethren. The brotherhood accuses them of witchcraft when the two old friends confess, but while Maldonado is convinced that he is cursed, Lucero is apprehensive because he dreams up his plots of robbery when drunk and then enacts them when he is conscious. On one occasion, Lucero breaks into the local mission church and steals a large chalice *de oro mexicano* from the sacristy, but he is quickly apprehended, jailed for ten months, and released under Maldonado's political machinations. In the end, however, Maldonado cannot, or will not, rescue his friend from an angry lynch mob that strings up Lucero for stealing the horse of an Anglo villager. Before Lucero perishes, though, he reveals that Maldonado killed Doña Encarnación—a representative of old Spanish gentility—for his share of her estate. Upon hearing this, her nephew shoots and kills Maldonado at point blank. The story thus ambivalently concludes with Lucero's final act of betrayal that both redeems him as the good thief and punishes him for participating in the corruptible machinations of the state's new political regime.

Chicano literary critic Genaro Padilla accurately surmises that Chávez's narratives are double voiced with a surface narrative and a subtextual one. "On the surface narrative," says Padilla, "Chávez's tales are genial, easy to read, written in a style that draws upon the rich resources of informal storytelling in the Hispano communities of New Mexico, as well as the more formal *cuento* tradition in the Southwest" (xi). Noting Chávez's socio-historical references, Padilla argues that, "specific historical and cultural issues remain hidden somewhere in the background of each tale's morality structure" (xii). "The Penitente Thief" can be read as an allegory of class struggle that laments the demise of New Mexico's folk culture, but it also implicates the native Hispano population for its complicit role in the commodification, theft, and reproduction of the region's conflicted history. As Padilla notes, Chávez's narratives are double-voiced social allegories that speak for and against a dominant Anglo audience, yet Chávez's triptych work moves beyond dualism: it enacts social allegories that recall, revise, and reproduce New Mexico's tri-cultural predicament(s). We might think of Chávez work as tripartite historical fictions in the sense that they provide a surface narrative for Anglo consumption; a counter *cuento* narrative, to follow Padilla, that speaks for New Mexico's Hispano population; and a subtextual narrative that critiques both colonial histories by calling the category "native" into question. The myth of tri-cultural harmony, in other words, becomes in Chávez's work a mode of triptych cultural critique.

The Courthouse Raid, the Civil Rights Movement, and *The Lady From Toledo*

Chávez's 1960 historical novel *The Lady From Toledo*, a narrative about the 1680 Pueblo Revolt written at the dawn of the Civil Rights era in New Mexico, is an exemplar of Chávez's triptych literary mode. The novel narrates the Pueblo Revolt in three separate but interrelated stories and through three black-and-white drawings that narrate visually the (multi)story of New Mexico's Pueblo Revolt; the three stories converge in the final showdown between the Pueblos and the Spanish in the Santa Fe plaza. The novel concludes at the San Lorenzo colony where the High Sherrif's daughter, María Romero, retells her story about the revolt and her statue, a small replica of the Toledo Virgin from Spain, to a Mexican lay brother who takes the statue back to Mexico where Aztec neophytes subsequently worship it and rename the statue "Our Lady of the Macana" to commemorate the Pueblo Revolt. The three *cuentos* correspond to the three major historical eras that inform the text—the Spanish colonial, the Spanish Revival, and the Civil Rights era—and the novel's narrative unfolds within and against New Mexico's tri-culturalism. In this sense, *The Lady From Toledo* becomes a socially symbolic act, as Fredric Jameson phrases it, both exposing and containing the political forces and ideological fissures that generate the need for its particular narrative in the first place.[3] The main image, the Lady From Toledo, in other words, becomes a contested feminine site of competing ideologies that collapses history and geography to comment on the Civil Rights era and the politics of ethno-racial identity that shape the historical moment of the novel's publication.

On June 5, 1967, at three o'clock in the afternoon, twenty armed members of La Alianza Federal de Mercedes (a/k/a the Federation of Free City States) stormed through the Rio Arriba County Courthouse in Tierra Amarilla, New Mexico, to make a citizen's arrest of District Attorney Alfonso Sánchez. *The Santa Fe New Mexican* reported the dramatic events of the Courthouse Raid over the next week, including the dispatch of 350 National Guardsmen to Northern New Mexico; the search for Tijerina and four other men; Peter Nabokov's exclusive interview with the fugitive; and, finally, Tijerina's apprehension and arrest in Bernalillo on June 10, 1967. The enigmatic leader from Texas and the Courthouse Raid certainly brought New Mexico into the foreground of the Civil Rights Movement in 1967 and generated local, state, and national visibility for Northern New Mexican poverty, the land grant struggle, and civil rights.[4] The *SFNM* expressed both disdain and admiration for Tijerina and his cause, while many native Hispanos were outraged by local, state, and federal treatment of Spanish-American residents in the aftermath of the raid. Charles S. Knowlton, sociology professor at the University of Texas at El Paso and long-time friend of Tijerina, wrote to the *SFNM* editor lambasting the violation of civil rights in New Mexico. "The civil rights movement in New Mexico that shows so much concern for civil right violations in the South should be ashamed for their strange and tardy reluctance to come to the assistance of the members of the Alianza whose rights have been victimized" (Knowlton 4). Another letter echoes Knowlton's geo-racial link between the civil rights in New Mexico and the Civil Rights Movements across the country: one native New Mexican characterized the situation by calling Tierra Amarilla "the Watts area of Northern New Mexico" (Tapia 4).

Indeed, Northern New Mexico momentarily took on the face of the racial unrest plaguing the South and the country's urban centers with the Courthouse shoot-out, the governor's dispatch of the New Mexico National Guard, and the detainment of Alianza members—men, women, and children alike—corralled in the outdoors of Canjillon, New Mexico for an entire night. New Mexico's uncanny resemblance to the nation's racial unrest and political crises in 1967 generated discomfort for its native residents and its liberal Anglo journalists. Even Tijerina was conscious of the discomfort. In 1967, Tijerina claimed that the Watts riots "were a preview of what could happen up and down the Rio Grande valley if his people didn't get a fair shake.'" Conscious of his people's aversion to "foreign" politics, however, Tijerina added "'But I don't want to copy the Negroes. . . . I tell my people the best way to get our rights is through the courts" (Windes 9). The Watts analogy expressed the depth of social and political unrest in New Mexico, but it also revealed deep-seated contradictions in the state's civil rights struggle. Despite the similarities between black civil rights and the land grant struggle in New Mexico, there was no clear racial division between authorities and militants in New Mexico; rather, the authorities in New Mexico were largely native-born Hispanos, as were the members of the Alianza who stormed the Tierra Amarilla Courthouse in 1967. The land grant conflict of the 1960s, in other words, highlighted the divisions that historically fracture native New Mexico and the state's collective identity.

In the aftermath of the Courthouse Raid and at the height of the nation's

Civil Rights radicalism, Chávez announced his aversion to Tijerina when he called the Tiger a "demagogue" and maintained that his followers were "poor descendants of Genízaros who still hold grudges from long ago, or some few people of recent Mexican origin who now live in the northern part of the state (And let us not forget the Anglo instigators)" ("A Look at the Background of New Mexico Culture" A-5). Chávez implied that Tijerina and his followers were foreign to New Mexico's Spanish Americans in the North, and like urban black activists, Tijerina threatened to instill racial rebellion in Northern New Mexico and to overturn the state's decades-long revival of Spanish colonial art and history.[5]

In response to New Mexico's activism, Chávez produced three separate but interrelated narratives about the Pueblo Revolt between 1959 and 1967; the three pieces reflect a general shift from the 1950s nuclear era to the 1960s civil rights struggle. In 1959, Chávez wrote "Our Lady of La Macana," an article about the Toledo virgin who played a prominent role in the Pueblo Revolt; then in 1960 he penned *The Lady From Toledo*, which centers on the Pueblo Revolt; and in 1967 he produced the article "Pohé-yemo's Representative," in which he maintains that a black fugitive slave from Veracruz, Mexico, was responsible for inciting the Pueblos to revolt against the Spanish in the seventeenth century. As the novel tells it, the black fugitive slave that succeeded in carrying out the 1680 Pueblo Revolt is from southern Mexico, but this fugitive slave can also potentially represent the black Civil Rights Movement. Centered originally in the U.S. South, the Civil Rights Movement fueled similar struggles across the country, and as the *Watts-cum-Courthouse Raid* suggest, New Mexico was also radically influenced by the nation's racial conflict.

Indeed, *The Lady From Toledo* is Chávez's revisionist history of the Pueblo Revolt based on real historical figures that played prominent roles during the indigenous revolt and siege of Santa Fe in 1680, but it is also Chávez's reactionary vision of the Civil Rights Movement that unsettled New Mexico in the 1960s. In the novel's prelude, Chávez explains that his narrative is a mixture of fact, folklore and fiction about the "ordinary folk whom conventional history overlooked," including a runaway slave, a crippled young girl, a martyred priest, and a conflicted Galisteo Indian who betrays both his Pueblo and the Spaniards who adopt him as a young man (Chavez 1960 7). The text's subject and its historical context are interrelated, and Chávez uses the Pueblo Revolt to comment on New Mexico's civil unrest in the 1960s.[6] *The Lady From Toledo* synthesizes myth, folklore, and history to reveal the Pueblo Revolt's untold stories, and to generate a modern-day triptych prophecy that warns against New Mexico's emergent racial unrest. Chávez's omniscient narrating voice in the pre- and postludes lends the novel historical authenticity, and the drawings, which accompany the text, point to the novel's triptych politics. The novel's jacket opens to a hand-drawn, black-and-white map of Southwestern Spain and the Americas with a Spanish coat of arms in the upper left-hand corner and a caption in the lower right-hand that reads: "The Voyages and Sojourns of the Lady From Toledo." The prelude thus begins:

> *In the enchanted heart of the great City of Mexico there is a very old stone church, sculptured once by human hands and molded ever since by the fingers of centuries. Its name is San Francisco del Convento Grande. Somewhere underneath the lofty yawns of its age-worn ceiling, or in some nook of what remains of the once extensive friary, may be found the little figure of* Nuestra Señora de la Macana, *which literally means, "Our Lady of the Aztec War Club." The original title, however, was* Nuestra Señora del Sagrario, *which is the ancient patronal Madonna of old Toledo in Spain.* (Chávez 1960 3)

The prelude gives the Lady statue a physical as well as a spiritual identity, and it narrates in a nutshell the historical events that unfold in this literary triptych. The postlude, on the other hand, provides the novel with a post-Pueblo Revolt history and links the statue to the U.S.-Mexico border (162). The Toledo statue thus crosses political and aesthetic borders in Chávez's literary triptych.

The novel consists of three parts: "The High Sheriff's Daughter"; "The Padre and the Slave"; and "Kingdom's End." Each part narrates from a different spatial perspective and from the vantage point of divergent characters, and each part could stand alone as a short story. María Romero, the sheriff's daughter, born paralyzed in Santa Fe, miraculously cured after the Toledo statue's apparition, is subject of the first story. The second *cuento* tells of Fray José de Trujillo's martyrdom at the Moqui (Hopi) Pueblo and takes the perspective of Diego Naranjo who travels to New Mexico as a fugitive slave from Veracruz to become the god Pohé-yemo at Taos Pueblo. The novel returns to Santa Fe as the city is sieged during the Pueblo Revolt and concludes with the brutal lynching of Juan el Tano, a Galisteo native who betrays both his Pueblo of origin and his adoptive Spanish culture during the revolt. The statue's apparition, María's healing, and the virgin's prophecy against the "sins of the kingdom" is what links these three stories, and the novel concludes at the San Lorenzo colony where María retells Fray Buenaventura the story of the Pueblo Revolt. The statue thus becomes a symbol of myth, history, and folklore for New Mexicans and Mexicans, Indians and Spaniards alike.

Chávez opens each of his *cuentos* with a black-and-white sketch that narrates visually the novel's spatial movement. *The Lady From Toledo* is an example of what Ellen McCracken calls Chávez's "imagetext," or a composite text that bridges the verbal and the visual. As McCracken argues, "[Chávez] expects that the words he employs will 'add color' to his own black-and-white drawings and the photo [of Our Lady of the Macana] at the end [of the novel], not vice-versa, as is usually assumed to be the case in illustrated texts" (McCracken 55). Yet, where McCracken sees a "harmonious, nonconflictive relationship" between the two modes of expression (visual and verbal) in Chávez's work, New Mexico history and social conflict color the *The Lady From Toledo's* simple pictures. The first section, "The High Sheriff's Daughter," begins with Chávez's drawing of a Spanish señorita standing amidst Santa Fe's adobe structures and the San Miguel Church, the edifice that the Tano insurgents will eventually take over and transform into a kiva after routing the Spaniards during the siege of Santa Fe. Part two, "The Padre and the Slave," begins with an image of Taos Pueblo to establish it as a the seat of racial unrest in New Mexico history and as a site of regional romance in the nation's symbolic imaginary. Finally, the last drawing is a hybridized sketch of the previous two landscapes: the mountainous backdrop is similar to the first image of Santa Fe, but the third image's foreground resembles the second one of Taos Pueblo. A young woman stands on the unpopulated mesas, but unlike the first figure—indisputably a Spanish lady—this figure has no facial features or distinguishable dress. The final drawing prefigures the novel's closure at the San Lorenzo colony, and the young woman's ambiguity seems to suggest that her identity—indeed, New Mexico's civil rights history—is yet to be written.

The novel's three main characters—María, Diego, and Juan—are loosely based on factual people and events that appear in the colonial documents recounting the Pueblo Revolt. Isolated from the outside world, María is completely dependent on her family and her family's company for her survival because she cannot move from her bedroom where the Toledo statue is enshrined. María's family members include her father, Bartolomé Romero, Aunt Ana Robledo, and cousin Francisco Gómez Robledo, real historical figures whom played prominent roles in the Pueblo Revolt. The Toledo statue is a Romero family heirloom, as Aunt Ana reveals in the novel, and it is María's connection to the Pueblo Revolt, as Chávez reveals in his 1959 article, "Our Lady of la Macana." The statue, formerly known as *Nuestra Señora del Sagrario de Toledo* because it was a copy of the patron Madonna of the city of Toledo in central Spain, was brought to New Mexico with the Oñate colony and was a family relic that belonged to a crippled girl. As legend has it, the virgin appeared to the little girl, cured her, and prophesized the Spanish kingdom's demise (Chávez 1959 174).

During the siege of Santa Fe in 1680, an Indian from Galisteo "raised his macana and cut off the head of an image of Our Lady" (Bancroft 195). The image was the little girl's statue and its decapitation gave the statue a new name and identity. The Toledo statue escaped to El Paso with the Spanish colonists and was subsequently taken into Mexico City where Aztec neophytes repaired and worshipped the virgin statue. "Presumably at this same period the little replica of an Aztec macana of wrought copper was made for it, and this popularized a new name and title which came to supplant that of the Sagrario of Toledo" (Chávez 1959 96). The Aztec converts venerated the Macana statue at the mission of Tlalnepantla until 1754, when it was transplanted to the Convento Grande in Mexico City, where it remains to this day (Chávez 1960 160).[7]

The identity of the Indian captain who decapitated María's Virgin is unknown, though Chávez maintains that it was one Juan el Tano (or Tagno, as it appears in the official records).[8] The Tanos from Galisteo were especially visible in the uprising against the Spanish, for after routing the Spanish, the Tanos took over the Santa Fe capital and transformed the San Miguel Church into a kiva where they re-instituted their native religion. Spanish colonial documents reveal how the Spanish had come to rely on Indians like Juan el Tano and were relatively surprised by their uprising:

> A troop of [Spanish] soldiers going out to reconnoiter them saw the said Tagno, Juan, on horseback, wearing a sash of red taffeta which was recognized as being from the missal of the convent of Galisteo, and with harquebus, sword, dagger, leather jacket, and all the arms of the Spaniards. He was summoned and persuaded with fair words to enter the plaza of the villa to talk with the señor governor and captain-general, and being asked how he could do such a thing when his lordship had placed confidence in him, he said that there was now no help for it; that everything he had said about the deaths of the father custodian and all the other Spaniards and religious was true, and that the Indians who were coming with him and those whom they were awaiting were coming to destroy the villa (Hackett and Shelby 14).[9]

Juan initially threw his lot with the Spanish and was sent off to negotiate with his native tribe, but instead he returned in command of a rebel army. The Indians took up Spanish arms against the colonists and revealed that they too had come to rely on Spanish forms of warfare and military organization. In this particular battle, Governor Otermín temporarily routed the Tanos and Queres Indians and took forty-seven prisoners to be executed, but before Otermín gave the order he demanded to know the identity of their leader. They replied that "they had the mandate of an Indian who lives a very long way from this kingdom, toward the north, from which region Montezuma came, and who is the lieutenant of Po he yemu [sic]" (Hackett and Shelby 16).

The god of Pohé-yemo is what Richard J. Parmentier calls a "pan-Pueblo culture hero," a religious icon that constitutes the Pohé-yemo/Montezuma/Jesus triad (Parmentier 609). Pohé-yemo's universality temporarily subdued inter-tribal warfare in seventeenth century to unite the Pueblo Indians and to establish an alliance with raiding Apaches in exchange for Spanish plunder.[10] On August 9, 1680, two Tesuque Indians testified to Maestre de Campo Francisco Gómez Robledo (María's cousin) that "there had come from very far away toward the north a letter from an Indian lieutenant of Po-he-yemu [sic] to the effect that all of them in general should rebel. . .It was reported that this Indian lieutenant of Po-he-yemu was very tall, black, and had very large yellow eyes, and that everyone feared him greatly" (Hackett and Shelby 4-5). Two reports on Pohé-yemo identify the god differentially to underscore the fact that the god did not literally exist for the indigenous rebellion but functioned instead as a symbol of power. As Parmentier explains, Pohé-yemo is a powerful symbol in Pueblo mythology because he represents a cross-cultural socio-religious triangle that negotiates three different figures: Pohé-yemo, Montezuma, and Christ.[11] The figurative triangle, as Parmentier explains, underscores the connection of Pueblo mythology to the Aztec emperor Montezuma and the Christian son Jesus Christ. For Chávez, Pohé-yemo both reflects and refracts the Southwest's tri-culturalism to foster a layered cultural critique of the state's conflicted histories.

The Pohé-yemo legend was manufactured in Mexico and imported to New Mexico, a foreign commodity that confused the Spaniards because of its illusiveness; this is the thesis that Chávez expounds in his 1967 article. As Chávez has it, Diego Naranjo, a black fugitive slave, masked his identity as Pohé-yemo's lieutenant in a Taos oracle near Blue Lake where he secretly planned the Pueblo Revolt. Chávez argues that only someone close enough and yet foreign to the Spanish colonial system—a slave—could know how to manipulate the myth of Montezuma at once to control the Pueblo Indian leaders and to destroy their Spanish masters. The myth of Pohé-yemo frightened Spanish folk but infuriated the crown's officers despite, and because of, its basis in myth and not fact. For instance, in *The Lady From Toledo* María questions her father Bartolomé about "the mysterious gigantic black god, Pohé-yemo," and the narrative explains:

> The Mexican Indians whom the earliest Spaniards left among the pueblos had taught them their own ancient myth about their hero-god, Huitzilopochtli, founder of the City of Mexico. These pueblo Indians then confused him with the Emperor Moctezuma [sic]—whom they called Pohé-yemo in their own manner of speaking. And they further claimed that he dwelt by the blue mountain lake near the pueblo of Taos. Such an unreal being posed no problem for the authorities—it was the underground temples and the secret dances that were the high sheriff's headache. (60)

Pohé-yemo's oracle was myth even to the Spaniards who paid little attention to the symbolic value of the Pueblo Revolt's leadership. As the novel tells it, Governor Otermín executed forty-seven Pueblo prisoners in the Santa Fe plaza because they insisted, "one and all, that their rebellion had been planned and caused by a giant who lived far to the north, and that this giant was the *teniente* Pohé-yemo. Governor Otermín wanted facts, not fables, and so he had them all shot" (148).

The Lady From Toledo conflates myth and history, collapsing the distinction between the two genres altogether to generate a social allegory that blames a slave—a barbarian, fugitive, and foreigner—for the Pueblo Revolt. Chávez's Pohé-yemo, for instance, is a black barbarian—literally a foreigner—that can also be read as a mask or social allegory that warns against the threat of (foreign) racial rebellion in the state, be it rebellion that mirrors the Watts Riots, the rallies in the South, or, eventually, the raid in Tierra Amarilla. María embodies the feminine trappings of Santa Fe's twentieth-century Spanish revival movement and New Mexico's regional isolation. Chávez literally and symbolically recovers María's body, in his words, from "*the ferment of historical and political change*" by returning to the Pueblo Revolt exactly when the nation is feeling the reverberation of the black Civil Rights Movement (8). Pohé-yemo's threat, then, is layered, triple-voiced as the rest of Chávez's work: just as the black foreigner incited racial rebellion in 1680, the Civil Rights Movement of the late 1950s and early 1960s threatened to instill the same agitation among Native and Mexican American communities in New Mexico. Chávez combines Fray de Trujillo and Diego's narratives to highlight their difference and to emphasize New Mexico's cross-cultural and interdependent histories of accommodation and resistance. While Trujillo effeminately dreams of the Orient in the confines of Mexico City and Spain's adobe missions, Naranjo escapes slavery and Mexico's *barrios* in search of the lost homeland that Chicano nationalists would reclaim at the height of the Chicano Movement.[12] The second story symbolically resolves New Mexico's shift from the (Anglo) Orient to the (Chicano) Aztlán homeland, and Naranjo emerges as the text's political unconscious: though Chávez's digs through the archives to prove Naranjo's literal existence, this enigmatic figure attests to the radical influence of ethno-racial discourses across the nation and specifically in Chávez's work.

The third *cuento* begins as the Spaniards learn about the Franciscan martyrdoms, and the governor's appeal to his native allies like Juan el Tano, "*un indio con calzones*, an Indian living the white man's way" (119). While the first and second *cuento* in this literary triptych maintain the ideological and cultural distinctions between Trujillo and Naranjo, the third story collapses their distinctions altogether in "The Confused Chieftan," the tale of Juan el Tano and his role in the siege of Santa Fe. Chávez characterizes Juan as a conflicted ethnic subject who is charged with protecting the Spanish Villa, but in the end is coerced into siding with the Pueblos after the elders promise him Spanish loot. Juan enters the battlefield dressed as a mounted Spanish soldier, fires his musket, kills Andrés Gómez Robledo (Francisco's brother), and is thrown from his horse where "he found himself once more a primitive Indian, in spite of his uniform and sash, fighting for his very life with the *macana* of a fallen comrade" (130).[13] Indeed, the novel blames Naranjo for the Pueblo Revolt and redeems María, but Juan is the punishable subject that paradoxically becomes the novel's ultimate martyr. After all, Juan, in a fit of rage, strikes the statue with his *macana* and decapitates the virgin, only to gather up the statue's pieces and return them to the Spanish military with instructions to have the statue returned to María. The Pueblo shamans then order Naranjo to hang Juan from a tree, and Chávez revises the Southern lynch narrative by inverting the slave's position to reinforce the threat of black Civil Rights in New Mexico and to quell its social dissent. The lynched body becomes a signal, a public event of brutality, betrayal, and retribution that, in Chávez's narrative at least, befits any subject tempted by racial rebellion.

The novel closes at the San Lorenzo colony on the border, where María meets Fray Buenaventura, a lay Third Order Franciscan brother who travels up the *Camino Real* with provisions for the colony. María tells Buenaventura the story of the decapitated Toledo statue, and he returns to Mexico City with the statue in arms and an embellished account of the Pueblo Revolt. The Toledo statue connects Hispanic New Mexico to indigenous Mexico as Buenaventura heads south to deliver the Toledo/Macana statue across the border; his Good Voyage thus warrants his name. The final *cuento* collapses the voices of María and the friar to generate a prophetic text that attempts to contain the contradictions of the Pueblo Revolt and New Mexico's hybrid colonial histories. But the novel's warning against racial rebellion in New Mexico is ambivalent, for Juan's sacrilegious act ironically sanctifies the statue, just as the Pueblo Revolt affirms the virgin's prophecy and enables María to walk again, a literal if not symbolic recuperation of New Mexico's Spanish body politic. Juan figuratively displays New Mexico's hybrid colonial history and internecine conflicts—thus the ambiguity of the third picture's identity. Like Juan el Tano, the Toledo/Macana statue is a hybrid, cross-cultural representation of competing ethno-racial and national ideologies: Aztlán and the Orient; feminine and masculine; indigenous and catholic; New Mexican and Mexican. Thus *The Lady From Toledo* uses the Pueblo Revolt to negotiate New Mexico's shift from the Spanish Revival to the Chicano Movement, and it regenerates in the process New Mexico's Spanish colonial history.

Postlude

As the 1970s rolled into New Mexico, the state's land disputes peaked, as did its Civil Rights reform and discord. While members of the Alianza demanded fair legal representation for those awaiting trial for their roles in the Courthouse Raid, Taos Pueblo regained trust title to Blue Lake, 48,000 acres in the Kit Carson National Forest, a landmark decision that gained President Nixon's support and altered the nation's federal Indian land policy (Rodríguez 96). While the federal government recognized Indian land rights it also denied Chicano land claims, thus it isn't ironic that Taos Pueblo is at the center of *The Lady From Toledo*. Taos Pueblo is an ambivalent symbol of revolt because it is central to the U.S.'s conception of the Southwest. Indeed, Chávez's second drawing in his literary triptych—a sketch of Taos' archetypal, multi-leveled Pueblo—plays off of the state's Anglo-dominant tourist industry and prefigures, in some ways, the Blue Lake decision. Taos Pueblo's Anglo-inflected undertones are not far from the surface of the novel, for Chávez's sketch, on the one hand, and Trujillo's Oriental visions, on the other, certainly recall New Mexico's Anglo Southwesternism. Yet, even as *The Lady From Toledo* (re)produces New Mexico's regional romance, the novel forewarns—and even forgives—the emergence of Chicano nationalism and its myth of Aztlán.

Chávez's literary triptychs fall outside of the binaries that define the Anglo Orient and the mythical Aztlán; in fact, his triptychs work to collapse the distinction between Chicano and Anglo literary practices and their romantic ideology of New Mexico's indigenous history. The triptych is a hybrid cultural critique that troubles both Anglo Southwesternism and Chicano/a literary history, and it points to at least three layers of history, culture, and ideology shaping New Mexico regionalism in general and Chávez's work in particular. Chávez's triptych mode challenges its own historical production while it simultaneously calls the Civil Rights Movement into question. Yet, paradoxically the Civil Rights era fostered a shift in Chávez's work that mirrors María's recovery from a crippled girl to a border woman. *The Lady From Toledo* facilitates Chávez's shift from romantic to historical genres, from his feminine poetic tropes in the pre-Civil Rights era to his historical biographies in post-Chicano New Mexico, and the novel becomes a symbolic reclamation of New Mexico's history from the effeminate trappings of the Spanish Revival.[14] The Civil Rights era marks the culmination of Chávez's triptych mode of cultural critique and the last vestige of the dominant feminine voice in much of his literature. The 1960s is the symbolic central panel in Chávez's literary career because it provided an alternative platform to engage in New Mexico's history; the emergence of Aztlán, in other words, symbolically liberated Chávez's writing from the effeminate trappings of the Spanish Revival era.

Chávez's triptych mode of cultural critique is a useful methodology for recovering U.S. Hispanic literature because it points to the Southwest's triple-voiced literary history, its hybrid colonial histories, and contested cultural icons. The triptych compliments, and in some ways foreshadows, what Chicana feminists call the "third space," but Chávez's triptychs, and his feminine icons in particular, shore up the limitations of oppositional ideologies. Chávez's triptychs work within and against Anglo tri-culturalism, Chicano nationalism, and Chicana feminism, and they demonstrate in the process the overlap between traditional and radical conceptions of the Southwest. Chávez's work in particular, and U.S. Hispanic literary history in general, sits both inside and outside of multiple literary histories, colonial encounters, and cultural ideologies, and the triptych mode of cultural critique expands the dualistic and double-voiced paradigm of Chicano Studies while at the same time it connects the emergence of Chicana literary history to Anglo Southwesternism and the feminine tropes of New Mexico's tri-culturalism. The triptych as a methodology recovers the marginal voices in mainstream histories and shores up the mainstream assumptions in oppositional ones. Chávez's triptych cultural critique weaves together the dialectics of difference and collapses, the real and symbolic forces, the secular and religious ideologies that shape the U.S. Hispanic literary history.

Notes

[1]For a discussion of New Mexico's historical pageantry and the theme of Spanish conquest, see Chris Wilson's *The Myth of Santa Fe*, Charles Montgomery's *The Spanish Redemption*, and particularly Marta Weigle and Peter White's *The Lore of New Mexico* for a detailed discussion of the Coronado Cuatro Centennial.

[2]For more on the history of Chávez's artistic development and iconography, see Ellen McCracken's article, "Iconicity and Narrative in the Work of Fray Angélico Chávez: Toward the Harmonious Imagetext."

[3]Jameson explains that literary texts are also social allegories in the sense that "ideology is not something which informs or invests symbolic production; rather the aesthetic act is itself ideological, and the production of aesthetic or narrative form is to be seen as an ideological act in its own right, with the function of inventing the imaginary or formal 'solutions' to unresolvable social contradictions" (79). Chávez symbolically resolves the impending Civil Rights era with the novel's allegorical revision of the Pueblo Revolt.

[4]*The Santa Fe New Mexican* reported the Courthouse Raid on June 6, 1967 and followed closely the events leading to Tijerina's arrest on June 10, 1967. See the

June 8, 1967 issue for Peter Nabokov's interview, "The New Mexican's Reporter Interviews Tijerina" (A-1-2).

[5]Charles Montgomery lays out a critical history of the Anglo-dominant Spanish colonial arts revival movement in the early twentieth century and the racial undertones that elevated the *español* in his book *The Spanish Redemption.* I support Montgomery's thesis that Anglo American artists constructed an image of the Southwest that redeemed native Hispanos from their Mexican past, but because Montgomery does not analyze native New Mexican texts that challenge and affirm New Mexico's connection to Mexico, he reproduces the erasure of native subjects from the discourse of Spanish redemption.

[6]Chávez's 1967 article, for instance, maintained that one Diego Naranjo was the fugitive slave of Mexican-Indian ancestry who acted as the Pueblo god Pohéyemo and staged the Pueblo Revolt. Stefanie Beninato critiques Chávez's controversial thesis for ignoring multiple leadership roles and Pueblo Indian agency, but Naranjo is largely a symbolic figure for Chávez, despite the documentary evidence supporting Naranjo's genealogy in New Mexico. The article coincides with the 1967 Courthouse Raid in Tierra Amarilla, when a key player—the High Sheriff, no less—was none other than Benny Naranjo. While perhaps coincidental, this irony of history is significant because the Naranjo name highlighted New Mexico's internal conflicts both historically and symbolically in the 1960s. Chávez first asserted his Naranjo thesis in the 1959 article about the Macana/Toledo statue, but the socio-literary conditions in 1967 proved ripe for Naranjo's recovery, just as the Spanish Revival was a proper setting for the virgin's appearance. Chávez's three pieces on the Pueblo Revolt thus allegorize New Mexico's discursive shift from an Anglo-dominant Spanish revival movement to the ethno-racial politics of the Chicano Movement.

[7]This local-national-international triad with which Chávez concludes the novel is characteristic of Chávez's cultural work itself. In 1959, an editorial house in San Pablo, Buenos Aires ostensibly translated and published Chávez's book of New Mexican short stories, *From An Altar Screen*. Although Chávez never received a translated copy of the book, the *SFNM* nonetheless reported the Buenos Aires publication as fact ("Translation Set For Fr. Angélico Stories" 24). The event demonstrates how Chávez's work—symbolically if not literally—traversed local, national, and international borders like the sacred Virgins he wrote about in the 1950s. See also Chávez's 1959 poem *The Virgin of Port Lligat*, which opens with Salvador Dalí's surrealist painting of the same virgin; moves into a poetic description of the painting; and concludes with a line-by-line interpretation of the poem.

[8]According to James Brooks in *Captives and Cousins*, Juan el Tano was "a renegade 'Christian' Tano Indian" who negotiated on behalf of the Pueblo Indians

and "made clear the extent to which slavery figured prominently in the grievances of Indian peoples throughout the region" (53). Whether or not Juan el Tagno from the historical record is the same Indian who decapitated the Toledo statue is not at issue. What Chávez accomplishes with his version of Juan el Tano's role in the Pueblo Revolt is best understood at the symbolic level.

[9]This *auto* is dated August 20, 1680 and relates the events of August 13-20. Juan gave Otermín a choice between two crosses: the red one signified war, and the white one meant peaceful submission. Otermín did not entertain such a proposition and encouraged Juan to re-consider peace. Juan led his forces against the Spanish, an "encounter [that] lasted nearly all day, during which many of the enemy were killed and they wounded many of our men, because they came with harquebuses and the arms which they had taken from the religious and the Spaniards, and were very well provided with power and shot, with which, fortified in the houses, in which they made embrasures, they fought all day" (Hackett and Shelby 14).

[10]A report dated August 9, 1680, just days before the uprising, states, "All the nations of this kingdom were now implicated in it, forming a confederation with the heathen Apaches so that, on the night of the thirteenth of the current month, they might carry out their disobedience, perfidious treason, and atrocities," (Hackett and Shelby 4).

[11]Parmentier maintains that the Pueblos consistently linked Pohé-yemo to Montezuma in the sixteenth and seventeenth centuries, and Pueblo mythology used the Aztec god in the nineteenth century to mediate the incorporation of Jesus Christ into Pueblo religion.

[12]John R. Chavez suggests that the Southwest is Aztlán, a figurative trope that constitutes the Mexican-American "lost homeland" and their birthright. See *The Lost Land: The Chicano Image of the Southwest.*

[13]As Chávez has it, the elders manipulated Juan as the Spanish manipulated their Indian allies and informants. Governor Otermín made many promises and offered many gifts to those Christian Indians who foretold of the Pueblo Revolt, and according to John L. Kessell, many Pueblo leaders fashioned themselves in the manner of Spanish rule as a means to power. "El Popé was a paradox," says Kessell. "He lashed out against everything Spanish, and he did it as only a Spaniard would." As for political unification, the Pueblos had none outside of Spanish governance. "Thus El Popé, in his effort to hold together what had been wrought against the Spaniards, ruled in the manner of a Spaniard. He even swaggered like one," (238). See Kessell's *Kiva, Cross, and Crown: The Pecos Indians and New Mexico, 1540-1840.*

[14]I am referring here to Chávez's biographical trilogy of New Mexico's mid-nineteenth century Mexican priests: Martínez of Taos; Gallegos of Albuquerque; and Ortiz of Santa Fe.

Works Cited

Anonymous. "Translation Set For Fr. Angelico Stories." *The Santa Fe New Mexican* 15 February 1959: 24.

Anonymous. "Fray Anglico Chavez Named Recipient of Newman Award." *The Santa Fe New Mexican* 15 April 1959: 19.

Bancroft, H. H. *History of Arizona and New Mexico, 1530-1888*. Albuquerque: Horn and Wallace, 1962.

Beninato, Stefanie. "Popé, Pose-yemu, and Naranjo: A New Look at Leadership in the Pueblo Revolt of 1680." *New Mexico Historical Review* 65.3 (1990): 419-35.

Brooks, James. *Captives and Cousins: Slavery, Kinship, and Community in the Southwest Borderlands*. Chapel Hill: University of North Carolina Press, 2002.

Chávez, Fray Angélico. "Adventurers in Cibola." *Clothed with the Sun*. Santa Fe: Writer's Editions, 1939: 33.

______. *But Time and Chance: The Story of Padre Martínez of Taos, 1793-1867*. Santa Fe: Sunstone Press, 1981.

______. *From An Altar Screen: Tales From New Mexico*. New York: Farrar, Straus & Cudahy, 1957.

______. *The Lady from Toledo*. Fresno: Academy Guild Press, 1960.

______. "A Look at the Background of New Mexico Culture." *The Albuquerque Journal* 18 December 1970: A-5.

______. *New Mexico Triptych: Being Three Panels and Three Accounts: 1. The Angel's Wings; 2. The Penitente Thief; 3. Hunchback Madonna*, 2nd Ed. Santa Fe: William Gannon, 1976 [1940].

______. "Nuestra Señora de la Macana." *New Mexico Historical Review* 24.2 (April 1959):80-97.

______. "Pohe-Yemo's Representative and the Pueblo Revolt of 1680." *New Mexican Historical Review* 42.2 (1967): 85-126.

______. *Trés Macho—He Said: Padre Gallegos of Albuquerque, New Mexico's First Congressman*. Santa Fe: William Gannon, 1985.

______. *The Virgin of Port Lligat*. Fresno: Academy Library Guild, 1959.

______, and Thomas E. Chávez. *Wake For A Fat Vicar: Father Juan Felipe Ortiz, Archbishop Lamy, and the New Mexican Catholic Church in the Middle of the Nineteenth Century*. Albuquerque: LPD Press, 2004.

Chávez, John R. *The Lost Land: The Chicano Image of the Southwest*. Albuquerque: University of New Mexico Press, 1984.

Cosman, Madeleine Polner. *Medieval Wordbook*. New York: Facts on File, Inc., 1996.

García, Nasario. "Introduction: Fray Angélico Chávez: A Man of Many Talents." In *Cantares: Canticles and Poems of Youth*. Ed. Nasario García. Houston: Arte Público Press, 2000.

Gutiérrez, Ramón A. "Charles Fletcher Lummis and the Orientalization of New Mexico." *Nuevomexicano Cultural Legacy: Forms, Agencies, and Discourse*. Ed. Francisco A. Lomelí, et al. Albuquerque: University of New Mexico Press, 2002: 11-27.

Hackett, Charles Wilson and Chairman Clair Shelby. *Revolt of the Pueblo Indians of New Mexico and Otermín's Attempted Reconquest, 1680-1682*. Albuquerque: University of New Mexico Press, 1970 [1942].

Jameson, Fredric. *The Political Unconscious: Narrative As a Socially Symbolic Act*. Ithaca: Cornell University Press, 1981.

Kessell, John L. *Kiva, Cross, and Crown: The Pecos Indians and New Mexico, 1540-1840*. Albuquerque: University of New Mexico Press, 1987.

Knowlton, Charles S. "A Tortilla Curtain?" *The Santa Fe New Mexican* 13 June 1967: A-4.

McCracken, Ellen. "Iconicity and Narrative in the Work of Fray Angélico Chavez: Toward the Harmonious Imagetext." In *Fray Angélico Chávez: Poet, Priest, and Artist*. Ed. Ellen McCracken. Albuquerque: University of New Mexico Press, 2000: 53-90.

Montgomery, Charles. *The Spanish Redemption: Heritage, Power, and Loss on New Mexico's Upper Rio Grande*. Berkeley: University of California Press, 2002.

Padilla, Genaro M. "Introduction." *The Short Stories of Fray Angélico Chávez*. Ed. Genaro M. Padilla. Albuquerque: University of New Mexico Press, 1984: vii-xx.

Parmentier, Richard J. "The Mythological Triangle: Poseyemu, Montezuma, and Jesus in the Pueblos." In *The Handbook of North American Indians, Southwest Volume 9*. Ed. Simon Ortiz. Washington: Smithsonian Institution, 1979: 609-22.

Rodríguez, Sylvia. "Art, Tourism, and Race Relations in Taos: Toward a Sociology of the Art Colony." *Journal of Anthropological Research* 45.1 (1989): 77-99.

Tapia, Tim. "A Loss of Pride." *The Santa Fe New Mexican* 25 June 1967: A-4.

Rudnick, Lois. "Re-Naming the Land: Anglo Expatriate Women in the Southwest." *The Desert Is No Lady: Southwestern Landscapes in Women's Writing and Art*. Ed. Vera Norwood and Janice Monk. New Haven: Yale University Press, 1987. 10-26.

Weigle, Marta "Southwest Lures: Innocents Detoured, Incensed Determined." *Journal of the Southwest* 32.4 (1990): 499-540.

______, and Kyle Fiore. *Santa Fe and Taos: The Writer's Era, 1916-1941*. Santa Fe: Ancient City Press, 1982.

______, and Peter White. *The Lore of New Mexico*. Albuquerque: University of New Mexico Press, 2003 [1989].

Wilson, Chris. *The Myth of Santa Fe: Creating a Modern Regional Tradition*. Albuquerque: University of New Mexico Press, 1997.

Windes, Vina, "Research Reveals Little About 'King Tiger.'" *The Santa Fe New Mexican* 8 June 1967: A-9.

Part II

Voicing Dissent, Staging Identity, Speaking into Time

El discurso político y la construcción de la identidad: El ejemplo de *La Voz del Pueblo*

Patricia Gubitosi
University of Houston

La discusión acerca del periodismo y la literatura no es nueva ni desconocida. Pero no es sino a partir de los postulados del análisis del discurso que tenemos una comprensión del género periodístico en toda su dimensión. El periódico, entonces, es visto como una unidad estructural llena de voces diferenciadas donde cada una de ellas representa una porción de la realidad que se trata de describir, y donde la no-uniformidad está planteando, precisamente, la necesidad de describir un mundo múltiple y diverso; diferente, en el cual no existe una única voz. De este modo, el periódico:

> Comunica lo que pasa, acerca a todo ello y lo hace ver, sentir y comprender, abre ventanas para que lleguen impresiones de lo que ocurre en diversos lugares del espacio y en diversos sectores de la vida social, da cuenta del desarrollo de los actos y analiza y enjuicia las obras que se ofrecen al público y recoge las diversas opiniones y puntos de vista bien especializados, o aquellos con los que la opinión reacciona ante los hechos que pasan y las noticias y comentarios que se publican; y completa el ciclo con la opinión misma del periódico (editorial). Todo es interpretación, de la noticia al editorial, pero interpretación en diversos grados y por distintos medios. (Gutiérrez Palacio, 1984:17)

El propósito de este trabajo es esclarecer, desde un punto de vista lingüístico, el tipo de relaciones que se establecen a través de los editoriales de *La Voz del Pueblo* entre los distintos actores de la realidad nuevomexicana de fines del siglo XIX y principios del siglo XX. La década de 1890, en que da comienzo la publicación de *La Voz del Pueblo* (más precisamente, en 1889) fue la de mayor florecimiento de la actividad periodística en el estado de Nuevo México (Meléndez 1997: 23). La prensa en español, en este sentido, jugó un significativo papel en la formación de esta nueva comunidad lectora nuevomexicana que compartía una visión del mundo propia muy diferente de la angloamericana. El papel que le corresponde a *La Voz del Pueblo* en esta empresa es privilegiado a juzgar por la cantidad de ejemplares semanales publicados (que en 1889 llegaron a 3000, representando la mayor tirada de todos los periódicos publicados en el territorio) (Fernández Gibert 2001: 84).

Nuestro análisis abarca desde su creación hasta el año de 1912, año en que Nuevo México logra, por fin, su incorporación como estado a los Estados Unidos de América. Creemos que nuestro aporte, al revelar las prácticas del lenguaje utilizadas en este periódico, contribuirá a iluminar los presupuestos culturales, ideológicos y políticos que subyacen en esta comunidad.

El discurso político

Las investigaciones realizadas por distintas disciplinas de las Ciencias Sociales reconocen al discurso no sólo como un vehículo destinado a transmitir información sino como un medio de acción que permite construir y modificar las relaciones entre los interlocutores; y entre éstos y la realidad. El lenguaje, entonces, no es sólo un sistema de signos que describen el mundo sino un medio por el cual los individuos se relacionan e interactúan con el mundo. El reconocimiento de la centralidad del discurso en la vida social ha permitido que el análisis del discurso se transforme en una propuesta teórico-metodológica de investigación social que permite captar y describir discursos de dimensiones específicas como lo son el ideológico y el político develando no sólo al emisor de dichos discursos sino también el contexto y la situación coyuntural en que éstos son emitidos. En este sentido, el discurso no nos brinda por sí mismo la información de la realidad, pero sí nos da las claves necesarias para poder reconstruir esa realidad. Como señala Bordieu (1998) "el trabajo político se reduce a un trabajo sobre las palabras, porque las palabras contribuyen a construir el mundo social".

Hablar de discurso político, entonces, supone que existe otro tipo de discurso no político. Definimos como político a cualquier discurso que se refiera al poder, al control, a la dominación (Wilson 2001: 399). En líneas generales, se reconoce que el discurso político no se dirige tanto a convencer al adversario sino a reconocer, distinguir y confirmar a los partidarios; es un discurso estratégico en la medida en que define propósitos, medios y antagonistas. Tiene una base esencialmente polémica, donde la enunciación política es inseparable de la construcción de un adversario; y, por último, es un discurso que busca validar la propia conducta. El siguiente párrafo nos ilustra de cómo opera esta identificación:

> El pecho de los héroes que tanto han sido calumniados descansan con la plácida satisfacción que la pobreza del justo es más gloriosa que la riqueza del traicionero movido por motivos de avaricia y envidia. (*La Voz del Pueblo*, 20 de diciembre de 1890; p. 2 col. 2)

Se asume, entonces, que los discursos son formas de acción e interacción social, situados en contextos sociales en los cuales los participantes no son tan sólo hablantes/ escribientes y oyentes/ lectores, sino también actores sociales que son miembros de grupos con una cierta identidad; la cual se vislumbra en nuestros textos a partir de la oposición *nosotros (el pueblo) —ellos*:

> Anticipando ellos por medio de grandes esfuerzo que van á hacer y mucho dinero que intentan gastar, poder llegar á las urnas electorales á todos sus aliados. De esa manera intentan los titiriteros derrotar la voluntad del pueblo. (*La Voz del Pueblo*, 30 de agosto de 1890; p. 1 col. 1-2)[1]

Por otra parte, las reglas y normas del discurso son socialmente compartidas; las condiciones, funciones y efectos del discurso son sociales. La competencia discursiva supone, en definitiva, el conocimiento implícito (o explícito) de las reglas culturales y sociales presupuestas —y a la vez requeridas— para la comunicación.

Uno de los principales propósitos del análisis del discurso político será, entonces, indagar sobre los modos del lenguaje que operan y hacen posible esta "manipulación" lingüística para conseguir determinados efectos políticos. ¿Qué niveles, qué estructuras se verán afectadas en la prosecución de este objetivo? Responder esta pregunta, y revelar a través de qué operaciones lingüísticas nuestro periódico, *La Voz del Pueblo,* construye su red de adhesiones y participantes, será nuestra principal tarea.

Discurso y contexto social

Cualquier acercamiento a un texto concreto no puede llevarse a cabo sin conocer el marco discursivo del mismo, es decir, las características sociales y de género en las que el texto se enmarca y que son imprescindibles para comprender su significado y su valor dentro del *orden del discurso* existente.[2] Esta necesidad es mucho mayor cuando se trata de un discurso ubicado en una época lejana a la actual, donde se desconocen todos los referentes interpretativos; ya que la comprensión de un texto periodístico depende del conocimiento, por parte de los lectores, de una serie de convenciones genéricas, presuposiciones, significados implícitos, etc. insertados tanto en la sociedad del momento como en los hábitos discursivos que los periódicos poseen para hacer referencia a su actualidad.[3]

El periódico que nos ocupa, *La Voz del Pueblo*, fundado por Enrique H. Salazar y Néstor Montoya, y posteriormente dirigido por Félix Martínez,[4] se publicó en Nuevo México entre los años 1889-1924; y aunque inicialmente apareció en Santa Fe; en 1890 se trasladó a la ciudad de Las Vegas, sesenta millas al noreste de Santa Fe (Meléndez, 1997: 28). Irónicamente, el periódico que desde un comienzo se propuso como misión el defender los intereses del pueblo hispano, ubicó sus oficinas en el Este de Las Vegas, en *New Town,* pleno territorio angloamericano. Las razones eran fundamentalmente económicas, como bien señala Fernández Gibert (2001:84):

> Detrás de la legítima voluntad de representar los intereses de aquellos nativos hispanos menos poderosos, los que no podían hacer llegar su voz hasta la opinión pública, *La Voz*, al mismo tiempo, servía a otros intereses bien distintos, que tenían mucho que ver con importantes empresas de negocios en la que estaban representados tanto anglos como hispanos.

Los motivos de la mudanza son explicados por el periódico en su edición del 7 de junio de 1890:

> Somos soldados del pueblo que velamos por sus derechos, de esta manera, creyendo que la lucha se acerca, deseamos plantar nuestras baterías donde tengan más efecto y hagan más daño al enemigo. Este es, en fin la razón por la cual nos trasladamos á Las Vegas.

Como muchos otros periódicos hispanos que se publicaron en el siglo XIX, *La Voz del Pueblo*, tomó para sí, desde un comienzo, la misión de defender los intereses de los nativos:

> Ya es tiempo para que la población nativa de Nuevo Méjico tenga un periódico que represente fielmente sus intereses y opiniones, un periódico que no se pueda cohechar ni atemorizar [...] Nuestra pluma siempre y en toda ocasión, sin temor alguno, estará lista para rechazar cualquier calumnia arrojada en contra del buen nombre y honor del pueblo de Nuevo Méjico. (2 de febrero de 1889; p. 4, col.1.)

Esta misión puede comprenderse en un contexto en el cual los ciudadanos de Nuevo México (al igual que el resto de los territorios que quedaron bajo el poder de Estados Unidos después del tratado de Guadalupe Hidalgo en 1848) fueron poco a poco despojados de sus derechos y de sus tierras bajo argumentos tales como el del *Destino Manifiesto*:

> Hispanic were subjected to more than a century of 'racialization' through such doctrines as Manifest Destiny and the Spanish Black Legend [...]; they subsequently conquered and/ or incorporated into the United States through territorial purchase and then treated as colonial subjects, as were the Mexicans of the Southwest, the Hispanic in Florida and Louisiana (Kanellos and Martell 2000: 75-76).

Como bien señala Leal (1989) después de la Guerra México-Americana los periódicos del Sudoeste se vieron en la necesidad de defender los derechos de los habitantes mexicanos del territorio ahora estadounidense cuando éstos parecían estar amenazados. *La Voz del Pueblo* no es la excepción, por eso proclama desde el primer número: "La imprenta es la antorcha de la libertad; sin ella los pueblos vivirían envueltos en las tinieblas, y en el manto execrable de la esclavitud" (2 de febrero de 1889; p. 4, col. 1).

Por otro lado, consciente del rol social que le corresponde a la prensa en el desarrollo del territorio, declara:

> La palanca poderosa semejante á la de Arquímedes, en sentido metafórico, en todos los países republicanos, especialmente, es la prensa: primero, porque ella siempre ha sido y será el final refulgente que con los suaves rayos de su ténue luz, lleva por doquiera el estandarte de la verdad, la ilustración y la enseñanza general en todo sentido. ("Libertad de la Prensa", 2 de marzo de 1889; p.3, col. 1-2).

El periódico es, por lo tanto, el instrumento que garantiza la democracia y la libertad:

> De que los periódicos son los mejores educadores nadie puede contradecirlo, en ellos se encuentra y se sabe cuanto pasa en el mundo desde un confin hasta el otro, las ideas y pensamientos del hombre en ellos se explican ya sea sobre Comercio, Política, Religion, Ciencias, Artes ó Invenciones, todo se encuentra en las columnas ya sea de los periódicos diarios ya sea semanarios. ("Los Mejicanos deben leer los periodicos", 9 de febrero de 1889; p.2, col. 4).

Estrategias del lenguaje

La interacción social no debe ser vista como un hecho independiente al lenguaje. El lenguaje produce relaciones intersubjetivas y, paradójicamente, es producto de estas mismas relaciones. Al decir de Lozano:

> El lenguaje inscribe en su propia naturaleza las coordenadas del mundo intersubjetivo; orienta, regula y transforma los modos de correspondencia

> entre los sujetos, además de servir a la objetivación de las distintas experiencias de la realidad y a la creación y actualización de mundos. (2004; 171)

A continuación, examinamos las estrategias discursivas sostenidas por el periódico a lo largo de sus editoriales con la convicción de que es a través del lenguaje donde las relaciones de poder se explicitan y dirimen; constituyéndose el lenguaje, al mismo tiempo, en el instrumento por medio del cual se construye y se forja la identidad. En nuestro análisis trataremos de explicar cómo las estrategias lingüísticas y las estrategias discursivas operan conjuntamente mediante implicaciones y presuposiciones que contribuyen a dar sentido total al texto.

1) Estructuras subordinadas:

Este tipo de estructuras, muchas veces, resta claridad al conjunto total del párrafo, pero es funcional a una estrategia determinada de antemano. Así, en numerosas ocasiones, en los editoriales de nuestro periódico vemos que este tipo de secuencia no lineal (mientras se está hablando de A se inserta B que a su vez permite la inserción de C) se utiliza para describir a los opositores los cuales son descritos con una serie de sustantivos y adjetivos de connotación negativa; mientras que una estructura clara, lineal, es usada para referirse a los nuevomexicanos.

Como ejemplo de lo que acabamos de decir, citamos estos dos fragmentos tomados del editorial del 20 de diciembre de 1890, publicado bajo el título "El dia se acerca"; en el primero de los casos inmediatamente después de la expresión "en Nuevo México y en los nativos sus habitantes" se nos aclara que ocurre una excepción; y esta excepción, la de la conducta execrable de los traidores, será descrita en un largo párrafo circular donde resaltan los sustantivos *traición, villanía, menosprecio, gracia temporaria*. En el segundo párrafo, en cambio, para hablar del honor de "los caballeros" no hace falta ningún circunloquio, ningún rodeo:

> Pero parece que en Nuevo México y en los nativos, sus habitantes, hay una notable excepción, oimos decir y leemos en los periódicos diariamente de la traicion y la villania exemplificada por los hombres de mas rango en el universo, pero no obstante todo esto parece que la indulgencia siempre está en su mano, y el estigma del menosprecio comun no es mas que una materia momentaria el que suele caer de la gracia temporariamente con muy pocas excepciones de pronto concurre al artificio y empaq[c]ona de nuevo y para el aprecio del mundo queda como si fuese inmaculado, pero este no es el caso en Nuevo México, desgraciadamente tenemos la prueba en la mano en la actualidad.

> Por nuestra parte con toda sinceridad aseguramos que hay mas honor individual en el pié de cada uno de los caballeros aquí mencionados que en toda la composición espiritual y natural del atrevido que trata de corromperlos.

La misma técnica se observa en el siguiente editorial del 7 de octubre de 1893 en el cual se trata la admisión de Nuevo México a los Estados Unidos, donde a los legítimos intereses de los hispano-americanos "legítimos poseedores de este suelo" se oponen los de "algunos individuos" a los que se califica a través de subordinadas adjetivas. Es claro el contraste entre la simplicidad discursiva que sirve para calificar a unos, en oposición a las estructuras utilizadas con el otro grupo:

> Se nos ha negado ese privilegio [de entrar en la Unión] no porque se creyera que nos faltaban los recursos ó populación que nos intitulase a ello; mas si parece que ha sido por la mala información que algunos individuos, de esos preocupados que hay, que no pueden ver más adelante que la punta de sus narices, han dado y dan en contra de los hispano-americanos, legítimos poseedores de este suelo.

Esta estrategia se repite más adelante en el mismo editorial donde contrasta en la misma oración el largo circunloquio que acompaña la caracterización de esos "individuos", con las cinco palabras con las que se refiere a la comunidad hispana: "pueblo Hispano-Americano de este Territorio":

> Son personas que han venido, y todavía si no nos equivocamos, estan viniendo, con el único fin de hacer fortunas á costa del sudor y trabajo de otros; y luego que han sido frustrados en sus designios, se han vuelto unos verdaderos liones y han vociferado, hablado y escrito en contra del pueblo Hispano-Americano de este Territorio.

2) Uso de *pasiva con se*[5]:

Estas construcciones requieren siempre un agente implícito o una causa externa que no se menciona porque no interesa destacarla. En general, se admite que el uso de la pasiva con *se* en español tiene la función de desfocalizar al agente (García 1975; Bogard 1999). De esta manera, el agente de la acción es quitado de la escena y el paciente, que es quien realmente interesa destacar, se proyecta a un primer plano. Obsérvese cómo, además, los adjetivos acompañan los sujetos pasivos: "la digna órden de Caballeros de Labor", "el pobre pueblo", etc.

> Se vé por lo de arriba que no hay cosa que se mueva hoy en día en el territorio que no se culpe por ello á la digna órden de Caballeros de Labor, la

> persecución es nuestra suerte y debemos arrostrarla hasta vencer y lograr nuestra justa y merecida vindicacion (16 de agosto de 1890)

> En esos tiempos el pobre pueblo se sometía —no había ninguna alternativa— pero hoy, ¡que se cuiden los pillos y bribones! ¡que los amos tomen precaución y escondan su cara llena de vergüenza! (23 de agosto de 1890)

> Se nos ha negado ese privilegio, no porque se creyera que nos faltaban los recursos ó populación que nos intitulase a ello. (7 de octubre de 1893)

> Con lógica inflexible y fraces elocuentes se demostró la falsedad de las imputaciones que al pueblo de Nuevo México le hacen en el Oriente, tachándosele de poco ilustrado y por consiguiente inhábil para gobernarse a sí mismo. (3 de noviembre de 1906)

3) Uso de pasiva perifrástica:

Según Mendikoetxea (1999) este tipo de oraciones coexisten con aquellas que utilizan la *pasiva con se* pero se caracterizan por "una cierta tendencia a la 'especialización' en acciones de carácter puntual con un sujeto implícito determinado". Este sujeto implícito determinado puede, o no, ser explicitado; aunque, frecuentemente, esta información es elidida de modo intencional. Este proceso de inversión sintáctica puede ser explicado pragmáticamente dado que la información que aportaría el sujeto-agente encabezado por la preposición *por* es información ya conocida por los lectores[6]:

> Los reportes oficiales demuestran que el promedio fue reducido más que 20 por ciento en cinco años, y su gobernador actual, en una carta reciente al Presidente le aseguró de que "en ninguna comunidad se han hecho esfuerzos más persistentes y con mejor exito para la promocion de educacion pública que en el Nuevo Mexico durante los últimos cinco años." (25 de febrero de 1889)

> su atrevimiento en todas las empresas arduas y difíciles ha sido bien probado en todas ocasiones y de todas maneras como la historia lo recita, el índole del Mexicano es suave y fino, hospitalario hasta rayar en prodigo y generoso por naturaleza. (2 de marzo de 1889)

> Esta sociedad es presentada al escarnio y aborrecimiento del país por el órgano Republicano de Santa Fé, siendo acusada la órden por ese periódico de ser culpable de ultrajes ilegales cometidos, los cuáles están aterrorizando al pueblo del condado de San Miguel. (16 de agosto de 1890)

> el carácter de formalidad Mexicano ha sido puesto á prueba y bajo las mismas circunstancias no hemos visto su igual en ninguna nacionalidad, la

> debilidad por supuesto existe en cierto grado tanto en la raza Latina como en la Anglo-Sajona (20 de diciembre de 1890)

> esta es la primera vez que tan perniciosa doctrina es adoptada por una persona que pretende civilizar y moralizar á los que ella considera sus inferiores. (26 de octubre de 1901)

> A las 7 P.M., llegó el Hon. Larrazlo á la Opera Barber, seguido de más de 600 personas siendo saludado con aplausos estrepitosos. Acto continuo el Sr. Antonio Lucero, con palabra fácil y castiza hizo la presentación del candidato. (3 de noviembre de 1906)

4) Introducción de citas en forma de discurso directo.

En general se considera que la introducción de las palabras de otro en forma de *discurso directo* permite un mayor grado de objetividad, y esta estrategia se utiliza para reforzar la opinión del *nosotros* discursivo; de este modo, entonces, las palabras de otro son empleadas para expresar la propia opinión. En nuestro texto, en algunas ocasiones, se incluyen discursos completos dentro del editorial con el fin de autorizar y convalidar la opinión política del diario:

> El senador Casimiro Barela pronunció un elocuente discurso a favor de la adopción del Memorial para conferir gobierno de estado al Nuevo Mexico, y consiguió su adopción unánime por la Legislatura del Estado de Colorado. [...] El Senador Barela dijo: [y se inserta aquí el texto completo del discurso] (23 de febrero de 1889)

Sin embargo, muchas veces se cita la palabra del otro para calificarlo (o descalificarlo). Con esta estrategia el que cita también logra una aparente objetividad, pues él sólo acompaña con el gesto la calificación que el citado se merece a través de sus palabras. Este el objetivo que persigue la publicación de una carta escrita por Francisco Chavez en Socorro, Nuevo México el 16 de abril de 1890, dirigida a Don Juan Trujillo; y que el diario publica en su edición del 25 de octubre de 1890, página 1, columnas 2-3-4 y 5 bajo el ampuloso título "Donde hablan Letras callan Barbas". Luego de la reproducción facsimilar de la carta, el periódico inserta su opinión:

> A según ven por la carta de arriba, ese es el modo como manejan y se burlan los Jefes Republicanos de la justicia. De esa manera manchan y pisotean los tribunales de honor. Esa es la regla que siguen para satisfacer sus caprichos depravados. Lean con cuidado la carta escrita por el puño del Coronel J. Francisco Chavez, de Valencia; y verán como prostituyen los Republicanos las cortes para hacer sus maldades. No tienen escrúpulo, no se detienen por

> nada, y se valen de los métodos más sucios y bajos para lograr sus negros intentos. Todavía con éstas pruebas patentes, ¿podrá el pueblo de Nuevo Mexico creer en un partido tan corrompido en cuyas filas existen hombres, métodos y planes tan viles, ponzoñosos y traicioneros? ¿Podrán creerse de un partido cuyo corazón es tan negro, cuyos principios se valen de armas ocultas y corrupción para fines vengativos. Creemos que no, y estamos ciertos que en la próxima elección quedará derrotado ese partido miserable, y que en el Condado de Valencia el autor del documento presentado arriba, le mostrará al pueblo el aborrecimiento que le tiene, derrotándole para la posición que aspira. Tales víboras debe quebrárseles la cabeza. Tales monstruos deben ser aniquilados. Donde hablan letras callan barbas.

La objetividad, sin embargo, es muchas veces una construcción discursiva con la cual el periódico responde a disputas ideológicas (muchas veces agresiones insultantes) que ocurren en el seno de la sociedad, y de la cual son víctimas los nuevomexicanos. Un episodio que merece la pena considerarse es el ocurrido en Las Vegas en octubre de 1901 (Fernández Gibert 2001: 361) cuando las palabras vertidas por la misionera protestante Nelly Snider —y reproducidas por *The Review*— motivó una protesta masiva del pueblo de Las Vegas. El editorial de *La Voz del Pueblo* condenará obviamente los excesos verbales de la citada misionera a partir de la introducción de las citas completas de aquellos párrafos más lacerantes. A través de esta técnica, el periódico se reafirma como defensor de los derechos de los hispanos acercándoles en traducción los párrafos más sobresalientes del ataque sufrido por la comunidad; pero, fundamentalmente, confirma frente a los ojos de la misma comunidad su papel moderado, objetivo y confiable. Es interesante observar cómo la aparentemente fría introducción está, desde el principio, salpicada de connotaciones negativas que preanuncian la posición editorial: “insultante”, “ramera”, “lupanar”, “atrevido”, “soez”:

> Ha llamado mucho la atención del pueblo de habla español de Las Vegas un artículo insultante contra el pueblo neo-mexicano de este Territorio publicado en el número del periódico semanario “The Review” correspondiente al Domingo último, y escrito, no por una ramera, ni por uno de esos caracteres depravados que se crean en los lupanares, según se creyó al principio juzgando por su lenguaje atrevido y soez, sino por una de esas que pretenden se agentes de Cristo en la tierra. Su nombre es Nellie Snider y segun estamos informados estuvo hasta últimamente “convirtiendo almas” en la misión protestante [...] Pero antes de hacer nuestra refutación, extractaremos del referido artículo aquellas partes que nos son más insultantes. Helas aquí: [aquí se inserta la traducción de *The Review*] (“Insultos Gratuitos”, 26 de octubre de 1901)

5) Uso de la negación como reforzador discursivo de la propia voz.

El argumento es introducido por el adverbio de negación *no* para hacer más fuerte la afirmación que sigue. Esta estrategia constituye una clara figura de manipulación comunicativa: el emisor empuja al destinatario hacia una posición extrema donde no es posible no aceptar las razones expuestas por el emisor. En palabras de Greimas (1980: 80) se trata de la construcción de un discurso cuya función no es el *decir verdadero* sino el *parecer verdadero*. En esta manipulación discursiva, el uso de la negación como introductor aparece, entonces, como un recurso eficaz dirigido a garantizar la adhesión del lector:

> ¿Qué no ha dado el pueblo Neo–Mejicano suficiente prueba de su abilida? ¿Qué sus hijos no poseen la capacidad? ¿Qué somos indignos á causa de que en nuestras venas surca la sangre Española? ("El ciudadano Hispano-Americano de Nuevo Mejico", 16 de febrero de 1889)

> Nuestra raza Hispano-Americana posee cualidades que no son segundas á las de ninguna otra raza en el mundo: su atrevimiento en todas las empresas ardúas y difíciles ha sido bien probado en todas ocasiones y de todas maneras como la historia lo recita. ("El tiempo se ha llegado", 2 de marzo de 1889)

> no hay cosa que se mueva hoy día en el Territorio que no se culpe por ello á la digna órden de Caballeros de Labor, la persecución es nuestra suerte y debemos arrostrarla hasta vencer y lograr nuestra justa y merecida vindicación ("Los Caballeros de Labor y Los Habladores", 16 de agosto de 1890)

> No es necesario pensar mucho para convencerse que el autor de tan viles insultos y bajas difamaciones no puede ser sino uno que está poseído de un odio y preocupación dignos de la ralea más baja que puede haber en toda la extencion del mundo, un degenerado charlatán, sin escrúpulo y sin pizca de vergüenza. ("Un egoísta degenerado", 2 de junio de 1906)

6) Uso de narrativas que dan luz y ejemplifican el propio discurso.

Según Blakemore la ejemplificación es "un camino común para proveer evidencia de algo o, simplemente, para brindar razones para creer algo". [(2001; 109)] Una de las maneras más típicas de ilustrar un texto es utilizando narrativas que generalmente apelan a la autoridad y que, además de ejemplificar, arrojan luz sobre el discurso propio.

> el horizonte refulgente de la libertad, extenderá sus rayos dorados, como cuando el Espíritu Santo, que nos refiere la Historia Dogmática, del Empireo Celeste [y se introduce la anécdota] (2 de marzo de 1889)

> La persecución de Los Caballeros de Labor nos recuerda de un parrafito que aprendimos hace muchos años, éste es: -'Había en una familia rica [y se introduce aquí la historia]' (16 de agosto de 1890)

Es frecuente que estas prácticas discursivas no aparezcan aisladas sino entrelazadas unas con otras. Es el caso del ejemplo que sigue donde para hacer su defensa del idioma español se introduce la voz de la autoridad (se cita otro periódico, en este caso *El Águila de Puerto Rico*) y además se introduce una narrativa para ejemplificar el punto de vista propio:

> Cuentan que Amadeo, rey de España, le preguntaba á su padre, el rey de Italia: ¿Cómo se puede gobernar en España? Y el rey "galantuomo" le contestó: "para gobernar en España hay que empezar por hablar español!"
>
> Es un hecho indiscutible que el que gobierna un país, debe saber hablar el idioma de aquel país. (5 de agosto de 1911)

7) Uso de la ironía como medio de desacreditar a los opositores:

La ironía representa una distancia enunciativa del emisor respecto de su enunciado, donde el que recibe el mensaje (para nosotros, el lector) percibe que lo que se dice *es lo contrario* de lo que se quiere decir. En este caso, para que la inversión de significado propuesta por la ironía cumpla con su cometido es necesaria la participación del lector que interprete el enunciado como irónico. En los ejemplos que proporcionamos, se advierte la no-adhesión del emisor a sus palabras a través de distintos mecanismos que operan como pistas para poder comprender la burla que dichas palabras contienen:

> *quienes saben de nosotros tanto como saben de los habitantes de la luna*[7] causan graves daños propagando sus equívocas nociones sobre asuntos y tocante á un pueblo que por su propio querer ignoran ó pretenden disminuirle en la estimacion de aquellos con quienes por casualidad conversan acerca de nosotros. ("Hispano Americano", 15 de febrero de 1890)
>
> Oradores por docena vertieron sus *almibaradas palabras en oídos sordos* —porque no quisieron oír sus necedades y propuestas ridículas— tocante al peregrino y singular documento que ellos llaman "La Constitución de Nuevo México" ("La Farsa", 30 de agosto de 1890)

8) Implicaciones y presuposiciones

Toda práctica discursiva implica una relación dialéctica con los otros participantes sociales caracterizada por la noción de hegemonía. En palabras de

Fairclough, una práctica discursiva es "an articulation of diverse social elements within a relatively stable configuration (2000: 168)". Así, el discurso incluye representaciones de cómo las cosas son, o cómo han sido, y cómo éstas deberían ser. Y, dado que el discurso es una práctica social, las representaciones deben ser, necesariamente, compartidas por el resto de la sociedad. Una presuposición es una información no requerida porque se asume como parte del conocimiento común (Ward, 2001; 121). De este modo, en los siguientes ejemplos es innecesario explicitar los nombres y apellidos de los personajes mencionados:

> según recientes entrevistas tenidas por ciudadanos de nuestro Territorio con algunos de los miembros del presente Congreso, parece que aún á esta fecha consideran á los ciudadanos nativos Hispano-Americanos, como una turba de ignorantes (15 de febrero de 1890)

> Los miembros de la Convención Constitucional de la trasera, en obediencia á un edicto expendido por su alteza el Conquistador de los reinos del triste y sangriento condado de Valencia (30 de agosto de 1890)

El siguiente ejemplo editorial publicado el 30 de septiembre de 1911 bajo el título "Los politiqueros tienen la culpa de que el pueblo no haya hecho mayor progreso" hace mención a la reciente historia del Partido Republicano, así como también a su situación actual; en ninguno de los casos es necesario hacer nombres porque ellos están presentes en la memoria colectiva:

> [Es notorio] que el Partido Republicano en Nuevo México ha estado dominado desde tiempo inmemorial por una corruptela podrida é ignorante que se ha cuidado más de mantenerse en el poder que del desarrollo del pueblo y sus intereses. El probar esto es cosa fácil. Las disenciones ahora existentes en el partido y los argumentos de los disidentes, es una prueba. Otra prueba convincente é irrefutable se tiene en el hecho que en el Partido Republicano; según ahora constituido, tienen mayor prestigio y más que decir los politiqueros arbitrarios, desconocedores de los derechos de otros, y sus compinches, los criminales, que los industriales hombres de bien.

9) Nodos semánticos

Es interesante señalar que los campos semánticos se articulan en función de oposiciones, construyéndose de este modo, la propia identidad. Así, desde el título seleccionado para cada uno de los editoriales se vislumbra la posición del artículo: "Hispano-Americano" se opone a los angloamericanos (15 de febrero de 1890); "Los Caballeros de Labor y los Habladores" (16 de agosto de 1890); "La verdad" cuyo título supone la existencia de su contrario *la mentira* (23 de agosto de 1890); "La Farsa" que vuelve a remitir al par *verdad-mentira* (30 de agosto de 1890); "Los Déspotas y el Ciudadano" (1 de noviembre de 1890); "Un egoísta degenerado" que supone la existencia de un *pueblo generoso* (2 de junio de 1906); "Los politiqueros" que enfrenta dos maneras de hacer política: la honrada y la criminal (30 de septiembre de 1911), etc.

La construcción de la identidad se realiza, entonces, a partir de contrastes que marcan claramente cuál es el lugar que cada grupo tiene en la representación social. Esta identidad, como bien señala Fernández Gibert (2001: 378) es debatida y negociada a través de las páginas de *La Voz del Pueblo.* El periódico, de este modo, resulta mediador y partícipe de esta negociación.

Conclusiones

Hemos definido el discurso como un sistema de referencias sociales que son inconscientemente aceptadas por la comunidad, y que funciona como un mecanismo que controla y regula la circulación de significados posibles que se establecen en toda comunicación. En este sentido, el periódico no sólo busca hacer circular la información sino que forma parte de la legitimación de ese discurso; discurso que, a su vez, es compartido por el resto de la sociedad que "lee" el periódico. El análisis de los elementos lingüísticos ofrecido aquí ha tratado de demostrar cómo el discurso acompaña la construcción de la identidad desde un punto de vista estratégico, semántico y gramatical. Esta construcción se ha mantenido constante en el periódico a lo largo de los años que preceden el ingreso de Nuevo México como un estado de la Unión Americana; en ese sentido, los ejemplos citados muestran que a pesar de las distintas circunstancias políticas de esos años, las prácticas del lenguaje fueron un elemento esencial en la construcción de la identidad neomexicana que acompañaría a los ciudadanos del estado a negociar su ingreso como parte de los Estados Unidos.

El lenguaje, entonces, es el que edifica, arma y ordena el mensaje llevando a un primer plano a los actores colectivos que merecen destacarse: "el pueblo nuevomexicano", "el pueblo Hispano-Americano", "la voluntad del pueblo", "los ciudadanos de nuestro territorio"; y desdibuja bajo la fina ironía o la indiferencia atroz la figura del adversario cuyo nombre particular casi nunca es rescatado más que por la sola mención de su representación política: "partidas de bandidos sostenidas y amparadas por los amos Republicanos"; "el órgano Republicano de Santa Fé", "los politiqueros del Partido Republicano", etc.

La construcción de la identidad no sólo se realiza a través de un gesto político. El lenguaje acompaña este gesto brindando todos los elementos y estrategias a su alcance en beneficio de esta dura pero eficaz tarea. El ejemplo de *La Voz del Pueblo* resulta paradigmático, no sólo por su importancia en la sociedad dada por la amplia circulación que el periódico tenía; sino porque en sus páginas es posible ver cómo operan, de una manera clara e inconfundible, todas las prácticas y estrategias lingüísticas propias del discurso político. Es en ese sentido que *La Voz del Pueblo* se transforma en un periódico ejemplar.

Notes

[1]En todos los casos respetamos la ortografía original del periódico.

[2]Siguiendo a Foucault (1999), se admite que cada sociedad configura determinados mecanismos que afectan a la producción de los discursos (restringiéndola a determinados individuos, seleccionando los temas que puede abarcar, o controlando su distribución, por ejemplo) así como a su recepción (limitando el acceso al mismo, o seleccionando determinados valores de verdad para ellos), de tal manera que el conjunto de discursos que la sociedad genera deben ser considerados como "prácticas discontinuas que se cruzan, a veces se yuxtaponen, pero que también se ignoran o se excluyen" (Foucault, 1999: 53) conformando un *orden* determinado.

[3]Para ampliar la noción de *marco discursivo*, consultar Fairclough 1992: 73.

[4]Sobre la historia del periódico, consultar Meléndez *So All Is Not Lost. The Poetics of Print in Nuevomexicano Communities, 1834-1958.*

[5]No entraremos en una discusión sobre la naturaleza de las oraciones pasivas; para una descripción más detallada consultar Bosque y Demonte 1999, volumen 2, capítulos 24 a 27.

[6]Sobre los efectos que la *pasivización* tiene en el manejo de la información, puede consultarse Gregory Ward and Betty J. Birner "Discourse and information Structure", p. 130-131.

[7]La bastardilla es nuestra y tiene como objetivo resaltar el mecanismo que provoca la ironía: en el primer ejemplo, la expresión exagerada "los habitantes de la luna" predispone la lectura del lector; en el segundo caso, el mismo efecto lo consigue la contraposición de *almibaradas palabras* vs. *oídos sordos*.

Referencias bibliográficas

Blakemore, Diane. "Discourse an Relevance Theory". Deborah Schiffrin et al. (eds.) *The Handbook of Discourse Analysis*. Oxford: Blackwell Publishers, 2001.

Bordieu, P. "A Reasoned Utopia and Economic Fatalism". *New Left Review* 227 (1998): 25-30.

Bosque, Ignacio y Violeta Demonte *Gramática descriptiva de la lengua española*. Madrid: Espasa Calpe, 1999.

Fairclough, Norman. *Discourse and Social Change*. Cambridge: Polity Press, 1992.

_____. "Discurso Social Theory and Social Research: The Discourse of Welfare Reform". *Journal of Sociolinguistics* 4 (2000): 163–195

Fernández Gibert, Arturo. *"La Voz del Pueblo*: texto, identidad y lengua en la prensa neomexicana, 1890-1911". Diss. U of New Mexico, 2001.

Foucault, Michel. *El orden del discurso*. Barcelona: Tusquets, 1999.

Greimas, A. J. "Le contract de véridiction". *Le vrai semblable et la fiction*. Gómez Moraina, ed. Montreal: K.R.Gürtller, 1980.

Gutiérrez Palacio, Juan. *Periodismo de Opinión*. Madrid, Paraninfo, 1984.

Kanellos, Nicolás, and Helvetia Martell. *Hispanic Periodicals in the United States. Origins to 1960. A Brief History and Comprehensive Bibliography*. Houston: Arte Público Press,1984.

Lozano, Jorge, Cristina Peña-Marín, y Gonzalo Abril. *Análisis del discurso. Hacia una semiótica de la interacción textual*. Madrid: Cátedra, 2004.

Meléndez, A. Gabriel. *So All Is Not Lost. The Poetics of Print in Nuevomexicano Communities, 1834-1958*. Albuquerque: University of Mexico Press, 1997.

Mendikoetxea, Amaya. "Construcciones con *se*: Medias, pasivas e impersonales". *Gramática descriptiva de la lengua española*. Ignacio Bosque y Violeta Demonte, eds. Madrid: Espasa Calpe, 1999. 2, 1631-1723.

Ward, Gregory and Betty Birner. "Discourse and Information Structure". *The Handbook of Discourse Analysis*. Deborah Schiffrin et al, eds. Oxford: Blackwell Publishers, 2001.

Wilson, John "Political Discourse". *The Handbook of Discourse Analysis*. Deborah Schiffrin et al, eds. Oxford: Blackwell Publishers, 2001.

La “construcción” de una nación puertorriqueña en la prensa escrita

Edwin Karli Padilla Aponte
University of Houston-Downtown

Este trabajo pretende retornar al Nueva York de los años cuarenta y “filosofar” utilizando como fuente la producción periodística de puertorriqueños que escribieron en *Pueblos Hispanos* (1943-1944) durante los años de la Segunda Guerra Mundial. Partían de la premisa de que en Puerto Rico existía desde el siglo XIX un grupo nacional,[1] y a través de estas columnas periodísticas se dieron a la tarea de legitimar la existencia de esta nación.

El inminente desenlace de la Segunda Guerra Mundial, durante la primera mitad de los años cuarenta, anticipaba para las colonias en Asia, África y América el fin de su estatus político, y este grupo de escritores puertorriqueños buscaban crear los consensos necesarios para que Puerto Rico formara también parte de los nuevos acuerdos. El concepto de la *autodeterminación de los pueblos*[2] que sostiene la idea de que todo gobierno extranjero es ilegítimo se esparce por todos los rincones del mundo colonial, y estos periodistas amparados en las promesas de Inglaterra y Estados Unidos en la Carta del Atlántico (1941)[3], anticipaban una pronta independencia para la isla. Bernardo Vega recoge el sentir popular en Nueva York antes y después de la guerra en sus *Memorias* señalando:

> Con el fin de la guerra, todos los puertorriqueños, no importa el lugar del mundo donde estuvieran, pensaban que el problema de la soberanía de Puerto Rico habría de resolverse pronto. Una de las cuestiones más importantes en discusión en los foros internacionales era, precisamente, la abolición del colonialismo. Quién iba a pensar que se iniciaría su desaparición rápidamente en África y demás continentes, y en la misma región del

> Caribe, con Jamaica, Trinidad y Barbados, sin salir Puerto Rico de su condición colonial.(265)

Estos periodistas puertorriqueños contemplaban muy de cerca el desenlace de la guerra y sus inmediatas repercusiones y, por tal motivo, dedicaban muchas páginas a preparar a los lectores para enfrentarlos a este crucial momento. Aparecen durante estos años el Proyecto Tydings[4] y el Proyecto Marcoantonio[5] como opciones de acción política y económica una vez se alcanzara la independencia de Puerto Rico. En fin, ante la esperanza de que ocurrieran cambios políticos para la isla durante estos años surgieron expectativas entre estos periodistas en Nueva York, y no se desperdició oportunidad alguna para reafirmar la existencia de la nación puertorriqueña. La definición Estalinista de nación popularizada a principios de siglo les sirvió como un modelo teórico para probar ante los lectores que Puerto Rico, desde la segunda mitad del siglo XIX en adelante, se había convertido en un grupo nacional, al cual España y Estados Unidos le habían arrebatado el derecho a su soberanía. Señala un editorial:

> A la hora en que el ejército de los EE.UU. invadió y sometió por la fuerza la patria de los puertorriqueños al yugo de su dominio, Puerto Rico habiendo logrado ya comunidad de idioma, de vida, de trabazón económica, y de comunidad sicológica expresada en una cultura común era una nación, ya que "nación es una comunidad estable, históricamente formada, de idioma, de territorio, de vida económica y de psicología manifestada ésta en la comunidad de cultura. (*Pueblos Hispanos*, 22 de abril de 1944)

Las constantes luchas entre puertorriqueños por motivo de clase social, ideología política y raza, que habían protagonizado muchas de las columnas anteriores,[6] pasaron a un segundo plano durante este crucial momento histórico, y gran cantidad de los escritos en *Pueblos Hispanos* se concentraron en unificar, engrandecer y glorificar la nación puertorriqueña. Señala un editorial:

> Para la unión nacional todos hemos de sacrificar algo. El doctrinarismo intransigente, no importa cuan hermosa sea para la depuración interior de almas las más excelsas o las más pervertidas, es lesivo a la unión nacional, y, por ende, de la independencia de Puerto Rico. Sólo en esto debemos ser intrasingentes: en el frente nacional pro independencia no cabe ningún fascista, no cabe ningún enemigo de la clase trabajadora: Puerto Rico es una nación de campesinos y obreros y esa razón basta. En el frente nacional deben estar a la vanguardia los sindicatos obreros. Pero también es necesaria la adhesión servicial de muchos otros grupos. Curas católicos y azucareros también caben en el frente nacional pro independencia, junto a comunistas y socialistas y nacionalistas, con tal que todos comprendan que

la independencia se hace para dar a los puertorriqueños la oportunidad de ser felices . . . (*Pueblos Hispanos*, 25 de marzo de 1943)

En otras palabras, para que existiera la nación puertorriqueña era necesario que los lectores echaran a un lado sus diferencias internas y dejaran de difundir la *literatura de la docilidad*[7] con raíces en la *muchedumbre sin alma* que Rosendo Matienzo Cintrón[8] dejó inscrita a principio de siglo, en la *masa amorfa* que denunció Vicente Géigel Polanco[9] a la llegada de los estadounidenses en el noventa y ocho y en los *aplatanaos* que Antonio S. Pedreira[10] ridiculizó en los años treinta. Por el contrario, cada una de estas percepciones negativas del puertorriqueño desaparecen en los cuarenta, y las columnas en *Pueblos Hispanos* se comprometen a legitimar la existencia de la nación puertorriqueña.

Construcción de la nación

La primera tarea de los constructores de la nación fue legitimar su nacimiento o establecer unos orígenes, y la revuelta armada de Lares (1868) frente al ejército español les sirve como ese imprescindible punto de partida. Entre la abundante cantidad de escritos en *Pueblos Hispanos* que glorifican uno de los episodios más oscuros en la historia de Puerto Rico se encuentra una narración de Gabriel Aracelis[11] en su columna semanal titulada *Viñetas*:

> En Aguadilla. Siglo pasado. Una mujer lucha con los últimos dolores de parto. Es bella esta mujer . . . El niño va a nacer. Declara su derecho a la vida con agudo chillido. Pregunta la madre por primera vez alterada. ¿Es varón? Sí. Es un varón. Este varón ha nacido en una cárcel . . . Esta mujer es la primera mujer de la patria borincana. Su nombre es Mariana Bracetti. En su tiempo la llamaron Brazo de Oro.

Agrega,

> Meses antes de este parto Mariana Bracetti cosía en su hogar. Es decir, antes de haber dado a luz en la cárcel a su hijo, había dado a luz en sus habitaciones a la bandera del naciente pueblo. (*Pueblos Hispanos*, 12 de junio de 1943)

El periodista intenta crear con este nacimiento una metáfora o el símbolo del natalicio del primer puertorriqueño usando al hijo de la mujer que tejió la bandera de la revuelta en Lares (bandera de Puerto Rico). El ser varón y haber nacido en la cárcel crea la imagen poética de una nación y una bandera prisioneras por un poder invasor. Apunta Walter Connors que la creencia del grupo en la existencia de un origen compartido es necesaria para la psicología nacional y precisamente es lo que Gabriel Aracelis aspira al dramatizar el supuesto nacimiento del primer puertorriqueño (185). Los mitos nacionales —apunta Connors— engendran su propia realidad, y apelan a los sentimientos del grupo, sin tener que ser explicados racionalmente. Agrega que a partir de estos mitos colectivos surgen conductas que no se inspiran en la realidad, sino en lo que los participantes del mito creen que es real (135).

En este ejercicio por legitimar la existencia de la nación puertorriqueña se escriben pasquines, pancartas o publicaciones que el estudioso no toma en serio por considerarlas como propaganda política que ni siquiera convencía a sus autores; sin embargo, lo que interesa resaltar en este trabajo no es la credibilidad de este material propagandístico sino el sentimiento nacionalista que despierta en sus seguidores. Por ejemplo,

> Vamos otra vez en Peregrinación Patriótica a Lares. Vamos a jurar otra vez nuestra consagración a la independencia de nuestra patria. Vamos a jurar, ante el reposo de los Inmortales, nuestra lealtad a su descendencia. Vamos a jurar, ante la serena mirada que desde la eternidad nos miran los Padres de nuestra Patria, como restauradores. Vamos a jurar, ante las generaciones venideras . . . A Lares, nacionalistas puertorriqueños, es el 23 de septiembre. (*Pueblos Hispanos*, 18 de septiembre de 1943)

Aparecen proclamas, frases patrióticas e imágenes que evocan la familia, los hermanos, la sangre, las bellezas de la isla y el deber patriótico hacia los mártires que derramaron su sangre en Lares. En estas proclamas se exhorta al lector a cumplir con estas promesas patrióticas con la esperanza de que las generaciones venideras disfruten algún día del fruto de estos sacrificios. Por ejemplo, en *Mujer y Borincanidad* (*Pueblos Hispanos*, 23 de septiembre 1944) Consuelo Lee Tapia[12] enfatiza el deber de la mujer en la lucha por la libertad de Puerto Rico y, por supuesto, Mariana Bracetti se convierte nuevamente en el arquetipo que toda mujer debe seguir.

> Nosotras las puertorriqueñas tenemos una promesa que cumplir, una promesa sagrada, una promesa de madre. Ya es tiempo que nosotras las madres puertorriqueñas agarremos la bandera y con todo el derecho, el valor, la abnegación y el sentido de justicia y deber nos pongamos cara a cara al enemigo y hundamos su resistencia en una ola de protesta hasta libertar nuestra patria . . . Ahora que el mundo entero lucha por el principio por el cual nuestra propia Mariana Bracetti tuvo su hijo en una prisión española, luchemos para que ningún puertorriqueño que dio su sangre en la lucha por la libertad la haya dado de balde, para que ningún puertorriqueño que hoy da su sangre para asegurarnos el derecho de unirnos al conjunto de naciones en la post guerra como nación que ha luchado por la democracia, deje su vida en lares extraños, sin la seguridad de que todas las madres puertorriqueñas son responsables por esas vidas puertorriqueñas . . . ¡Puer-

> torriqueños oid el Grito de Lares! ¡Oid la voz de Mariana Bracetti! ¡Cumplid la promesa de Lares!

¿A qué promesa se refiere la columnista? ¿Qué realmente dijo Mariana Bracetti en el mil novecientos sesenta y ocho? En caso que hubiera dicho algo, ¿estuvo consciente de la transcendencia histórica de sus palabras? No existe ningún documento escrito por Mariana Bracetti que exprese un mensaje trascendental, y Consuelo Lee Tapia en este fragmento recurre a lo que Benedict Anderson (274-278) denomina como ventriloquia o el escribir en nombre de los muertos.

Gabriel Aracelis va aún más allá que Consuelo Lee Tapia y en otra de sus viñetas (*Pueblos Hispanos*, 21 de agosto de 1943) presenta detalladamente un presunto levantamiento revolucionario en 1898 donde los insurgentes toman la comandancia del pueblo de Ciales a sólo días de que ocurriera el cambio de soberanía. El columnista narra detalladamente la batalla en que se apoderan del pueblo, y nombra a cada uno de los rebeldes por nombre y apellido, lo cual otorga historicidad a un suceso que no aparece —hasta lo que yo he investigado— en la historia oficial de Puerto Rico.[13] Se mencionan escopetas, fusiles, balas, machetes hasta que finalmente se anuncia el triunfo y el control del pueblo. Señala el cronista en señal de triunfo: *Ciales había dejado de ser español para ser puertorriqueño*. Posteriormente arriban refuerzos del ejército español y aplacan a los conspiradores una vez se les agotan las municiones. Señala Gabriel Aracelis que Pedro González —nieto de un tal Manuel González, excombatiente de Lares (1868)— prefiere morir antes de ir a la cárcel, lo cual no sólo establece continuidad sanguínea con los patriotas que derramaron su sangre en el mil ochocientos sesenta y ocho sino que también establece una conexión ideológica al elegir la muerte a la sumisión colonial. Irónicamente la columna finaliza aludiendo a la entrega de Puerto Rico a Estados Unidos solo unos días después, sin que los españoles dispararan un solo tiro.

En este tipo de columna se establece que la naciente nación puertorriqueña había estado próxima a liberarse de España cuando la Guerra Hispanoamericana (1898) interrumpe este proceso natural y Puerto Rico pasa a formar parte del botín de guerra. Los periodistas examinan la ilegalidad en que se produjo tal adquisición, y se exhorta a los lectores a acabar con la colonia mediante una participación conjunta. En otras palabras, los periodistas buscaban crear los necesarios consensos de manera que los lectores apoyaran los proyectos que buscaban terminar el status colonial una vez se pusiera sobre la mesa el caso de Puerto Rico. La prensa de este período mostraba en sus páginas que a pesar de cuarenta y cinco años de civilización estadounidense, Puerto Rico no había salido del sub-desarrollo económico, y sólo se había convertido en una plantación de azúcar que ni siquiera les pertenecía a los puertorriqueños. Señala el editorial:

> Con franqueza patriótica, con conciencia internacional, colocamos el caso puertorriqueño en el Programa de las Naciones Unidas y repetimos que EE.UU. no tiene derechos sobre Puerto Rico. Así se despertó, por medio de más de un año de lucha en este periódico, la iniciativa puertorriqueña, aquí y allá. Los que no querían hablar, se atrevieron. (*Pueblos Hispanos*, 22 de abril de 1944)

Con el propósito de presionar al gobierno estadounidense se buscaba apoyo de la política liberal norteamericana, de manera que se reconociera a Puerto Rico como una nación, y muchos de los escritos de Earl Browder —Secretario General del Partido Comunista en los Estados Unidos— fueron traducidos al español en *Pueblos Hipanos*. En *Puerto Rico en la victoria y después* (*Pueblos Hispanos*, 6 de marzo de 1943), Earl Browder señala:

> Esa isla es uno de nuestros puestos de avanzada militar. Tan completamente hemos olvidados como nación que Puerto Rico no es sólo una "posesión" sino también una nación de cerca de dos millones de hombres, mujeres y niños [. . .] Cierto que Puerto Rico no puede conmover la conciencia como lo hace la India, con el ruido de titánicas convulsiones, porque Puerto Rico no es un gigante. Pero las naciones pequeñas tienen también sus medios para probar que la opresión lleva consigo su propio castigo, como los irlandeses le han demostrado a Inglaterra y al mundo entero.

A pesar de que existía optimismo en que la historia se encargara finalmente de extirpar el coloniaje del mundo moderno, se desconfiaba de los grupos anexionistas puertorriqueños que ocupaban puestos políticos y presionaban al gobierno de Estados Unidos para que Puerto Rico se convirtiera en un estado más de la Confederación. De esa posibilidad nacía el desprecio hacia el político asalariado que servía a los intereses de la colonia y traicionaba los principios de la independencia. En la columna de Don Goyo aparece el poema *El gallo Malino* de Luis Lloréns Torres (*Pueblos Hispanos*, 16 de septiembre de 1944), dedicado a los gallos manilos o búlicos que se conforman con los granos de maíz que recibían sin pasar esfuerzo. El protagonista del poema, ave de nueve libras y figura central del gallinero, es caracterizado porque *No hay quien lo haga pelear*. Su carácter conformista aparece en versos como los que siguen:

> Huele a gallinero
> y a desperdicios de cocina,
> No hay quien lo haga pelear

Aletea y cocoroquea muchísimo
pero no dice nada,
como la mayor parte de nuestros
treinta o cuarenta mil oradores políticos.
No hay quien lo haga pelear

Da vivas a la Constitución Americana,
a la bandera de las franjas y estrellas
y a la mazorca de maíz.
Pero no hay quien lo haga pelear

El estribillo se repite en cada una de las estrofas del poema hasta que al final la ira del poeta interrumpe la monotonía del estribillo y exclama airadamente, ¡Pero ni Dios lo hace pelear!

Más desilucionada aún ante el conformismo y la pasividad de los líderes de la colonia aparece Julia de Burgos, y en *Canto a José Martí* (*Pueblos Hispanos*, 20 de mayo de 1944) le exige al mártir que despierte de su sueño y vuelva a la lucha para rescatar la isla menor. En este poema, la poetisa ha perdido toda esperanza en los líderes de la colonia y desesperadamente le implora al fenecido mártir el regreso a batalla.

Se reitera que la prensa puertorriqueña en Nueva York deseaba una y otra vez dejar clara la existencia de la nación puertorriqueña por encima de la condición de colonia, y las expectativas que se vislumbraban tras una victoria de los aliados durante la Segunda Guerra Mundial alentaban las esperanzas de su final liberación. Mientras este momento llegara, era imprescindible para estos intelectuales celebrar las fechas históricas que conmemoraban las hazañas de la nación puertorriqueña y *El grito de Lares* (1868) y *la Matanza de Ponce* (1936) —ocurrida sólo años atrás— respondían a estos propósitos patrióticos.

Identidad nacional

En lo que respecta a la identidad nacional, los *constructores de la nación* tienen la necesidad de rescatar las peculiaridades reconocibles que definan lo que es un puertorriqueño, y de ahí reiteran la noción de principios de siglo de que (1) el jíbaro es la base de la identidad nacional, (2) declaran el español como la lengua oficial de los puertorriqueños, (3) proclaman la música de Juan Morel Campos y Rafael Hernández como manifestaciones de ese alma nacional, y (4) hasta las comidas típicas y los paisajes de Puerto Rico se impregnan de significados nacionalistas. Señala Jesús Colón,

> Por fin se ha organizado un certamen que me gusta. Un certamen de algo que habla de mi alma puertorriqueña y me hace visionar agradablemente

> los "atrechos" y las hondonadas de mi isla querida, el bohío desafiando el precipicio; el jíbaro-espina dorsal de mi patria —*cantando así* por el eterno camino de nuestras esperanzas . . . Por fin un concurso puertorriqueño sobre una cosa puertorriqueña... Todos hemos oído hablar sobre certámenes de bañistas, de bailadores, concurso de comedores de "pie": pero nunca habíamos oído hablar sobre un certamen de cantadores de décimas jíbaras . . . El gran problema nuestro en Estados Unidos es el atrevernos a continuar siendo puertorriqueños [. . .] De ahí a afirmar que se siente más placer bailando un "fox trox" que una pieza de Rafael Hernández no hay nada más que un paso. [A éstos] no se le puede hablar de Juan Morel Campos, el que cristalizó para siempre toda la gracia de la mujer boricua del siglo diecinueve en una serie de inmortales danzas; no se le puede hablar de la poesía de Gautier ni del Río de la Plata, ni del Yunque de Luquillo, ni de Las Vegas de Comerío. Es un pobre diablo, que en su fanatismo por la americanización mal comprendida, cree que un "sandwich" de jamón sabe mejor que un plato de arroz con gandules.

En este fragmento el columnista deposita ese alma nacional en los paisajes, en las comidas y en la música popular de Puerto Rico, con el propósito de transmitirles a los lectores puertorriqueños el deseo por la lucha. La plasmación de este sentimiento a través de manifestaciones como las anteriores penetra donde las palabras o las explicaciones racionales no pueden alcanzar. Jesús Colón, en este tipo de columna, descontextualiza de su intrínsico valor los paisajes de la isla, las comidas y los exponentes musicales más celebrados durante el siglo XIX y XX, y arbitrariamente les estampa un sello nacional. ¿Acaso el Río de la Plata y el Yunque son portadores de significados que van más allá del topográfico? ¿Cómo el gusto por la comida y la bebida pueden crear marcas para definir sentimientos nacionalistas? Al mismo tiempo el columnista demuestra selectividad al apropiarse para sus propósitos de la danza de Juan Morel Campos y la música de Rafael Hernández, y excluye géneros musicales y autores de este proyecto nacionalista. En fin, la construcción de la identidad nacional puertorriqueña se va construyendo selectivamente por arte de su pluma con la intención de que se fuera transmitiendo a los lectores los sentimientos patrióticos. Una vez se crean las bases de lo que debe ser un puertorriqueño el columnista las contrasta con aquellos que en Nueva York manifiestan los síntomas de la transculturación. Agrega,

> Cuando a Ud. comienza a gustarle más una Coca-Cola que un mabí frío o una horchata de ajonjolí o cuando a Ud. comienza a saberle mejor un "rice pudding" que un "dulce" de arroz con coco hecho con azúcar prieta, Ud. está en un grave peligro de perder vuestra puertorriqueñidad. (123)

Sin embargo, se reitera que la nación puertorriqueña nunca podría existir a pesar de estos esfuerzos sin que se lograra un consenso entre el público-lector; de lo contrario, este proyecto nacional peligraba en sólo ser una *comunidad imaginada* con única existencia dentro del reducido círculo de periodistas. Por tal razón, Jesús Colón —al igual que otros columnistas— exhorta a toda la intelectualidad puertorriqueña en Nueva York a tomar una parte activa en la propagación de este proyecto nacional, de manera que Puerto Rico alcanzara su independencia junto a las colonias europeas que aún quedaban en las Américas. En *Puerto Rico es también una nación,* Colón señala:

> Una de las tareas que tendremos que imponernos todos los que escribimos o hablamos es el repetir durante todas las horas del día y siempre que se nos dé la oportunidad, el hecho histórico, la verdad palpable que debiéramos de saber todos —y actuar de acuerdo— de que Puerto Rico es también una nación, o sea, *una comunidad estable históricamente formada, de idioma, de territorio, de vida económica y de psicología, que se traducen en una comunidad de cultura,*[14] según la moderna definición del concepto. (141)

La misión de unir bajo una misma bandera a los puertorriqueños durante los cuarenta llevó a Jesús Colón a pasar por alto la existencia de prejuicios raciales, lo cual creaba unas contradicciones con sus columnas periodísticas antes y después de los años que escribió en *Pueblos Hispanos*.[15] En la misma columna señala:

> Otros de los momentos en que no se actúa como puertorriqueño es cuando se incitan odios y prejuicios raciales . . . Si algo tenemos los puertorriqueños —los verdaderos puertorriqueños— superior a los norteamericanos, es la completa ausencia de prejuicios raciales en nuestra personalidad como pueblo. El prejuicio racial que existe en Puerto Rico hoy, lo importaron los yanquis a Puerto Rico, junto con el absentismo que nos pauperiza, y el bilingüismo que nos embrutece. El prejuicio racial no es una característica puertorriqueña . . . (141)

Esta controversial declaración de un puertorriqueño negro dirigida hacia lectores que habían conocido directa e indirectamente el prejuicio racial en Puerto Rico no tiene otro propósito que el de "callar" las divisiones internas que siempre habían existido en función de la necesaria unidad que requería el momento histórico. Al mismo tiempo, Jesús Colón se hacía eco de Tomás Blanco quien también había negado la existencia de tales prejuicios en Puerto Rico.[16]

Comentarios finales

Esta breve investigación ha tenido entre sus propósitos el exaltar la importancia que ha tenido la prensa escrita para crear identidades. La prensa escrita, a diferencia de los géneros canónicos —novela, ensayo, poesía y teatro—, siempre se ha encontrado más cercana al ciudadano promedio y ha sido más eficaz en la creación de consensos. Sin embargo, la dificultad que ha habido para conservarla ha evitado que el estudioso le dedique la necesaria atención al emprender este tipo de investigación y, por tal razón, se han privilegiado los géneros asociados a los grupos letrados.

La investigación ha tenido que limitarse por razones de espacio a un sólo periódico y a un momento específico de la inmigración puertorriqueña, lo cual ha evitado que se haya podido examinar una mayor cantidad de periodistas y periódicos. Un estudio mayor tendría que tomar en cuenta toda la producción periodística de puertorriqueños en publicaciones como *Artistas Hispanos* (1948-19uu), *El Boricua* (194u-19uu), *Brooklyn, Colonia Latina* (1938-19uu), *Brújula* (1940-19uu), *La voz* (1937-1939), *Kan-de-la* (1949-19uu), etc., que dieran voces a todas las ideologías en este debate político-cultural. Sin embargo, a pesar de ser éste un estudio a pequeña escala, se han presentado unas bases teóricas que podrían servirles a los estudiosos en la investigación de este tipo de fenómeno.

Por otro lado, está por discutirse si la prensa escrita de puertorriqueños en estos años logró crear una *comunidad imaginada* en el sentido de Benedict Anderson. Ese sentimiento colectivo no pudo ni habría podido convertirse en una realidad a menos que las masas populares hubieran sido las únicas protagonistas. Es decir, los periodistas que escribieron en estos periódicos, al igual que la intelectualidad proveniente de las instituciones de cultura, no forman la nación ni tampoco la identidad nacional, y sólo pueden crear con sus plumas las condiciones para que tal identidad nacional y tal nación surjan. La misma lengua, los bellos paisajes, un territorio común, el gusto por la comida y la música, y la bandera no son equivalentes a la nación, pero preparan el camino para que ésta emerja.

Notas

[1]Walter Connors (21-23) señala que ha existido una inclinación a denominar a los grupos nacionales y a las naciones a través de manifestaciones tangibles como la lengua, la religión, las costumbres, la ubicación a un territorio específico y características de este tipo. Estas peculiaridades, a diferencia de las de índole psicológicas, son cuantificables y fáciles de explicar a la audiencia, y se

manejan fácilmente para crear diferencias de tipo 'nosotros-ellos'. Estas manifestaciones tangibles serán el blanco de en este estudio y se pretende demostrar que los periodistas en *Pueblos Hispanos* buscaban legitimar la existencia de una nación puertorriqueña, por supuesto, un grupo nacional.

[2]Según Walter Connors (4-26) la autodeterminación de las naciones fue un concepto destinado a las colonias que se encontraban bajo la soberanía de los países que perdieron la guerra; sin embargo, se propagó de tal manera que cualquier grupo que repudiara una dominación extranjera tenía el derecho a invocarlo.

[3]Juan José Benales señala en "La carta del Atlántico" (*Pueblos Hispanos*, 2 de octubre de 1943) *La Carta del Atlántico es de ahora en adelante una promesa y una esperanza para la nación puertorriqueña. La unión nacional de los puertorriqueños para conquistar sus fines, ¡Esa es ahora la tarea fundamental de todos los puetorriqueños!* Juan Marinelo apunta (*Pueblos Hispanos*, 10 de abril de 1943) *La Carta del Atlántico reza que a toda nación ha de darse el mando efectivo de su camino político. Excelente Venga ese mando, ya que por él hemos derrado sangre y sufrido estrecheces.*

[4]Independientemente de lo controversial del proyecto Tydings y de las divisiones que ocasionó entre la comunidad puertorriqueña, hay que verlo como una alternativa al estado colonial de Puerto Rico. Véase Otra vez la República de trapo (*Pueblos Hispanos*, 10 de abril de 1943) y *A Puerto Rico*: ¡Qué se Chupe el deo! (*Pueblos Hispanos*, 9 de octubre de 1943).

[5]A diferencia del proyecto Tydings, el Proyecto Marcantonio, según Bernardo Vega en sus memorias, propone un trato más justo para Puerto Rico. Véase el texto íntegro del Proyecto Marcantonio para la independencia de Puerto Rico (*Pueblos Hispanos* (10 de julio de 1943).

[6]Existió durante los años veinte y treinta una división entre los puertorriqueños por clase social, poder político e inclusive por color de piel, las cuales aparecen en las publicaciones de Joaquín Colón y Jesús Colón en *Gráfico*, *Vida Alegre* y *El Curioso*. Ver Lo que el pueblo me dice . . . y *Pioneros puertorriqueños en Nueva York.*

[7]Juan Ángel Silén plantea (57) que la literatura de la docilidad en Puerto Rico ha imperado en los períodos de crisis, y culpa a los sectores académicos de inicios de siglo por haber mantenido vigente esta concepción determinista que ha mantenido al puertorriqueño subordinado a la naturaleza. Ve a Pedreira e *Insularismo* como uno de los mentores y agentes propagandísticos de esta interpretación determinista que para el 1898 había sido una de las razones que justificaron la invasión norteamericana, en el sentido de que las razas más avanzadas estaban destinadas a conquistar.

[8]Rosendo Matienzo Cintrón pronunció en el 1903 las siguientes palabras: "Hoy Puerto Rico es solamente una muchedumbre, pero cuando la muchedumbre puertorriqueña tenga un alma, entonces Puerto Rico será una patria".

[9]Vicente Géigel Polanco responsabiliza (33) a la *masa amorfa* por no haberse revelado contra los norteamericanos en el 1898: "No teníamos pueblo. No había conciencia colectiva. Sólo teníamos muchedumbre sumida en la ignorancia. Un campesinado con la espalda corvada sobre el verdor de los sembrados, sin afanes de mejoramientos, ni esperanzas ni retención".

[10]Antonio S. Pedreira en *Insularismo* se dispuso a buscar ese alma nacional en los años treinta y el aplatanamiento del puertorriqueño (22-23) viene a ser un obstáculo para que ésta surja. Éste se define como "una especie de inhibición, de modorra mental y ausencia de acometividad. Es seguir, sin sofocarse, cómoda y rutinariamente, el curso de la vida, sin cambios ni inquietudes, cabeceando nuestras aspiraciones y en cuclillas frente al porvenir".

[11]No se ha podido investigar quién se esconde detrás del seudónimo, pero basado en la temática que aparecen en sus Viñetas y en la importancia que adquiere el pueblo de Ciales, se podría especular que se trata del mismo Juan Antonio Corretjer, uno de los fundadores y editores del periódico, oriundo de Ciales.

[12]Poeta patriota, nieta de Alejandro Tapia y Rivera y fundadora, junto a su esposo Juan Antonio Corretjer, de *Pueblos Hispanos*. Véase *En otra voz* para más información (313-315).

[13]Probablemente este episodio esté aludiendo a *Las Partidas Sediciosas* o, según Paul G. Miller —comisionado de Instrucción pública en Puerto Rico y autor del texto de *Historia de Puerto Rico*—, a un grupo de bandidos que asaltaban propiedades de españoles a finales del siglo diecinueve. Robaban las mercancías establecidas en los campos, asaltaban las haciendas, y cometieron algunos asesinatos. Juan Antonio Corretjer, (1-36) rechaza esta versión de Miller y señala que Las Partidas Sediciosas fueron grupos revolucionarios que surgieron a consecuencia de la entrada de las tropas estadounidenses a Puerto Rico. Señala Corretjer, "No se ha señalado todavía, que yo sepa, la enorme importancia de este movimiento espontáneo, alentado, en sus inicios, por algunos dignos conspiradores revolucionarios". (36)

[14]Nuevamente la definición textual de José Stalin.

[15]Vea *Invitación y Mis Cívica empolvada* (75-81) antes de los cuarenta y *Angels in my Hometown Church* (53-54) y *The Negro in Puerto Rico Today* después de los cuarenta.

[16]Probablemente la postura del cronista tenga relación con la de Tomás Blanco (43) quien durante estos años estableció una diferencia en el tipo de racismo que existía en Estados Unidos con la relación entre negros y blancos en Puerto Rico: "En Puerto Rico blancos y negros viven en perfecta armonía, se ha-

llan juntos en las escuelas públicas de todas las categorías, en la Universidad, y en todas las oficinas y profesiones".

Bibliografía

Anderson Benedict. *Comunidades imaginadas*. Madrid: Trama Editorial, 1997.

Blanco, Tomás. *El prejuicio racial en Puerto Rico*. New York: Arno Press, 1975.

Colón, Jesús. *Lo que el pueblo me dice*. Editado por Edwin K. Padilla. Houston: Arte Público Press, 2001.

_____. *A Puerto Rican in New York and Other Skeches*. New York: Mainstream Publishers, 1961.

_____. The Way It Was and Other Writings. Houston: Arte Público Press, 1993.

Colón, Joaquín. *Pioneros puertorriqueños en Nueva York*. Arte Público Presss, 2002.

Connors, Walter. *Entonacionalismo*. Madrid: Trama Editorial, 1994.

Corretjer, Juan Antonio. *La lucha por la independencia de Puerto Rico*. Ciales, Puerto Rico: Casa Corretjer, 1995.

Kanellos, Nicolás. *En otra voz*. Houston, Texas: Arte Público Press, 2002.

_____. *Hispanic Periodicals in the United States*. Houston, Texas: Arte Público Press, 2000.

Pedreira, Antonio S. *Insularismo*. Río Piedras: Editorial Edil, 1973.

Polanco Géigel, Vicente. *El despertar de un pueblo*. San Juan: Biblioteca de Autores Puertorriqueños, 1942.

Pueblos Hispanos. New York. N.Y., 1943-1944. (Newspaper in microfilm), Recovering the U.S. Hispanic Literary Heritage Project, Houston, Texas.

Silén, Juan Ángel. *Hacia una visión positiva del puertorriqueño*. Río Piedras: Editorial Edil, 1970.

Smith, Anthony. *La identidad nacional*. Madrid: Trama Editorial, 1997.

Vega, Bernardo. *Memorias de Bernardo Vega*. Editadas por César Andreu Iglesias. Río Piedras: Ediciones Huracán, 1988.

Josephina Niggli as a Regional Voice: A Re-examination of *Mexican Village* and *Step Down Elder Brother*

Donna M. Kabalen de Bichara
Tecnológico de Monterrey

Mexican-American writer Josephina Niggli was born in Monterrey, Mexico in 1910 where she lived until the start of the Mexican Revolution in 1913 when she and her mother left suddenly for San Antonio. Together with her parents she returned to Mexico in 1920. Her father took a position as the General Manager of the cement plant in Hidalgo, yet the family would decide to leave once again in 1925 because of further revolutionary turmoil. Niggli would often return to Mexico for visits, but the greater part of her life was spent in the United States. Thus, what is intriguing about Niggli's writing is her "fine grasp of the ironies and contradictions of Mexican culture," (Paredes, "Mexican-American Literature" 39) in spite of having lived in Mexico for only eight years.

On the basis of this family history, it is clear that Niggli's keen understanding and portrayal of her home country demonstrates more than a simple love of writing which she developed early on in life. Rather it would seem that the subject of Mexico evident in her literature is an expression of something deeper, that is, her sense of dual identity. As a means of exploring this issue, it is interesting to note that at the time of her birth, and according to Article 30 of the Mexican Constitution of 1857, Niggli would not have qualified for Mexican citizenship precisely because her parents were Scandanavian American and not Mexican. However, with the revision of Article 30 in the Mexican Constitution of 1917, which stipulates that "Son mexicanos por nacimiento: los que nazcan en territorio de la República, sea cual fuere la nacionalidad de sus padres," Niggli did indeed acquire a legal claim to Mexican citizenship. There is no evidence that she desired to claim that right; yet because her narratives demonstrate a depth of knowledge regarding Mexico, its values and traditions, as well as its people, she would seem to be expressing, through the written word, her sense of belonging to Mexico. Interestingly, it is Niggli herself who sheds light on this question. In a paper entitled "The Importance of History and the Novel for Better Relationships Between Countries" which she presented in 1949 at the Primera Reunión de Historiadores Mexicanos y Norteamericanos in Monterrey, Mexico, Niggli asserts that "the average North American from either the United States or Canada, does not know the ethical values of the Mexican," and she further notes that "there are, of course, plenty of half-way children like myself who do know" (199). It is precisely the notion of considering herself as 'half-way,' as situated between two worlds, that helps us to understand Niggli's own sense of dual consciousness which is both Mexican and American. Her description of herself as a "half-way" child corresponds to Juan Bruce-Novoa's sense of "the Chicano as an inter-space, that is, neither one of the poles . . . [but rather] a synthesis" (qtd. in Chabram 131). Therefore, because she sees herself as existing in that 'inter-space' between two cultures, between two countries, her literature can be seen as an expression of her own coming to terms with a dual identity. Thus, although she writes from the geographical space of the United States, the cultural memory of her homeland is constantly present in her narratives.

Niggli's work forms part of the early Mexican American literary tradition, and critics such as Hector Calderón and José Saldivar have classified her writings with those of Nina Otero de Warren, Cleofas M. Jaramillo and Fabiola Cabeza de Baca, all of whom have written in English. These texts have been described as "romantic" and "quaint", and they are perceived as presenting "conventional Anglo-American views of their culture" (4). Raymund A. Paredes, far from seeing Niggli's work as "quaint" describes *Mexican Village* as a "landmark in Mexican-American literary history" ("Mexican American Writers" 88). From this point of view the narrative which consists of ten related stories presents the reader with a chronicle of life in Hidalgo, Nuevo León. Tey Diana Rebolledo, like Paredes, points out that Niggli's "thematic use of Mexican folkways, history, and symbols . . . went beyond a mere quaint portrayal of Mexican life. She was eager to portray Mexico and its people in a complex manner so they would be better understood by Americans" (26). Gloria Louise Velasquez Trevino indicates that "Josephina Niggli's personal experience as an exiled Mexican growing up in San Antonio who is suddenly confronted with assimilation into American society, enables her to realistically portray the ideological conflicts that result from her dual identity" (128). Yolanda Padilla emphasizes Niggli's use of the folk in her writings which has its basis in "Mexican versions of the folk to connect established polarities of the historical and transhistorical, the political and the mythic"

(3). Besides a portrayal of Mexico, Padilla further asserts that Niggli's use of the folk in her literature is connected to the novel of the revolution which "often deploys the 'folk' not as myth but precisely to elaborate on the role Mexico's Indians play as producers and critics of history" (3).

From a Mexican and particularly "regiomontano" perspective, author Hugo Valdés has proclaimed Niggli as "la pionera de la narrativa regiomontana [and] precursora invisible de la narrativa femenina regiomontana del Siglo XX" (1). This commentary came shortly alter the Niggli's novel, *Step Down Elder Brother* (1947) was published by CONARTE (Consejo para la Cultura y las Artes de Nuevo León) in Spanish translation as *Apártate, hermano* (2003).What seems to endear her to the Monterrey author and critic is the fact that "Niggli ve a la Ciudad como lo que es, como una extranjera, a la distancia, pero con nostalgia, con afecto" (2). Indeed, he would seem to be recovering her text which he sees as having been "rescatado del olvido y del idioma inglés" (2). By including this novel as part of a corpus of "narrativa regiomontana", Valdés has also noted that it is necessary to undertake "un profundo trabajo de revaloración y de reivindicación de la obra de Niggli" (3). It is precisely within the framework of this commentary that the present discussion will focus on a reexamination of two works by Josephina Niggli: *Mexican Village* (1945) and *Step Down, Elder Brother*, which can be seen as regional indices of the early history and culture of Hidalgo and Monterrey, cities located in the state of Nuevo Leon. As a means of approaching these aspects I refer to portions of Yuri Lotman's theory regarding the semiosphere, as well as M.M. Bakhtin's notion of the folkloric chronotope. I also look at the imbedded commentary within the narrative which points to Niggli's perspective on the future of Mexico and her people, a perspective which is directed to a particular reading public. Finally, I discuss how Niggli's vision can be viewed in relation to present-day social and cultural realities of Monterrey, Nuevo León.

Niggli's Narratives and the Concept of Cultural Space

Mexican Village and *Step Down Elder Brother* can be located in what Yuri Lotman defines as the semiosphere, "an abstract space where the realization of the communicative process and the production of new information" (*Semiósfera I* 22) takes place. It is within the semiosphere that we encounter semiotic formations, such as isolated texts, which when they intervene with canonical texts as different or as 'other', often function as catalysts for the purpose of meaning formation. Both of the narratives considered here function as catalysts in bringing about meaning with regard to the "text" which is Mexico, and Niggli draws on the memory of her own cultural experience from her years in Mexico as the basis for filtering commonly-held notions about Mexico. She then translates these notions into a cultural "other" that fits more precisely with her own sense of identity, one that involves two cultural spheres. More precisely, however, she translates this cultural "other" as a means of representing a Mexico that can be more positively appreciated by an American reader. Thus, by examining this cultural memory regarding the northern region of Nuevo León, Mexico that is evident in these narratives, we are able to perceive what is hidden, what can be considered as an "extraordinarily complex controversy among different semiotic worlds" (79).

The controversy between two semiotic worlds is a mental one for Niggli. Although she was born in Mexico and lived there for a short time, in reality she writes from the semiotic space of the United States. Here it is important to realize that the text acts as an informer which brings to light things that are hidden, thus acquiring features of a model of culture, and as such it becomes much like an autonomous person, one that reads and interprets culture. How is it that we are to "read" Josephina Niggli's texts and their meaning? The texts were published in 1945 and 1947 respectively yet it is relevant to locate these narratives within a particular historical period. The period from 1898 through the first forty years of the Twentieth century marks the broadening of American imperial interests into the areas of Hawaii, the Samoan islands, the Philippines, Puerto Rico and the Canal Zone. However, American response to expansion and intervention into these areas was marked by blatant racism. For example, with respect to annexation of the Philippines, labor leader Samuel Gompers feared that annexation would result in cheap labor. He also warned about the "half-breeds and semi-barbaric people" (qtd in Divine et. al. 662) who would have a negative effect on the labor movement. Other anti-imperialists argued against the assimilation of different races. Thus, the audience that is the recipient of Niggli's text, is a United States that does not understand the unknown "other" or what Lotman terms as "extrasystemic", or "alosemiotic" (*Semiósfera II* 148), that which pertains to another system.

The dust jacket of the second edition of *Mexican Village* is said to contain "a set of brilliantly written sketches which [bring] to life and to the attention of a very wide public the manifold facets of Mexican village life". The dust jacket of the first edition of *Step Down Elder Brother* describes Niggli as having "set before the English-speaking world the story of change, change sweeping over a land, and change stirring in a people". Indeed, *Step Down Elder Brother* is introduced as a modern novel that deals with the "story of a great Mexican family whose modern sons and daughters through love and rebellion bring it new life and blood and find in industry new lands to conquer". The novel is said to deal with "the changing process which is remaking Mexico and her people, and the life they live". Thus Niggli, through her art, filters this American notion of Mexico as the "other", as an exotic space populated by Indians and people of color who are the result of racial mixing. Instead she presents the country of her birth, the home of her childhood to her readers, a Mexico that she nostalgically appreciates, a Mexico that is metaphorically "in the blood." She addresses the English speaking world on the basis of her own mental perspectives which are expressed in two texts which, I believe, can be seen as a continuum, a repository of her ideas which are set in counter-position to a nucleus of American beliefs regarding racial mixing and connotations of barbarity.

Niggli presents her vision of Mexico in such a way so as to free it from the ideological framework of the United States which traditionally has defined people of color as inferior. She does so by presenting us with two heroes as well as two related regional spaces in Nuevo Leon—Hidalgo and Monterrey. Both of these elements are relevant in communicating Niggli's perspective regarding Mexico's future. *Mexican Village* uses a literary form, the folkloric chronotope as defined by M.M. Bakhtin, and there are two elements of his definition of this literary form that are of interest here: historical inversion and the folkloric man. As noted by Bakhtin, "the essence of this inversion is found in the fact that mythological and artistic thinking locates such categories as purpose, ideal, justice, perfection, the harmonious condition of man and society and the like in the *past*" (147). Essentially by referring to much of Mexico's folkloric past in *Mexican Village* and then by leading the reader into the world of *Step Down Elder Brother* where we discover a Monterrey which is moving toward a future of modernity, the reader is presented with what Bakhtin sees as "a thing that could and in fact must only be realized exclusively in the *future* [that] is here portrayed as something out of the *past*, a thing that is in no sense part of the past's reality, but a thing that is in its essence a purpose, an obligation" (147). For Niggli, that future, that obligation, has to do with change, with transformation, and it is through the characters of Bob Webster in *Mexican Village* and Mateo in *Step Down Elder Brother* that the reader is presented with "the folkloric man" who is transformed into the new man who will propel Mexico into its modern future. Each of these men will become other than what he was, but each man will also be presented in close relationship to a Creole past. The Creole, Joaquín in *Mexican Village* and Domingo in *Step Down Elder Brother*, will take on a lesser role and it is the *mestizo* who will be portrayed as the key to Mexico's future progress. It is through these characters that we are able to perceive the author's broader vision regarding the new man, and therefore, the new country. As a means of doing so she takes us from the village of Hidalgo to the metropolis of Monterrey. Thus her vision is one involving the man, but the country as well.

A Critical Analysis and Interpretation of Two Heroes

Mexican Village is situated in the cultural sphere of Hidalgo, Nuevo León. The main character and hero, Bob Webster, undergoes a life process which allows him to become a man transformed, a man who finds himself within a particular socio-cultural framework which contributes to his knowledge of self and his sense of identity. He is the text of the folkloric man because "the folkloric man *is* the great folk, great in his own right" (Bakhtin 151). Initially, Bob Webster is unaware of his greatness. We find him recalling his father's voice: "You have the impudence to call yourself Bob Webster? Do you think I'd admit an Indian is a son of mine? Damn it, I'm a white man" (*MV* 40). He is rejected by his American father, because his blood is not pure. Symbolically this is the voice not only of Anglo America, it is also the voice of a Spanish past which emphasizes purity of blood and nobility. For the Hidalgo community Bob is a *Yanqui*, but he, "possesses Spanish. Some of the words are strange, and the accent is unfamiliar, but he speaks the language" (*M V* 14). The gradual change in Bob's sense of identity continues throughout the narrative as he becomes more involved in village life and with the Castillo family as well. It is his use of the Spanish language which first contributes to his acceptance into the sphere of village life, and the fact that he acquires and then rides *El Caballo Blanco* is a further step toward Bob's transformation. As he rides onto the mesa, mounted on his white horse, the Indians are astonished. Some are fearful that this mythical *Caballo Blanco* will take them to Hell, but it is Anselmo who refers to a proverb: "If someone tells you he saw a horse ridden by a king, ask him the color of the horse, and if he says 'white', believe him" (*MV* 43). Bob asks Don Anselmo if that makes him a king, and we see that "secret glances passed across the crowd like wind rippling a field of barley. Don Anselmo shrugged. Are you not the *patrón*? It was not a question but a statement. And Bob Webster knew with inner exultation that he was now, in truth, *jefe* of the quarry" (*MV* 43).

This *Yanqui* of mixed blood, this *jefe* is one who respects the Inditos and respects their method for mining and taking rocks to the train. Bob becomes linked to Hidalgo as he becomes more closely involved in village life and actually takes part in a contrived scheme of a cockfight which is to end the feud between Hidalgo and San Juan de Iglesias. It is during this moment of community life that Bob acts like a Mexican rather than an outsider. He gives a speech in which he allies himself with the men of Hidalgo, and "in that moment he spoke with a Mexican, not a North American, mind. In that moment Bob Webster truly became part of the valley" (*M V* 212).

It is through the character of Bob Webster that the reader is able to understand Niggli's perspective regarding identity and the mixing of blood, and it is in his relation to the Castillo family that this is most evident. Time and time again we find the concept of "blood" mentioned in the narrative. For example, it is the Castillo "blood [that] was thin with restraint" (*MV* 422). Indeed, it was those of Spanish origin, the conquerors who had received "the hereditary decoration of conquest . . . by Phillip II of Spain" (*MV* 449) who were fearful of mixing their blood with the villagers. Yet it is interesting that it is Don Saturnino Castillo who ultimately comes to consider Bob as a third son—this after his favorite son Alejandro's death and because his other son, Joaquín, is considered to be a revolutionary. Don Saturnino intuitively recognizes an air of similarity between his son Alejandro and Bob as he notes, "You have the Castillo hands. Perhaps it is an omen. You believe in omens Roberto?" (*MV 453).* It is at this moment when Bob Webster hears his name spoken in Spanish, his name that had not been pronounced as such since his mother's death, that he felt "as though at last he had come into his inheritance, as though he had found for himself a fixed position. A sense of security came into him" (*MV* 454). This sense of coming into his own is once again reinforced by Don Saturnino who ultimately comes to perceive of Bob as the only one capable of taking care of the Castillo estate.

It is later in the narrative that Bob travels to Monterrey and meets with his half sister Sofía who gives him an envelope with papers that are meant for him. After reading a letter that had been written by his grandmother, he comes to realize his true identity as the descendent of Isabela Castillo, the woman who dared to marry a man of Indian blood. Bob Webster is in reality Roberto Ortega Menéndez y Castillo, Duque de Huachichil, and it is "an Indian [who comes to] be true heir to the Castillo title and estate" (*MV* 475). However, even after discovering his ancestry, it is interesting to note that he does not reveal who he is after returning to Hidalgo. Thus, Bob Webster's greatness as the folkloric hero is evident as he does not attempt to place himself at the same social level as Joaquín Diego Sanchez Castillo Buentello, y Vizcon de Mogollón Castillo, son of Don Saturnino Castillo. Instead, he simply asks Joaquín to call him Cousin as "he had found his dignity of being and his place in an ordered society" (*MV* 486). Bob has come to understand his own identity and place in the history of Hidalgo, yet he recognizes Joaquín's historical place in the Sabinas valley, as well as his love of the land. As Joaquín had told Bob,

> "my ancestors for over three hundred years have ruled this valley. In the beginning they had the power of life and death. Their word was law. [. . .] Up here the Castillos recognized one God, their own, and one king, themselves. And in spite of revolutions and the breaking away from Spain, and later from Maximilian, the outside world had little to do with Castillo power in the Sabinas. The Great Revolution changed all that. It was time to change. It was not good for one man to say, 'This one shall be rich and that one poor—this one shall live and that one die.'" (*MV* 479)

The cultural memory of Spanish nobility and its role of power can be seen here as the center of a semiotic system, one that over time must interact with the cultural space of a new experience, a new text. Bob Webster functions as that new text which moves from the periphery closer to the center of Mexico's semiotic space. Yet it is interesting to note that Bob, the man of mixed-blood, does not reveal his identity but simply defers to Joaquin's position of power, and ultimately, the two young men "linked arms, and walked—Bob, earth-solid and firm, Joaquín, air-light and arrogant—out of the patio" (*MV* 491). Joaquín as a descendent of the landed class represents the memory of Spain that still occupies a central position in the cultural space of Mexico, but he can only find his true future by accepting the participation of Bob Webster and thus the rightful place of those, who are of mixed blood. This is Josephina Niggli's proposal, a new Mexico, one that will be based on the "solid" heroic position of the *mestizo* who must break away from the Spanish and European past and move forward.

Niggli's focus on the future of Mexico is clarified further in *Step Down Elder Brother*. Just as Joaquín in *Mexican Village* represents the Spanish past and the deterioration of Creole dominance, so too does Domingo Vázquez de Anda in *Step Down Elder Brother* represent the old tradition in Monterrey that must find a new expression. Domingo, the eldest son of this Creole family, is a man who had dreamt of becoming a doctor, but is forced by his Uncle Agapito to go into the family real estate business. He finds no pleasure in the business, unlike his childhood friend Tito who sees Monterrey as a place of industry, a place of business. Domingo represents the Monterrey of old, the Monterrey of tradition. And it is his sister Sofía who notes "we are too inbred, we old families, too proud of our grandeur. There is no shame in having been a servant. Honest labor wears its own dignity" (*SDEB* 72). Sofía is the voice of change, and it is she who breaks with the Creole family tradition of aristocratic notions by marrying Mateo, someone not of her own social position.

Mateo stands in contrast to Domingo and the Creole tradition. Unlike Bob Webster, however, Mateo is not as colorful a figure, yet he represents the *mestizo* who will make up the new working class in Monterrey. Mateo begins working as a chauffer for the Vázquez de Anda family, and he slowly becomes involved in the family real estate business. He is able to understand that "the new rich [. . .] they're hunting for fine corners. Real gentlemen corners" (*SDEB* 118), yet he is aware of his class difference. Mateo is not a gentleman of Monterrey society, but it is Sofía who will encourage "the bleak spaces of his inquiring mind" (*SDEB* 121), it is she who is responsible for encouraging his entrance into the family real estate business as she realizes only Mateo is capable of bringing about the changes that are necessary. Mateo brings a new sense of economy to Domingo's world as well. He criticizes a large tip that Domingo leaves after a meal in a restaurant and Sofía points out, "Remember, Mateo, Monterrey is Domingo's home, but Monterrey's spirit is not in his blood" (*SDEB* 122). Thus Sofía recognizes Mateo's potential and the way in which Monterrey's spirit of business is part of his blood. Domingo, however, is troubled with what Mateo is becoming. He becomes an excellent real estate salesman, true to the spirit of Monterrey and we are witness to the transformation of this new type of hero:

> That man's no servant," Irineo said. "Didn't you notice the way he sat in his chair? He was on a level with us in that moment, and he knew it. That's why he left when he did. He's had luck, so far, and he knows enough to push it. As yet he's not ready to be on level with us. He still has things to learn, but when he learns them—well, I for one will vote for his entry to this club, and I am sure the rest of you will, too." (*SDEB* 179)

Thus, Mateo has become more sure of himself as he continues to develop new areas of real estate, yet Domingo and others of his social class who are members of the Casino, the elite country club of Monterrey, are having difficulty coming to terms with this change. This is evident as Irenio Mirando notes,

> As a historian, it worries me a little. We have grown too fast in our social order. From feudalism to socialism in one step with no middle ground to cushion us. We old ones from the past, we don't know how to stand aside. These young ones from the future, they push against us, wrap themselves like vines around our trunks. We try to fight, but what good is fighting? The vines always win in the end, and the trunks die. (*SDEB* 180)

It is here that we are keenly made aware of Josephina Niggli's commentary that is imbedded in the text, and it is here that she makes clear her vision of what Mexico is to become. The old ways, the old class lines must be done away with to pave the way for modernity, a modernity that must include those democratizing elements which will result in a new Mexico. Indeed, Niggli's perspective is clear here as we note Domingo's thoughts: "To the Lawyer, to the Engineer, even, in a measure to himself, the world they had known was tumbling around them, and it was the Mateos who were causing the earthquake" (*SDEB* 180). This is the true revolution that the author sees taking place in Mexico, a revolution that has brought about changes that cannot be contained. Mateo's position as a hero is evident in his final transformation. It is his marriage to Sofía which presents us once again with the link between Creole and *mestizo*. He has risen from the position of chauffeur to businessman and resident of the Obispado, a residential area where the old elite families of Monterrey resided after the 1940's. Again, just as Bob Webster and Joaquín move forward together, so too does the marriage between Sofía and Mateo represent Niggli's proposal for Mexico's future, a future where the *mestizo* not only will have his equal place in society, but a position of authority as well. This is evident symbolically in Sofía's deference to her husband as head of their middle-class household, which is a change in social position that Sofía freely accepts.

Niggli's Vision of a Beloved Mexico

How is it that we are led by the author to understand her personal vision of Mexico? In *Mexican Village* we are confronted with a series of ten stories which present us with situations of romantic love, town traditions and conflicts. Niggli, however, focuses much of the narrative on a semiotic space that is one of order and structure. For example, when describing the members of the ruling council of Hidalgo we find that: when the "little professor" is made a member of the ruling council, the author's imbedded comment becomes clear: "the men on the council were not men to the village, but symbols. Don Nacho represented the people; the priest, religion; the doctor, health; and Don Rosalio money. To these four had been added learning" (*MV* 379). Thus Hidalgo, in spite of Tía Magdalena's witchcraft, and the Indians who often revert to superstitious practice, is a place which has an economic system based on the quarry, and the town life is guided by a ruling council which involves a hierarchy of governing members who will be responsible for moving Hidalgo towards progress. However, Niggli does not simply provide the reader with literary descriptions of Hidalgo. From the very beginning of this series of stories, she points to Monterrey as an important place, a cultural and economic sphere beyond the confines of Hidalgo. Indeed, Monterrey is a place, a life to be looked up to. For instance as the stranger, Bob Webster, comes into the town of Hidalgo, the *Yanqui* is received as "your grace" by Anselmo, a man wearing "a dirty blue shirt and gray trousers belted with rope" (3). Bob Webster is taken to his office, yet he seems distracted. Indeed, rather than pay attention to what is to serve as his office for the year he plans to spend in Hidalgo, he instead "strolled to the mesa edge and was staring across the great cut in space that was the valley" (5). He is told by Anselmo "there lies Monterrey", and of course as Anselmo points out, "you can see the smoke from the smelters. It is a very great city . . . it is the third largest in all the Republic" (6). Anselmo and the *Yanqui* look at the Saddle Mountain, "the mountain of Monterrey. . . . the distant purple smudge of rock with the double peak" (6). One might think that Niggli is simply praising her place of birth; however, the world of Monterrey is mentioned time and time again in the narrative. Rock is mined in the quarry of Hidalgo, but sent by rail to the factory in Monterrey. Monterrey is home to the brewery from which Hidalgo receives ice twice a week. It is also known for the Quong Lee grocery, "the finest in the Republic" (*MV* 38). Monterrey symbolizes progress, whereas in Hidalgo, progress has not been fully achieved.

When Bob Webster travels to Monterrey, he observes the many people in the dining room of the hotel where he stays, and he muses about the "unconscious sophistication . . . [that] symbolized Monterrey, that strange city of contrasts, which industry had transformed into a Texas suburb, and which had yet remained so essentially Mexican that it was hated and envied by the entire Republic" (*MV* 462). This same theme regarding Monterrey as a "strange city of contrasts" runs through *Step Down Elder Brother* where Niggli points to Monterrey's history. For example, the street named Hidalgo is described as the "old Camino Real. Along it rode messengers from the Viceroy with orders for His Christian Majesty's most loyal governor of the Province of Nuevo León" (*SDEB* 51). Here we are introduced to the Spanish past which forms part of the cultural system of Monterrey. Part of the essential process or self-organization of this cultural system involves the North's concern with purity of blood. As we have seen, this notion is presented to us first in *Mexican Village* in the character of Bob Webster whose mixed blood is rejected by his Anglo father. The question of blood, status and identity are elements that permeate this entire area of Nuevo Leon, the village as well as the city.

Mexican Village presents Hidalgo as a minor participant in the road to progress, however, Monterrey is the depicted as the epitome of industrial progress. In *Step Down Elder Brother*, Domingo Vázquez de Anda contemplates this city, especially Avenida Madero which he sees as the "real heart of Monterrey" (*SDEB* 43). This street for Domingo symbolized Monterrey "clanging with music from a thousand radios and victrolas. It was as hard and garish as a painted woman, as full of laughter, as full of warmth. Lacking the subtlety, the charm, the sweet placidity of the south, it was frankly interested in only one thing: money" (*SDEB* 44). It is precisely the figure of the elder of the Vázquez de Anda family, Don Agapito, who describes Monterrey as the "Stingy City", and it was he who "was so certain of his city's industrial future, of her power as one of the key cities on the great highway that soon would stretch from Canada to Brazil" (*SDEB* 207).

Hidalgo represents village life in Mexico, but it is Monterrey that symbolically functions as Niggli's vision regarding Mexico's future. The *mestizo* is presented as the man of power, and we observe this through Domingo's eyes,

> Domingo looked around at Mateo. The muscular young man was relaxed on the bed, his face [. . .] was the mask the *mestizos* had inherited from the Indian, the mask that had strengthened them, given them power to fight the

> tempestuous blood of their Creole ancestors, the mask of patience. (*SDEB* 315)

It is interesting to note here too, the role of Sofía:

> Sofía-Monterrey, Monterrey-Sofía, the one the symbol of the other. Not Sofía Vázquez de Anda, but Sofía the entity, the new generation who, like Saddle Mountain, rejected the conservative line of the ranges, and stood alone, in solitary grandeur, dominating the valley, with her hands on her hips, her head pressed against the sky, her arrogance flaunting in the wind, masking the enmity of the rest of the Republic . . . (*SDEB* 317)

Here we see Sofía as the new woman, a symbol of those who would have a hand in reshaping and changing Mexico from its traditional perspective to one of progress and modernity. And once again, it is through Domingo that Niggli emphasizes her vision in a moment when Domingo reaches across the table toward Mateo. As Mateo takes Domingo's hand, we are confronted with Domingo's sense of what is to come: "to Domingo's Spanish mind it was an emotional moment. The hand of the Creole lay in the hand of the *mestizo* and between the palms lay the happiness of Sofía" (*SDEB* 317). It is here that the figure of Sofía takes on a larger dimension she; is *la madre patria* that will flourish as a result of the cooperation that will take place between the Creole and the *mestizo*. Mateo can be seen as the heroic figure who is transformed from the servant of the past to the new man who will take his place on an equal level with those who once saw themselves as "those from above". And the center, the nucleus where this will be played out is in Monterrey which symbolizes the benefits of future industrial progress that will come about with the growth of a middle class. This is the vision of Mexico that Niggli presents to her English-speaking reading public.

Step Down Elder Brother certainly gives us a clear look at Monterrey of the 1930's, and that is the importance of this narrative work as one that has been recovered as regional literature, *literatura regiomontana*. The question we might ask at this point is whether or not Josephina Niggli's vision regarding Mexico has in fact become a reality. Has the middle class of Monterrey flourished, and has the *mestizo/a* taken his/her rightful place in Monterrey society? Has the identity of the *mestizo* surpassed that of the Creole? Let us look to Mexico's historical project which is based on a liberal paradigm that initially was intended to promote the freedom of the individual together with equality in terms of human beings capable of reasoning. From this perspective Mexico can be understood as being born under *la Reforma*. However, as history has shown, the liberalism proposed under *la Reforma* was essentially an ideology taken up by the elite minorities who were totally out of touch with the religious and popular elements that were basic for the majority of Mexican society (Cristoffanini 65). The liberal model has not come to fruition, and as such, the Mexico of today has not become the Mexico that Niggli dreamed of. The distance between the rich and the poor remains great, and the continuity of the exercise of power that was practiced by the Aztecs and the Spaniards continue to find expression in Mexican society, in spite of the hope of progress in the direction of democracy that resulted from the defeat of the PRI in 2000.

In terms of economic growth, however, Monterrey does in fact continue to be the most important industrial center of the country. The Monterrey portrayed in *Step Down Elder Brother* in many ways resembles the Monterrey of today, and it is for this reason that the narrative is an important text which fills a vacant space in *regiomontana* literary history. Monterrey, as it has been poetically described, is still "an empire of industry and labor, the city where the man of above tends his hand to the man below [. . .] its sons are made of steel [. . .] but they dream with the grandeur of a small country" (Pedraza 5). Certainly, the *mestizo* has gained a position in Monterrey society, but this is a city that continues to be true to the text of its Spanish heritage. It is a city in which the *Casino* and *el Campestre* are the meeting places of elite families. Monterrey excels in industry and *el Grupo de los Diez* includes important industrial corporations such as CYDSA, VITRO, FEMSA, Grupo ALFA, Grupo Proeza, Grupo IMSA, Grupo CEMEX, Grupo COPAMEX, Villacero y RFC and Grupo Maseca (GRUMA). The heads of these companies are the industrial captains of Mexico who are courted by presidential candidates. This is the Monterrey that Josephina Niggli captures so well, the Monterrey, who after the days of the Great Revolution, "shook herself, exchanged her rags for a fine new dress, and strung a chain of factories about her neck" (*SDEB* 6). The past that is described here, is a description of the present. There are the families, who like Domingo Vázquez de Anda, hold positions of status and power within Monterrey. Today we continue to see a Monterrey that still honors the family name: Garza Sada, Garza Lagüera, González Sada, Sada González, Garza Medina, Zambrano Lozano, Clariond Reyes, González Barrera and so on. Thus, it is through the characters that make up the world of the fictional narratives presented by Josephina Niggli that the reader is able to look to the past so as to "rescatar del olvido las voces del tiempo, cantarle a la ciudad y reconocer en sus habitantes, su vocación por el trabajo y su ejemplo de honradez y franqueza" (Pedraza xv). *Mexican Village* presents us with a view of village life in the North, but it is the Monterrey of *Step Down Elder Brother* where Niggli writes of her place of birth—"her city [where] Saddle Mountain arrogantly reared cantle and pommel to the clear blue sky" (*SDEB* 374).

Works Cited

Bakhtin, M.M. *The Dialogic Imagination*. "Forms of Time and Chronotope in the Novel". Austin: University of Texas Press, 1981.

Calderón, Héctor and José David Saldívar, Eds. *Criticism in the Borderlands: Studies in Chicano Literature, Culture, and Ideology*. Durham: Duke University Press, 1991.

Chabram, Angie. "Conceptualizing Chicano Critical Discourse." Calderón and Saldívar 127-48.

Constitución política de los Estados Unidos Mexicanos: Comentada y concordada. Mexico: Editorial Porrúa, 1985.

Cristoffanini, Pablo R. "Identidad mexicana e interculturalidad en Octavio Paz." *Identidad y otredad en el mundo de habla hispánica*. Mexico: Universidad Nacional Autónoma de México, 1999.

Divine, Robert A. et.al. *America Past and Present*. New York: Addison Wesley Educational Publishers Inc., 1999.

Lotman, Yuri M. *La semiosfera I: Semiótica de la cultura y del texto*. Madrid: Ediciones Cátedra., 1996

_____. *La semiosfera II: Semiótica de la cultura, del texto, de la conducta y del espacio*. Madrid: Ediciones Cátedra, 1998.

Niggli, Josephina. *Mexican Village*. Chapel Hill: The University of North Carolina Press. 1945.

_____. *Step Down Elder Brother*. New York: Rinehart and Company, Inc., 1947.

_____. "The Importance of History and the Novel for Better Relationships Between Countries." *Historiadores Cincuenta Años de Reuniones Internacionales: 1949-1999, Edición Facsimilar Conmemorativa.* Monterrey: Universidad Autónoma de Nuevo León. 1999.

Padilla, Yolanda. "Nostalgia of the Blood: Race, Revolution and Genre in Josephina Niggli's *Mexican Village*". Proc. of PAMLA Conference, Nov. 2001.

Paredes, Raymund A. "Mexican American Authors and the American Dream". *MELUS,* 8.4 (1981): 71-89. *JSTOR*. 18 Aug 2004 <http://www.jstor.org/search>.

_____. "Mexican-American Literature: An Overview." *Recovering the U.S. Hispanic Literary Heritage*. Eds. Ramón Gutiérrez and Genaro Padilla. Houston: Arte Público Press, 1993.

Pedraza Salinas, Jorge. *Monterrey entre montañas y acero*. Monterrey: Villacero, 1996.

Rebolledo, Tey Diana. *Women Singing in the Snow: A Cultural Analysis of Chicana Literatura.* Tucson: The University of Arizona Press, 1995.

Valdes, Hugo. “Josephina Niggli: La precursora invisible”. *El Norte* 23 November 2002. *Proquest*. 17 August 2004.

Velasquez Trevino, Gloria Louise. *Cultural Ambivalence in Early Chicana Prose Fiction.* Ann Arbor: University Microfilms International, 1985.

Part III

Translating Latinidad, Hispanismo in the World

Resisting the "Fatal Allurement" of Local Color: María Cristina Mena's Mexico in *American Magazine* and *The Century Magazine*

Melissa Marie González
Columbia University

In 1913, the first Mexican-American woman to publish fiction in prestigious American magazines wrote to her editor at *The Century Magazine*, "When I received the manuscript, it was marked with many pencilled suggestions for changes. I followed all those which did not make me rebellious" (4 April).[1] As it turns out, many editorial decisions made María Cristina Mena "rebellious"—a fact that may seem unexpected given that her earliest critics read her creations as "obsequious" (Tatum 1982, 33). Mena occupies a significant, if problematic, place in the history of Chicano literature, and the reception of her stories has been colored by contrasting interpretations of her use of the local color genre (Simmen 1997, 147). As an interpreter of Mexican life for the upper class Anglo audience of the highbrow *The Century Magazine*, María Cristina Mena was initially dismissed by first-wave Chicano critics such as Charles Tatum and Raymond A. Paredes as a local color writer who merely caters to the exoticizing tastes of her Anglo audience.[2] Paredes, for example, maintains that Mena "knew what Americans liked to read about Mexico, so she gave it to them" (50). Certainly, the threatening proximity of the Mexican Revolution at least partly explains the appeal of innocuous, local color stories about Mexico but Mena is not the anxiety-quelling native informant her editors at *The Century* may have wished for. On the contrary, Mena's correspondence with her editors conveys her awareness of herself as a cultural translator who corrects the ignorant assumptions of her editors, and attentive readings of her earliest stories and one article reveal the ways in which she critiques and resists the local color genre from within it.

Accordingly, more recent revisionist readings of multicultural local color writers have offered more comprehensive analyses of Mena's works. Several critics, most notably Amy Doherty and Tiffany Ana López, have shed light on the subversions of Mena's texts—which range from proto-feminist explorations of the increasing liberation of women to negative depictions of the American cultural invasion of Mexico—in order to re-inscribe her as a "Latina literary foremother" (Johnson 2001, 191). As these critics note, Mena can be neither a radical subversive nor a full-fledged trickster because of the ways her gender, class, and ethnicity inform her identity in her historical moment.[3] Nevertheless, Mena's letters to the editors of *The Century Magazine* show that she asserted the authority of her intercultural perspective within the restricted space offered by a magazine that wanted only local color.

We may fairly speculate not only that the local color genre served as one of few possible vehicles for bringing Mexican-American voices to a receptive Anglo audience in the early twentieth century, but also that a basic adherence to the conventions of the local color genre serve to mask subversions of form and content. Mena wrote stories about Mexico in the local color mode with an Anglo magazine audience in mind, but these aspects of her writerly position do not preclude subversion. In fact, the magazine audience's desire for foreignness packaged as local color provides a forum, however restricted, for foreign perspectives, and the multiplicity of ethnic subjectivities traversed by Mena's narrator present the foreign in ways that alternatively reproduce, explore, and defy stereotyping of Mexico and Mexican-ness. If Mena "knew what Americans liked to read about Mexico . . . [and] gave it to them" (Paredes 50), she gave them a version of Mexico imprinted with the subjectivity of her own intercultural position and fraught with assertions of un-translatability. Similarly, the Spanish words in her stories represent more than elements of local color. In fact, the bilingualism of her texts is a little-studied but elucidating subversion, a resistance reflected both in her arguments and negotiations with the editors over the inclusion of Spanish words, and in the alienating potential of the texts' untranslated bilingualism.

At least a part of the reason that Mena was initially dismissed by Chicano critics as a merely local color writer can be found in her social origins, since the writings of upper-class women in popular magazines have been often dismissed as trivial and assimilationist. As an upper-middle-class Mexican teenager, Mena was sent to New York during the Mexican revolution by her "Spanish mother and Yucatecan father of European blood" and eventually became a naturalized citizen of the U.S. (Simmen 1992, 39).[4] In New York, she ran in elite literary circles, making the acquaintance of D.H. Lawrence and marrying the playwright and journalist Henry Kellet Chambers.[5] In 1913, at the age of twenty-one, Mena published her first short stories, "The Gold Vanity Set" and "John of God, the Water-Carrier" in *American Magazine* and *The Century Magazine*, respectively[6]. Although both of these stories problematically stereotype and idealize the indigenous Mexican, they also assert the autonomy and impenetrability of Mexican culture and protest the American economic and cultural invasion.

One of Mena's first stories, "The Gold Vanity Set", both parodies and performs the relationships between the local color writer, the local color subject, and the local color reader. Like the writer of local color narrative, Don Ramón wishes to offer Miss Young, the frivolous American tourist in Mexico, a glimpse of his native culture, especially as embodied by Petra, a young indigenous woman. Mena's narrative voice, however, does not align itself with a single protagonist. Instead, the narrator of "The Gold Vanity Set" traverses a multiplicity of ethnic subjectivities—a strategy revisited in Mena's later fiction for *The Century Magazine* and identified by Amy Doherty as "polyphonic" in her introduction to *The Collected Stories* (xxvii).

Towards the beginning of the story, an American tourist to Mexico, upon seeing a beautiful indigenous woman, exclaims,

> "I positively must have her picture!" exclaimed Miss Young.
> "Of course—at your disposition," murmured Don Ramón.
> But the matter was not so simple. Petra rebelled—rebelled with the dumb obstinacy of the Indian, even to weeping and sitting on the floor.
> (*The Collected Stories* 3-4)[7]

This passage showcases the representatives of three cultural groups: the American tourist, the wealthy Mexican of Spanish descent, and the indigenous Mexican. Throughout the story, Mena's narrative voice embodies the subjectivities of each representative, reading the other subjectivities through alternate critical lenses. Like Petra, Mena's narrator resists the fixedness of a snapshot. Specifically, Mena's narrator parallels the indigenous girl's resistance to being captured on film by resisting explanation, saying only "the matter was not so simple". The narrator does not deign to explain the reason behind the "dumb obstinacy of the Indian", which would be, possibly, a reference to the received idea that indigenous people believe that the taking of a photo constitutes the taking of a soul. Mena's role as local color interpreter for her Anglo audience also parallels that of the wealthy "*Patrón*" who hosts the American guests and interprets the ways of the indigenous people for them, aided by his knowledge of English, but ultimately unable (or unwilling) to give Miss Young the picture she wants (4)[8].

Interestingly, the challenge of the *patrón*'s inter-lingual position is suggested by his mistaken use of "disposition" instead of "disposal". Although Mena's own English is consistently free of such errors, her placing of the error in the mouth of the *patrón* both implies her awareness of the pitfalls of bilingualism and mocks the obliging land-owner who is "nervous, sensitively anxious about the impressions of his guest from the North" yet has not successfully appropriated the English language (10). But not all of the narrator's mockery of Don Ramón is easily accessible by a monolingual Anglo audience. Earlier in the story, Don Ramón's says, "The house is yours, Miss Young", a (implicitly) literal translation of "Mi casa es su casa", a joke accessible only to readers with a knowledge of the original Spanish idiom[9]. Indeed, Miss Young herself enthusiastically takes his invitation literally, probably charmed by its (perceived) outlandishness she cries, "Girls, do you hear that? This is my house—and I invite you all in." Miss Young's misunderstanding is implicitly mocked by Mena's narrator, and the entrance of her and her travel companions is described as an invasion: "Immediately the inn was invaded" (3). Mena's narrator suggests that the American tourist both misunderstands and invades.

Yet the narrator's implicit resistance to this "invasion" and depiction of multiple perspectives is not uncomplicatedly anti-imperialist. For instance, it is not clear which cultural perspective informs the prejudice behind the phrase "the dumb obstinacy of the Indian" in the first passage cited because, as Don Ramón explains to his American guest later on, "You may observe that we always speak of them as *Inditos*, never as Indios. We use the diminutive because we love them.

> They are our blood. With their passion, their melancholy, their music and superstition they have passed without transition from the feudalism of the Aztecs into the world of today, which ignores them; but we never forget that it was their valor and love of country which won our independence" (10)[10].

Although this romanticizing of the indigenous Mexican by an upper class Mexican character (and author) would be dismissed as condescending today, in1913 it does anticipate the championing of the indigenous Mexican and the valorization of indigenous mythology. Just as the character of Don Ramón attempts to educate the American tourist, Mena attempts to educate her Anglo reader about the upper class Mexican's perception of the role of the indigenous Mexican. Miss Young replies with characteristic shallowness: "They certainly are picturesque . . . and it's great fun to run into the twelfth or some other old century one day out from Austin" (10). Don Ramón's didacticism is met with the Anglo tourist's empty enthusiasm: what represents "passion" and "valor" to Don Ramón is merely "picturesque" and "fun" to Miss Young. The narrator thereby alludes to the local color genre that makes her culture palatable to an Anglo audience, a reality suggested by the fact that the local color genre was one of the few vehicles for bringing a Mexican-American voice to the Anglo masses. At the same time, this passage suggests that the reader of local color has poor reading skills—an indictment subversively aimed at the readers of *The Century* themselves. The indictment, however, is cloaked by the ever-present polyphony; it is never very clear what voice, what perspective, is being privileged. Here, as in other places, Mena's narrator delights in inhabiting the glib voice of the Anglo tourist and contrasting it with the solemnity of Don Ramón's English.

Earlier on, Mena's narrator offers more virtuoso polyphony in a passage that emphasizes the American's incomplete understanding of Petra's explanation for her theft of the gold vanity set—an explanation that comes via Don Ramón's translation, of course. Petra has the floor first, and she explains, "looking beneath fluttering eyelids", how taking and using Miss Young's cosmetics had set off a chain of events that culminated in her husband's swearing off of *pulque*, a miracle overseen by the blessed Virgin of Guadalupe. Clearly, this is a genuine religious experience for Petra. Mena's narrator continues, "All of which Don Ramón translated to Miss Young, who looked puzzled and remarked: 'Well, I just love the temperance cause, but does she want to keep my danglums to make sure of this Manuelo staying on the water wagon?'" (9). In this parody of local color, the message is that the reader of local color will always translate the story into her own terms. The story itself has been translated through the dialects and subjectivities of three classes: Petra, the indigenous *peon*, Don Ramón, the Mexican landowner, and Miss Young, the wealthy American tourist. Petra is the indigenous narrator; Don Ramón is the intercultural translator; and Miss Young is the "puzzled" American tourist who fails to understand Petra (9). A fourth subjectivity, the author's, performs all three subjectivities, refusing to give any single one authority; the story ends, in fact, with a melancholic folksong performed by Manuelo, the once-abusive husband.

Placing these representative subjectivities side by side without reconciling them, Mena's narrative voice explores the ways in which different cultural groups perceive each other but refuses to take sides. Representing intercultural mis-readings instead of digesting a single, "foreign" culture, Mena alters the conventions of the local color genre. At the same time, by parodying the local color genre within a local color story, Mena critiques the genre from within, questioning its ability to accurately transmit a picture of the foreign, the subject of local color narratives, to the tourist, the reader of local color narratives. By modifying reader's expectations instead of directing them, she transmits to the reader a gentle warning: Mexico defies easy comprehension.

Despite—or perhaps partly because of—its popularity, local color has been classified as "minor" literature and assigned a marginal space in the canon

(Ammons and Rohy 1998, xix). Furthermore, in the context of Chicano criticism, the local color story has been depicted as pandering to American stereotypes of Mexicans (Johnson 2001, 183). In the introduction to their anthology of the multicultural local color story, Ammons and Rohy assert: "Local color has the ability to challenge and deconstruct monolithic national, imperial, and racial agendas. The sheer display of diversity offered by local color, for all attempts to control and hierarchize it, speaks to a multicultural reality that defies homogenization and erasure" (1998, xviii). Indeed, in her non-fiction article on the Mexican musical prodigy Julian Carillo for *The Century*, Mena deconstructs the local color agenda:

> He was born in—well, I've forgotten the name except that it ends in 'huacan. It is a Mexican pueblo with a census of one hundred souls. Our hero was the youngest of a family of nineteen. His father was a saint, he relates, on eighteen *centavos* a day.
>
> This would seem to be a good place for "local color," but the writer resists that fatal allurement. Nor will she couple with her hero the august phrase "pure Castilian blood," chiefly because in Mexico most of our leading Castilians are money-lenders or something in the small grocery line. No; we must reconcile ourselves as well as we can to the fact that Julián Carillo's blood is pure Mexican, not a drop of it being traceable to any European fount, but all flowing to him from the vast and ancient reservoir of the indigenes, a fruitful source, it would seem, in the light of the fact that his father's family was not considered in that pueblo a scandalously large one.
>
> (Mar. 1915, 753)[11]

In this passage, Mena's voice oscillates between adherences to local color and protests against local color. The suppression of the town's name is not accidental: since Carillo "relates" the story to her and was living in New York at the time, it would have been easy to include the exact name. At the very beginning of the passage, Mena anticipates her explicit resistance of the local color genre later in the passage by resisting the specificity of place that is essential to local color, ironically making the anti-regionalist assertion that Carillo's birthplace is a Mexican town like many others. She then gives in to the local color impulse as she describes his humble beginnings, but corrects herself, suggestively labeling local color a "fatal allurement". Casting herself in the role of both Anglo reader and Mexican writer with plural first-person pronouns, Mena not only alludes to the valuing of Spanish bloodlines over indigenous bloodlines and the tendency to falsely attribute Spanish blood to any successful Mexican but also exposes the prosaic professions of the idealized Castilian. As a Mexican, she can attest to the fact that "most of *our* leading Castilians are money-lenders or something in the small grocery line" and as an Anglo she can recognize the need to "reconcile ourselves as well as *we* can to the fact". Her protesting assertion that "not a drop" of Carillo's blood is traceable to a European font is countered by a reversion to the local color mode: Carillo's family of nineteen "was not considered in that pueblo a scandalously large one". Her narrative voice continues to oscillate throughout the article, interrupting midway to proclaim with self-satisfaction, "You see, *we* do some things not so badly in Mexico" (756).

The oscillation of Mena's "we" from a Mexican "we" to a U.S. "we" context highlights the fact that, to some extent, she is writing from within and against two distinct regionalist traditions: U.S. local color and the Mexican *costumbrismo* she was exposed to as a child and teenager in Mexico.[12] Her stories do not contain the proliferation of "tipos" that populate the *cuadros de costumbres*—"photographic negatives from which a great number of images can be reproduced"; instead, she focuses her energies on particularizing her characters, showcasing nuances and inviting ambiguity (Alberto Millán Chivite, 27)[13]. If Mexican *costumbrismo* directed towards a Mexican audience aims to inspire recognition of the types it describes, Mena's stories, directed towards an Anglo audience, aim to showcase instances of misrecognition. By the same token, Mena refuses to paint the pretty picture of Mexico called for by the U.S. local color tradition, and her voice frequently takes on the ironic register demonstrated in the passage cited above.

Accordingly, Mena's short fiction for *The Century Magazine* is anything but homogenous; in fact, she often defies generic prescriptions. "John of God, the Water-Carrier" does characterize the "dear Indito" protagonists as noble, hardworking, and superstitious but also protests against the importation of American technology into Mexico. "Doña Rita's Rivals" outlines the trappings of Mexican castes, but mocks the protagonist for her class obsession. "The Emotions of María Concepción" begins with the yearnings of a young Mexican woman for a Spanish bullfighter and ends with the dissipation of her ardor in the face of the violent reality of the *corrida*.

T.S. Eliot, when he re-published Mena's story "John of God" in the October 1927 issue of *The Monthly Criterion*, noted that Mena had "written perhaps the most comprehensive stories of Mexican life published in English" (Simmen 1997, 148). Because Mena had been at an English boarding school, her emigration to America did not signal her first contact with English. To use Steven G. Kellman's terminology, Mena seems to be a "monolingual translingual", someone who has written in only one language that is not their native one (2000, 12). But, while Mena's stories for *The Century* are predominantly English, the presence of a few un-translated Spanish words make them bilingual texts.[14]

Although the classification of her texts as "bilingual" on the basis of a few untranslated Spanish words may seem questionable, it is justified by the exceedingly monolingual environment of *The Century.* Furthermore, the words left untranslated are not fully accessible to the monolingual reader; in fact, Amy Doherty, the editor of *The Collected Stories*, has added explanatory footnotes to all of the Spanish words not translated inter-textually in order to accommodate monolingual readers. On average, there are about twenty-one footnotes in each of the nine bilingual stories published between 1913 and 1916.[15]

Mena's instances of bilingualism involve all of the semantic fields identified by Ernst Rudin in his study of bilingualism in the contemporary Chicano novel: terms of address (e.g. *patrón, doña, señorita, benediciones, adios, buenos días*); high impact terms (e.g. *bruto, imbécil, caramba, ¡chist!, ¡por dios!, ingrato, ¡blasfemia!*) ethnographic terms (e.g. *plazuela, hacienda, cañon, sombreros, pueblos, maguey*); culinary terms (e.g. *pulque, tortillera, chillitos verdes, aguardiente, aguamiel*); groups of people (e.g. *aguador, papa, peladitos, portero, indito, Yanquis, caballero, torero, capeadores, padres*).[16] Whenever longer phrases in Spanish are introduced, they are usually followed by an intertextual translation; for example: "Still she would find her heart's ease in the intervals of acute distemper during which the poor profligate became once more her *bebecito, tierno retoño de su cuerpo*—tender sprig of her body" (78). Also, when writing dialogue in English that is intended to represent dialogue in Spanish, Mena often preserves the conventions of Spanish syntax and translates the formal "usted" as "thee", a strategy that stresses the foreignness of the dialogue.

Rudin explains that the "mimetic" use of Hispanicisms—in order to reflect that the narrative is set in a region in which the language spoken is not the language of the text—tends to add local color, while the "artificial" use of a secondary language is more common in experimental literature (14-15). Mena's texts, along with those of many Chicano authors, must be situated between the two poles of the literary avant-garde and the local color (15). Although Mena's textual bilingualism is not extreme, it is significant, because it places demands on the monolingual Anglo reader.[17] As Rudin notes, "In a text that builds its discourse on code switching, the reader . . . will take language switches as the norm [. . .] In a text that relies on one vehicular language, on the other hand, switches to a secondary language are much rarer, and therefore take the reader more by surprise. They may constitute, precisely because of their scarcity, a more radical foregrounding" (29).

Theodor W. Adorno seconds this observation by noting that writers can exploit "the tension between the foreign word and the language by incorporating that tension into his own reflections and his own technique" in order to "effect a beneficial interruption of the conformist moment of language, the muddy stream in which the specific expressive intention drowns" (Adorno 189). In other words, even modestly bilingual texts like Mena's showcase the tension between standard English and "foreign" Spanish, beneficially rupturing the conformity of homogenous English. Indeed, the potential for both the assertion of un-translatable cultural specificity and the defiance of the standard English code is provided by the local color genre. Joshua L. Miller examines a similar strategy of resistance employed by a standard language against a secondary one that sheds light on the genre's potential for subversion:

> Language, like national citizenship, has a double movement concealed within. On the one hand, standard English instills hierarchies, forcibly assimilating new speakers to an established power structure. At the same time, the purpose of a "standard" language is to resist new(er) speakers through accents. Pronouncing accents to be markers of inauthentic belonging, this process thus withholds the possibility of assimilation (268).

In her stories Mena demonstrates her virtuoso grasp of American colloquialism and formal discourse, asserting her assimilation of the standard language. At the same time, her prose is "accented" by Spanish words and phrases, only some of which are translated. Her "accent", however, is not read by her Anglo audience as a "marker of inauthentic belonging" but as a marker of local color. By exoticizing and commodifying the foreign, the local color genre sanctions such non-standard "accents" and opens the door to nonconformist moments of language that resist cultural and linguistic translation.

Indeed, in her letters to the editors of *The Century*, Mena uses the local color sanction to argue for the inclusion of Spanish words. Her writer's quest to represent two linguistically and socially disparate cultures through bilingualism in her fiction is an aesthetic venture that is elucidated by the political dimension of her epistolary arguments for the inclusion of Spanish words into her text. Her letters to the editors of *The Century* reveal that she believes in the integrity of bilingualism and that she is actively engaged in a struggle to preserve her own texts' bilingualism in the face of the hegemonic Anglophone discourse, compromised though she is by her financial and emotional reliance on the publication of her stories.[18] Within the compromised space of her letters to the Anglo editors of the highbrow magazine, she negotiates her linguistic subversions, balancing politely demure phrases with assertive claims: "[I have] cut out many of the Spanish words—but I must make a special plea for the few that remain, all of them having a definite value of humor, irony, local color, or what not" (Letter to Doty November/December 1914). Her "special plea" is compromised by the dismissiveness of the final "or what not" that forces us to re-read the sentence. A retrospective reading reveals that Mena, cunningly, concedes to the perspectives of the hegemonic discourse in order to appeal to the editor in his own terms. Specifically, her marketing strategy is to urge the inclusion of Spanish words on the basis of their entertainment value as exotic commodities (i.e. as "local color") although her real reasons may be more complex. As we have seen, in her article on Julián Carillo, Mena demonstrates both her awareness of and disdain for the "fatal allurement" of local color. Indeed, the dismissive "what not" of the letter contrasts strikingly with the assertion of the words' "definitive value" and betrays the subversion of the sentence—forcing us to discard again readings of Mena as merely a local color writer who panders compliantly to Anglo audiences. This subversive politics of language in her letters is complemented by fictional subversions that affirm the value of bilingualism.

Accordingly, Mena's narrative voice poses a markedly different argument for the inclusion of Spanish words in "The Birth of the God of War", a first-person narrative in which an adult narrator remembers how, as a young girl, she coaxed her *mamagrande* to re-tell the story of the birth of the Aztec god Huitzilopochtli.[19] Remembering her grandmother's story, the adult narrator writes, "Alas! The sonorous imagery of those well-remembered phrases loses much in my attempt to render them in sober English" (65). Here, she argues for bilingualism as maintaining integrity of meaning—a very different argument than the one intended to appeal to her editors. She also cheekily tells her Anglo readers that they are missing out. Indeed, her privileging of Spanish is present from the very beginning: this description of English as "sober" hearkens back to the first sentences of the story that, in contrast, cast Spanish as the "flowery and rhythmic" language in which "epic narrations" become "so precious" to our narrator (63). By privileging Spanish in this way, Mena tunes into the perception of the divergent characteristics of Spanish and English: Spanish is soft, romantic, and private while English is hard, sober, and public (Rudin 40-41).

Mena's challenges to the editors are not, however, limited to Spanish—she feels equally comfortable challenging the editors' criticism of her English and asserting the autonomy of her author's subjectivity in English territory as she does in bilingual territory. Just as Mena displays a virtuoso grasp of American colloquialism in her fiction, in her letters she displays a thorough grasp of academic English. In a letter to Robert Underwood Johnson, she writes, "When I received the manuscript, it was marked with many pencilled suggestions for changes. I followed all those which did not make me rebellious" (4 April 1913). Indeed, as the rest of her letter shows, several editorial changes made her "rebellious"—and, like Petra in "The Gold Vanity Set," Mena becomes obstinate when she is asked to perform something that she "did not understand."

> There were other corrections that I did not understand. For instance, where I wrote that the stairway was shaded by immense trees, the adjective there was changed to "huge". I looked up "huge" in the Imperial dictionary and found it defined as "having an immense bulk", which offered no shade of distinction as to meaning. The word "huge", to my Latin ear and throat, is a little, contracted, choking word, whereas "immense" is expansive, and fits perfectly the trees I remember at Guadalupe—and so I have taken the liberty of restoring my own adjective. Again, in the sentence telling of a horse charging through an Indian cabin, "beating down a woman who knelt in the doorway", the word "beating" was changed to "throwing"; but as the phrase "throwing down" was far from expressing the action, with its deadly finality, I decided, after anxious consideration, not to adopt it. And I did not feel that the word "giddiness" was an improvement on "sickness" in the passage about the earthquake—"with a twitching of houses, a spilling of fountains and a quick sickness to people's brains."

Although she begins by demurely pleading ignorance ("there were other corrections I did not understand"), she effectively defends her choice by citing the canonical *Imperial Dictionary*, thereby using mainstream discourse to support the subjectivity of her "Latin ear and throat". As the letter continues, she grows more bold in her assertion of her subjectivity, justifying her choices less comprehensively, and finally ending with the straightforward claim that she simply "did not feel that the word 'giddiness' was an improvement on 'sickness'". The final version indicates that a compromise was reached, as "great" replaces "immense" / "huge", and "striking down" replaces "beating down" / "throwing down". Mena won out on "sickness", however.

Towards the end of this letter, she challenges "the very best academic principles" that informed the editor's changes:

> Will you please ask the gentleman who marked the manuscript to forgive me for not having adopted all of his suggestions? I know that they were founded on the very best academic principles, and I wish to thank him for having drawn my attention to those vexing shalls and wills, and thats and whiches, and to my bad habit of putting the adverb before the verb. And yet—may I argue for liberty of judgment? I wrote that John of God "abruptly went out into the rain", and it was changed to "went out abruptly", and I changed it back again because I felt that his abruptness began before he got to the door—began with his first movement towards it—whereas with the adverb demurely following its verb I could not make myself feel that the action had any abruptness until the man was actually outside the door. . . . And so I make my excuses, with very great respect!

Again, Mena begins politely and demurely before countering the hegemonic discourse with her argument "for liberty of judgment." She concedes to the authority of "the very best academic principle," retracts this concession with "and yet," then subverts the authority of the academic principles with a linguistically sophisticated argument for the placement of the adverb before the verb. Tellingly, she does not attribute her vexing confusion of "shalls" and "wills" and "thats" and "whiches" to her bilingualism, and, indeed, the placement of the adverb in relation to the verb is more flexible in Spanish than it is according to (contemporary) "academic principles" of English. By not alluding to her own bilingualism in this section of the letter, Mena stakes her claim on purely English grounds. She is equally capable of asserting the integrity of her English and Spanish word choices.

In another portion of this lengthy letter, Mena defends her choices as author: "Some others of the suggested changes, although slight, would have marred little shades, perfumes, cadences, which to me were full of meaning" (Letter to Johnson 4 April 1913). Interestingly, Mena appears to cite this editorial tussle in "The Birth of the God of War", a first-person account published about one year later that seems to move away from the local color genre into the realms of autobiography and mythology. The narrator says, "'Ruge éste por la vez postrera,' as it rolled out in my grandmother's voice, the *éste* signifying that ill-fated cub, for which I always wept. I render the construction literally because it seems to carry more of the perfume that came with those phrases as I heard them by the blue-tiled fountain" (65). Translations of Spanish, like representations of Mexico, are not as good as the real thing. Mena consistently tells her Anglo readers that they are missing out, that translations are deficient—a stance definitely not taken by either U.S. local color narrative or Mexican *costumbrismo*.

Indeed, her letters to the editors at *The Century* also convey Mena's awareness of herself as a cultural translator who corrects the ignorant assumptions of her editors. In a letter dated September 28, 1914, Douglas Z. Doty asks, "I am wondering whether you would be interested to consider the idea of transplanting a Spanish character to this country; that is to say, using a Mexican character with an American background." Her response avoids referring to the editor's conflation of 'Spanish' and 'Mexican' characters but corrects it by substituting "Spanish speaking": "I have thought a great deal about the serial I outlined to you in response to your suggestion concerning the adventures of a Spanish speaking character in New York."

As an upper-middle class Mexican-American woman courting the highbrow Anglo audience of *The Century*, Mena is aware that her audience wants to see quaint depictions of "Mexicanness" and can pander expertly and subversively to the magazine's exoticizing tastes because she writes simultaneously from within and without the dominant Anglo culture. Interestingly, Mena's subversions, both in her fiction and in her letters to the editors of *The Century*, decline after the publication of "Doña Rita's Rivals" in September of 1914. Around this time, staff changes at *The Century* led to Mena's corresponding primarily with the less sympathetic editor Douglas Z. Doty[20]; furthermore, she seems to have been encountering financial difficulties at this time and asked for an advance on the story about the Mexican characters in New York.[21] Not surprisingly, her letters from this period are hardly the creatively assertive letters of before. Indeed, she seems eager to comply with Doty's request:

> I have in outline the personalities of a family of wealthy refugees from Mexico, with possibilities of rich comedy in their contact with American life, especially in relation to the gradual emancipation of their daughter, who in spite of the efforts of her parents to keep her in pious subjection in accordance with Mexican tradition, takes to American freedom like a duck to water and blossoms into an ardently independent young woman, with of course, a suitable romance to crown her adventures (September 1914).

Unfortunately for modern fans of Mena, this proposed story was never published; but even its preliminary outline tells us that Mena has changed. The easy synthesis of Mexican and American cultures implied by the phrase "like a duck to water" represents a shift away from the cultural incompatibilities explored in Mena's earlier stories.

In "The Education of Popo", Mena explores the clash between "Mexican tradition" and "American freedom" not by explicitly privileging one over the other but by suggesting their mutual attraction yet asserting their incompatibility. In this story, Mena again shows her Anglo readers how Mexicans perceive them when the adolescent Mexican protagonist studies the curious relationship of the visiting American mother and daughter: "By some magic peculiar to the highly original country of the *Yanquis*, their relation appeared to be that of an indifferent sisterliness, with a balance of authority in favor of the younger" (49). This bossy American daughter is "captivated by the native courtliness of his [Popo's] manners" (50). Indeed, young Popo foregoes the "dark-eyed, demure, and now despised damsels of his own race" in favor of the blonde, outspoken, virginal Miss Cherry—who turns out to be a hair-dying, heart-breaking, divorcee.

The proposed story about a wealthy family of Mexican refugees whose daughter takes to American life like a "duck to water" is precisely the type of story that readers of *The Century* would have appreciated, one which stereotypes "Mexican tradition" and ends in a conventional romantic plot, much like another *Century* story "The Transformation of Angelita Lopez" (Millard, 547-57). However, in "The Emotions of Maria Concepción" which was published several months earlier, Mena alters the conventionally romantic plot by ending with the heroine's disillusionment with her bullfighter crush. But this story is not free from stereotypes. Mena's narrative voice accuses Anglos of misreading Mexican women but unconsciously ends by conveying her own participation in the perpetuation of Mexican stereotypes. She describes her heroine's initial passion for the bullfighter as "all powerful, but also delicate, immaterial, and remote compared with that which the North too confidently assumes to read in the smoldering eyes of the South" (39). Here, Mena simultaneously accuses her Anglo audience of misreading Mexican women and demonstrates her own stereotyping of southern eyes as "smoldering", a description that hearkens back to the "land of wonderful eyes" that Paredes responds to with disdain (1982, 50).

As Amy Doherty points out in the introduction to *The Collected Stories*, Mena's stories defy generic classification: they are neither stereotypically made-to-order magazine stories in the local color mode, nor are they consistently subversive of hegemonic Anglo power structures. Although *The Century* seems to want only the gratification of stereotyped exoticization—as suggested by the many quaint travel narratives, local color stories, and even racist treatises published there around this time—many of Mena's stories place demands on their readers by showcasing moments of intercultural misrecognition and including Spanish words.[22] Indeed, her correspondence with the editors of *The Century Magazine* reveals a writer engaged in cultural and linguistic negotiations made all the more remarkable by their context. Undoubtedly, both Mena's historical moment and the authority of her editors place limits on her subversions. Still, many decades before the emergence of identity politics, Mena asserts the untranslatability of her native culture and language before early twentieth-century magazine editors and produces self-conscious local color stories that transcend generic prescriptions.

Notes

[1]The letters are in the Century Co. records held in the Rare Books and Manuscript Division of New York Public Library. Estimated dates are given in brackets in the bibliography. I am indebted to Anne Gebelein and Gustavo Pérez Firmat for their valuable insights into earlier drafts of this paper.

[2]The American local color, or "regionalist", narrative that was hugely popular in the decades after the Civil War depicted the unique features of a particular locale and the dialect and typical behaviors of its inhabitants. After the influx of new Americans in the early twentieth century, the genre gained a multicultural dimension, and local color narratives began to be defined also as narratives that depict a region foreign to their audiences. By this definition, local color writers become interpreters of the "foreign" locale, interpreters who

exploit the tension between the "native" and the "foreign" (Stephanie Foote, 3; 15-16). Indeed, Amy Doherty notes that *Household Magazine* dubbed Mena "the foremost interpreter of Mexican life" (xii). See the Introduction of Ammons and Rohy for a description and contextualization of local color writing in the U.S.

[3]In oral traditions worldwide, the trickster is a recurring figure who perpetuates subversions through wiliness, deceit, and/or magical powers during his picaresque travels. In her introduction to a collection of essays about multicultural trickster tales in turn-of-the-century American literature (a collection which includes Tiffany Ana López' essay on Mena as Malinche), Elizabeth Ammons notes, "Trickster strategies are not just a way to get 'in' or 'back at' the dominant culture. Tricksters and trickster energy articulate a whole other, independent, cultural reality and positive way of negotiating multiple cultural systems" (1994, xi).

[4]See Simmen's article in *The Journal of American Culture* for a more comprehensive biography of Mena.

[5]See Mena's article "Afternoons in Italy with D.H. Lawrence." *Texas Quarterly* 7.4 (1964): 114-120.

[6]In "John of God, the Water-Carrier", Mena takes up a subject tackled by Mexican *costumbrista* author José T. de Cuellar about three decades earlier in un *artículo de costumbre* in the newspaper *El Libertador*. Unlike Cuellar, Mena neither concludes that the water carrier's work is "costly and unhygienic" nor that Mexico should learn from the technological progress in the United States (Jefferson Rea Spell, 307). In fact, she seems to be lamenting the loss of the individual in the face of American-imported modernization. In his 1935 article on Mexican *costumbrismo*, Rea Spell identifies a shift in the focus of Mexican *costumbrista* writers in the nineteenth century that spilled into the twentieth century: the newer writers did not celebrate peculiarly local and picturesque customs, types, and manners so much as they scorned them (308). While Mena exhibits some gently satirical tendencies, they are often directed towards the North, and she does not participate in the ruthless satire of the progressive Mexican *costumbristas* in the latter half of the nineteenth century and early twentieth century who used regionalist narratives to call for the destruction of the local and the primitive in favor of the universal and advanced (308). Considered in light of these contemporary Mexican local color traditions, Mena's stories seem nostalgic.

[7]All page references for the stories will refer to *The Collected Works*.

[8]In the original, the Spanish loan word *patrón* is capitalized.

[9]In a talk on the history of Hispanism, James Fernandez notes that up until Pan-Americanism gained a great deal of Anglo attention during World War I, few

people studied Spanish as a foreign language (qtd. In Aronowicz, n. pag.). In his 1915 article "The Inevitable Trend in Mexico" David Lawrence confirms that "an effective stimulus has been given to Pan-Americanism not only in the United States, but in Central and South America, since the outbreak of war in Europe" (743). Indeed, in the November 1913 edition of *The Century Magazine,* a character in a serial novel by Frances Hodgson Burnett lists only French, German, and Italian as popular options for foreign language study (139).

[10]In a letter to one of her *Century* editors, Mena herself uses the diminutive when discussing the indigenous in the context of the Mexican Revolution: "I expect to write more stories of Inditos than of any other class in Mexico. They form the majority; the issue of their rights and wrongs, their aspirations and possibilities, is at the root of the present situation in my unhappy country" (letter to Yard, March 1913).

[11]Interestingly, this article of Mena's seems to be in dialogue with other *Century* articles about the Monroe Doctrine and the limitations it has placed on American intervention in Latin America, such as Lawrence's "The Inevitable Trend in Mexico" and Morgan W. Shuster's "The Mexican Menace" (also see: Whelpley's "Our Disorganized Diplomacy Service" in the November 1913 edition and Shuster's "Is There a Sound American Foreign Policy?" in the December 1913 edition). The Julian Carrillo article is subtitled "The Herald of a Musical Monroe Doctrine" and provides a pan-American reading of the Monroe Doctrine, claiming "In a waking vision he saw the Americas, North and South, become spiritually federated by the free evolution and jealous nurture of a music neither of North nor South, but of America" (759).

[12]See note 6.

[13]The translation is mine.

[14]The Spanish words appear in italics in *The Century*, but without any editorial explanation. NB. "The Soul of Hilda Brunel" is the only story by Mena that does not contain italicized Spanish words; its bilingualism is restricted to the Italian phrase *bel canto*. This story, however, was published in *Cosmopolitan*, not in *The Century*.

[15]In total, Mena published ten stories during these years, but, as noted, "The Soul of Hilda Brunel" (1916), is neither bilingual nor set in Mexico. Although Amy Doherty adds an average of twenty-one explanatory footnotes to the nine bilingual stories, she does not define words that are translated intra-textually, or repeated. The shortest story, "Birth of the God of War", contains only nine footnotes, while a longer story, "The Emotions of María Concepción", contains fifty-two footnotes.

[16]All examples are taken from Mena's stories and are intended to be representative, but they are not all-inclusive.

[17]Rudin writes, "The *monolingual reader*, or *monolingual English reader*, is a phantom in a way, a stereotype label that moreover does not cover the entire readership of Chicano texts in English. On the other hand, that phantom has a very real existence and is a factor of power in the United States. Furthermore . . . it exists, i.e., as the *implied reader* in Iser's sense" (60). In Mena's case, the monolingual Anglo reader is an even more pressing reality. See note 9.

[18]In a letter to Douglas Z. Doty, Mena alludes to her financial reliance on the publication of her stories: "You were good enough to say last time I saw you that you would consider the questions of making me and advance on a serial of this kind. If you can only manage to do so enough to free me from anxiety for a month of two—I can attack the work immediately and keep at it until it is finished" (September 1914). As evidence of the emotional gratification she received from publication, she writes to a *Century* editor: "Still your wonderful praises ring in my ear, and the afternoon I passed in your office remains in my memory as a moment of enchantment in a life that has not always been as happy as it is now" (Letter to Robert Underwood Johnson 20 March 1913).

[19]Only bilingual readers know for certain that the narrator is female because her gender is not revealed until the end, when the grandmother refers to her as "*chiquita*" (69).

[20]Under Doty, "The Son of His Master" was rejected by *The Century*. A revised version probably became "Son of the Tropics" published by *Household Magazine* in 1931.

[21]See note 18.

[22]See stories and articles by G. Millard, Edward A. Ross, Jacob A. Riis, Julius Muller, Charles Johnson Post, and Hugh Johnson for context. It would be interesting to consider whether Mena's early success (she published seven stories from November 1913 to December 1914) actually reflects her Anglo readers' desire, conscious or not, for more ambivalent local color.

Works Cited

Primary Sources

Doty, Douglas Zabriske. Letter to María Cristina Mena. 28 September 1914.

Hodgson Burnett, Frances. "T. Tembarom." *The Century Magazine* (Nov. 1913): 135-148.

Johnson Post, Charles. "At the Ebb-Tide." *The Century Magazine* (Mar. 1914): 760-67.

Johnson, Hugh. "Race." *The Century Magazine* (Aug. 1914): 616-23.

Lawrence, David. "The Inevitable Trend in Mexico." *The Century Magazine* (Sept. 1915): 737-44.

Mena, María Cristina. Letter to Robert Underwood Johnson. 20 March 1913.
_____. Letter to Johnson. 4 April 1913.
_____. Letter to Douglas Zabriske Doty. [October 1914].
_____. Letter to Doty. [November/December 1914].
_____. "Julian Carillo: The Herald of a Musical Monroe Doctrine." *The Century Magazine* (Mar. 1915): 753-59.
_____. *The Collected Stories of María Cristina Mena*. Houston: Arte Público Press, 1997.
Millard, Gertrude B. "The Transformation of Angelita Lopez." *The Century Magazine* (Aug. 1914): 547-57
Muller, Julius. "Among Caribbean Devils and Duppies." *The Century Magazine* (July 1914): 446-54.
Riis, Jacob A. "The Battle with the Slum." *The Century Magazine* (Nov. 1913): 49-53.
Ross, Edward Alsworth. "The Old World in the New: Economic Consequences of Immigration." *The Century Magazine* (Nov. 1913): 28-35.
_____. "American and Immigrant Blood: A Study of the Effects of Immigration." *The Century Magazine*. (Dec. 1913): 225-32.
_____. "The Lesser Immigrant Groups in America." *The Century Magazine* (Oct. 1914): 934-40.
_____. "Labor and Class." *The Century Magazine* (Mar. 1915): 760-68.
Shuster, W. Morgan. "The Mexican Menace." *The Century Magazine.* (Jan. 1914): 593-602.

Secondary Sources
Adorno, Theodor W. *The Jargon of Authenticity*. Evanston: Northwestern University Press, 1973.
Ammons, Elizabeth. Introduction. *Tricksterism in turn-of-the-century American literature: a multicultural perspective*. Eds. Elizabeth Ammons and Annette White-Parks, Hanover: University Press New England, 1994.
Ammons, Elizabeth and Valerie Rohy, eds. Introduction. *American Local Color Writing 1880-1920*. New York: Penguin, 1998.
Aronowicz, Yaron. "Fernandez Outlines History of Hispanism." 15 Dec. 2005. <http://www.wesleyan.edu/argus/archives/nov122002/dateyear/n4.html>.
Doherty, Amy. "Introduction." *The Collected Stories of María Cristina Mena.* Houston: Arte Público Press, 1997. vii-l.
Foote, Stephanie. *Regional Fictions: Culture and Identity in Nineteenth-Century American Literature*. Wisconsin: University Wisconsin Press, 2001.
Johnson, Rob. "'A Taste for the Exotic': Revolutionary Mexico and the Short Stories of Katherine Anne Porter and María Cristina Mena." *From Texas to*

The World and Back: Essays on The Journeys of Katherine Anne Porter. Ed. Mark Busby, Fort Worth: TX Publication, 2001. 178-98.

Kellman, Steven G. *The Translingual Imagination*. Lincoln: University Nebraska Press, 2000.

Millán Chivite, Alberto. *El costumbrismo mexicano en las novellas de revolución*. Sevilla: Universidad de Sevilla, 1996.

Miller, Joshua L. "Lingual Politics: The Syncopated Accents of Multilingual Modernism, 1919-1948." Diss. Columbia U, 2001.

Paredes, Raymund A. "The Evolution of Chicano Literature." *Three American Literatures*. Ed. Houston A. Baker, Jr. New York: MLA, 1982.

Rea Spell, Jefferson. "The Costumbrista Movement in Mexico." *PMLA* 50.1 (1935): 290-315.

Rudin, Ernst. *Tender Accents of Sound: Spanish in the Chicano Novel in English*. Tempe: Bilingual Press, 1996.

Simmen, Edward. "The Mountain Came Long Ago to Mohammed: The American Cultural Invasion of Mexico as Seen in the Short Fiction of María Cristina Mena." *Journal of American Culture* 20.2 (Summer 1997): 147-52.

_____. *North of The Rio Grande: The Mexican-American Experience in Short Fiction*. New York: Mentor, 1992.

Tatum, Charles M. *Chicano Literatures*. Boston: Twayne, 1982.

Translating, Smuggling, and Recovering Books in Nineteenth Century Mexico: Thomas Smith Webb's *El Monitor de los Masones Libres: ó, Illustraciones sobre la Masonería*

Guillermo de los Reyes Heredia
University of Houston

In the era of Globalization and high technology there is an anxiety about the disappearance of the printed text. Such anxiety has made us conscious of the crucial role that the printed text has played in our lives. Books have become invisible because we grew up around them; therefore we take them for granted. Books have been the instrument that human beings have used to perpetuate their cultural memory. This paper seeks to show that by recovering the written text we can learn more about our history. Further, the aim of this paper is to recover and explore a Masonic book that tells us a great deal of the political life of Mexico in the first half of the nineteenth century.

Thomas Smith Webb's *Freemason's Monitor* published in 1797 was the first Masonic book published in the United States containing the practice of Masonic degrees. These degrees were "then being conferred in various section of the nation, especially in New England, New York and Pennsylvania, and which were to form the nucleus of a new rite" (Leyland 74). The *Freemason's Monitor* established a new system that later was expanded into a rite of ten degrees and distributed around the United States and other parts of the world. Over twenty five years later, the same book was published in Spanish by the well know publishing house H.C. Carey & I. Lea. The first edition in Spanish was translated as *El Monitor de los Masones Libres: ó, Illustraciones sobre la Masonería* in

1822 in Philadelphia, this is arguably one of the first, if not the first, Masonic publications published in Spanish in the Americas.

On May of 1998, at an antiquarian book dealer's in Mexico City, a colleague and I[1] found a copy of the first edition of Thomas Smith Webb *El Monitor de los Masones Libres: ó, Illustraciones sobre la Masonería.* After finding such a treasure many questions and ideas came to mind, such as: Why was a Masonic book translated to Spanish and published in Philadelphia? How did the books get into Mexico and other parts of Latin America considering the rigid laws against Masonic publications? Who translated the book? What were the political implications of such an enterprise? After doing some preliminary research, I found out that there are two known Spanish editions of the book, both published in the United States in 1822. The one mentioned above and another version titled *Monitor ó Guía de los Franc-Mazones, Utílisimo Para la Instruccion de sus Miembros é Información de los que desean imponerse en sus principios* published in New York City. I discuss both of them here, although, most of the discussion will be focused on the Philadelphia version.

In this study, I analyze the Spanish translations of Webb's *The Freemason's Monitor* published in 1822. I argue that in Masonic translations the translator is twice invisible. This invisibility is created by the translation theories of the time, but more importantly, by the Masonic tradition of secrecy, antiquity and originality. In addition, I explore the Mexican political situation in the 1820s vis-à-vis the distribution and smuggling of Masonic books to Mexico.

Of Words, Secret Passwords and Other Demons

Freemasonry is a secret organization. The level of secrecy varies from country to country. In Spanish America, where I have done most of my research on Freemasonry, such organization is extremely hermetic. The public image of the society is not like that in the United States, where members of this institution appear in public and open their libraries to non-members. In Latin America, Freemasonry is an extremely political, often virulently anticlerical, and controversial institution. Thus, collecting material, analyzing and translating it can be like revealing the "X-Files" or discussing abortion with the Pope. In some countries the Masonic institutions are more open than in others. However, there is an area in which all of them keep their secrecy. In "The Short Talk Bulletin" titled "The Secret" published in December, 1941, by The Masonic Service Association of the United States (these pamphlets are sent to lodges for distribution to members), a discussion shows that there are certain secrets that are 'untranslatable' and cannot be told:

> The majority of those not Freemasons suppose that the Order has some Great Secret, some hidden knowledge the possession of which marks off the possessors from his fellows and, perhaps, gives him access to resources not possessed by the uninitiated. A majority of Freemasons undoubtedly consider that the secrets of the Order taught in a Lodge are the component parts of The Secret and find a contented satisfaction in their knowledge (3) [. . .] What then is The Secret? It is something, which cannot be told. He who has it cannot broadcast it to his neighbor. It is far too ethereal for words. None of the half million words in the English language are sufficient, either, alone or in any combination—not even if they are all used—to express music so another may hear it, the perfume of the rose so another may smell it, the glory of a sunset so another may see it. Music, perfume, color must be experienced to be known; they are not tellable. The Secret of Freemasonry is not tellable in words. (7)

A conundrum is that if one cannot experience something one can never judge whether it is or is not 'tellable.' Marie Mulvey Roberts points out that "secrecy is concerned above all with what human beings want to protect: the intimate, the dangerous, the profane, the fragile, the sacred, and the forbidden" (97). When we are dealing with secrecy, "one is struck by its elusive, amorphous and often invisible nature—it is to be found everywhere and nowhere" (97).

Mainstream academic publications lack references to Masonry. Perhaps one of the reasons is that scholars who are not members and who are interested in this topic are unaware of the considerable amount of literature about its history and about the rituals of Freemasonry. These ideas of secrecy and the belief that Masonic activities are completely secret have fostered the lack of information and the lack of consideration of Masonic motifs or symbols. Two good examples of this are Kipling's *Kim* (1901) and Manuel Rojas' *El hombre de la rosa* (1928). Paul Rich comments that "Kipling himself, often an institutionist in his writing, did not appreciate fully their significance. But the neglect in the literature about his reference to the so-called 'Royal craft' seems surprising given the fact that Kipling's interest in lodges and their ritual has been well documented" (323). Susan M. Linker points out that through the consideration and study of all the symbols we can have a better understanding of the texts. She argues that in order to fully appreciate *El hombre de la rosa* one has to "study Rojas' symbolism and allegory [. . .] Examined in detail, "*El hombre de la rosa* reveals itself as a superbly constructed synthesis of Masonic and Rosicrucian ideals and symbols" (27). In sum, while decoding these topics we will face problems that have to do with an esoteric subject's special vocabulary.

A key to understanding the peculiarity of Masonic vocabulary is to keep in mind that, although the fraternity sometimes is a political pressure group, and sometimes is involved in what currently might be called New Age activities, during its entire history it has been extremely ritualistic, and wherever it is established has been characterized by the importance attached to conferring degrees on initiates. These degrees can be likened to plays in which the candidate plays a principal part, undergoing numerous trials before he has gained full membership. Thomas C. Warden in an article titled "Whatever Happened to the Written Word?" points out that "Masonic ritual relies upon mouth to ear, as does Masonic education to some extent. But the preponderance of our responsibility —our Masonic tradition, heritage, and history—is essentially and necessarily dependent upon the written word. For the most vivid memory pales by comparison to the faintest ink on a printed page"(8).

Due to the great emphasis that Masonic members place on practicing their degrees and on legitimacy based on their past, there is an obsession for preserving the rituals unchanged. The vocabulary has in effect been sealed in a time capsule. Many of the words are invoked magically and are believed to confer power. This is particularly true of the passwords by which members identify each other. Although the degrees are usually presented in the vernacular,[2] the passwords are often universal. So every Mason can recall when he was given, under highly dramatic circumstances and after taking solemn oaths, the secret lexicon by which he can identify himself to the brethren.

Another aspect is that sometimes a word or phrase has become 'polluted' because the "profane world" (non-Masonic people) has appropriated some of their words or expressions. An example is the phrase 'giving someone the third degree,' which in contemporary English is used for the police roughing up a suspect, or even people commonly use that expression, but originally refers to the Masonic third degree (a degree which features the "Hiramic myth"). "Third degree" does not have the same connotation in Spanish, such expression is only used in the Masonic sense. These different aspects of legitimacy, secrecy, antiquity, and esoteric meaning that we discussed before will help us to understand the notions of invisibility and fidelity that Masonic translation enforced.

The Evolution of the Freemason's Monitor in the Nineteenth Century

Thomas Smith Webb (1771-1819) was one of the Founding Fathers of the York Rite of Freemasonry. The York or American Rite is a Masonic Rite created in the United States as a need of a "strong national and state organizations to preserve, invigorate and propagate the then detached, uncontrolled and sometimes nebulous ceremonies that now are known as the Capitular degrees and the Templar orders" (Leyland 69). Aware of this necessity Webb persuaded others to join him in creating this new Rite. Some other masons may have understood the need of creating a new Rite, however, they never translated this need into action.

Thomas Webb realized the importance of having the rituals printed in order to facilitate the practicing of the ceremonies. Consequently, he published *The Freemason's Monitor or Illustrations of Masonry in Two Parts*, by A Royal Arch Mason K.T., K. of M., (Albany: New York, Spencer and Webb) in 1797. With this book Thomas Webb contributed a great deal to the practice of Masonic ritual in the United States and other parts of the world. Since it first appeared in press, the *Freemason's Monitor* became a catechism for the York Rite ceremonies.

The different editions of the book published in the nineteenth century were different from the prefaces of the first edition. My research shows that the preface to the 'original' version is really the preface to the 1805-1818 editions. The most reproduced edition was the 1818 one, which is the last edition that Webb saw and revised.

Decoding the Invisible Translator

Freemasonry in Mexico during the first half of the nineteenth century played a key role in the different Independent movements throughout Latin America. In Mexico, the first political parties, the *yorkinos* and *escoceses*, were two different Masonic bodies that became the first political parties in Mexico that were fighting for the control of the new Republic after the Independence.[3] However Freemasonry was present in Mexico well before the Independence movement. The Mexican Inquisition hunted people with Masonic connections: in 1785 a Mexican, Manuel Zuralds, along with a Frenchman and an Italian, was tried for being a Mason. Masonry in Spanish America was regarded as a political threat. Freemasonry became politically significant in Mexico during the chaos of the 1820s, before and during Guadalupe Victoria's presidency.

There are many ways in which governments, organizations, and groups create internal unity. One of the most effective ways to pursue this objective is by creating a literary canon. This was one of the ways that the Masonic order used to expand its influence around the world. This process started with the members of the order who had to move to a different country and felt the necessity or interest in practicing Masonic rituals. Because of this, the order grew tremendously in the eighteenth and nineteenth centuries. The strategy was first to transmit the ritual orally, and then in a written form in order to create such a canon. Freemasonry used techniques similar to the nationalistic movements in order to create a sense of brotherhood, a universal movement sharing the same symbols, language, and rituals. These ideas are similar to those of the Romantic nationalists that Benedict Anderson describes in his book *Imagined Communities: Reflections on the Origin and Spread of Nationalism*. Many societies used translation as a useful method that can be helpful in building national culture (Scleiermacher in Venuti 100). Once these methods or "cultural artifacts" are created in the Masonic context they follow the patter of nationalism that Anderson describes: "they became modular, capable of being transplanted, with varying degree of self-consciousness, to a great variety of social terrains, to merge and be merged with a correspondingly wide variety of political and ideological constellations" (4). The nationalism described by Anderson and Scleiermacher viewed translation as an important practice in the different nationalistic movements: "it could enrich the German language by developing an elite literature and thus enable German culture to realized its historical destiny of global domination" (Scleiermacher in Venuti 99). The Masons have used this method to promote their rituals and to create and expand their influence in different parts of the world. A reason why the *Freemason's Monitor* was translated into Spanish apparently was to start a Masonic canon and promote its rituals.

The Spanish translations of Webb's book concentrates on two different aspects: 1) the traditional concept of translations which is fidelity, "the freedom of faithful reproduction and, in its service, fidelity to the word" (Benjamin 78) and 2) Invisibility, "the translators receive minimal [or non] recognition for their work" (Venuti 8). This invisibility is promoted by the Masonic obsession with originality, secrecy, and ancient tradition.

As remarked earlier, there are two versions of Webb's book in Spanish published in 1822. One is titled *Monitor ó Guía de los Franc-Mazones, Utílisimo Para la Instruccion de sus Miembros é Información de los que desean imponerse en sus principios* (New Cork, Joseph Desnoues), and the other *El Monitor de los Masones Libres: ó,Illustraciones sobre la Masoneria, por Thomas Smith Webb, Gran Maestro Pasado de la Gran Logia de Rhode Island. Traducido del inglés al español* (Philadelphia, H.C. Carey and I. Lea).

The title of the book was translated differently in both versions. The translation of the Philadelphia edition is closer to the English version. The New York edition is similar, but is not presented in its literal form. In this edition, the translator tries to show the purpose of the book in the title: a useful and informative manual for everyone who wants to be part of the order. A word from the title that deserves attention is the word Freemason. In the Philadelphia edition, this word was translated literally as "masones libres" (free = libre, masons = masones). In the New York edition the translator suggests a new word, *Franc-mazon*, similar to the word in French. This was probably one of the first times that this word was used in Spanish.[4]

These editions appear to be a translation of the 1818 edition printed by Cushing and Appleton in Salem, Massachusetts. Actually the majority of the English editions were taken from the same version. As I pointed out before, this was because it was the last edition that Webb edited and apparently, the one considered the best among the Masonic circles. It is intriguing that the Spanish editions have an illustration on the page opposite the cover page. This picture appears in many eighteenth-century and early nineteenth-century Masonic books. I think the editor included it with the purpose of showing a famous illustration that represents most of the symbols and elements that are used in conferring the basic Masonic degrees.

The *Monitor ó Guía de los Franc-Mazones* has a preface, unlike the Philadelphia edition. This preface is not a translation of the English version. The book contains no signature, or name of the translator anywhere. This edition has a note on the first page which writes "escrito en inglés por un Franc-mazon y traducido al Castellano" (written in English by a Freemason and translated into Spanish). We are dealing here with an *invisible translator*, a situation that was very common during that time. Venuti argues that 'invisibility' is one of the translator's characteristics that has prevailed in the United States and the United Kingdom since the seventeenth century (8). It is clear that the translator's invisibility is reinforced in the Masonic context. Masonic translations in the nineteenth century rarely show the name of the translators. The interest was in keeping the name of the author as if he or she was the only contributor. In doing this, the idea was that any translated text should be "judged acceptable by most publishers, reviewers, and readers when it reads fluently, when the absence of any linguistic or stylistic peculiarities makes it seem transparent, giving the appearance that it reflects the foreign writer's personality or intention or the essential meaning of foreign text— the appearance in other word, that the translation is not in fact a translation, but the original" (Venuti 1). This idea is still alive nowadays, particularly in Masonic circles.

The New York version's preface portrays Freemasonry as a universal order in which, "all men were born brothers": the differences in the languages they speak, the clothes they wear, the countries where they live in, and the position they have in society are accidental. They believe that "the whole world is just a replica, in which each nation is like a family, and each individual is like a son: having everything ready for the *sapientisimo* Grand Architect of the Universe." (iii). In this preface we can see the enormous appeal of Masonry that attracted men to the order and encouraged the creating of new lodges practicing the American Rite in the Americas.

There is evidence of considerable freedom in the way these books, particularly the New York edition, were translated. Indeed, it seems that fidelity was forgotten when the purpose of the work was to promote and attract new members. A purpose of the Spanish book is to transmit Webb's rituals to the newly born Latin American nations and the Spanish-speaking masons in the United States.

Now I will concentrate on the Spanish *Monitor* published in Philadelphia. Why would an American publisher produce a Masonic book in Spanish? Initially I was curious about Mathew Carey's's[5] Masonic affiliation, since he was a devoted Catholic who published religious books. However, at that time it was not uncommon to see liberal Catholics closely related to Freemasonry. In fact, some of them were both Catholic and Freemasons. Steven Bullock mentions that "The fraternity [Freemasonry] also provided aid in his other great passion, selling books. Masonic activities allowed him to beard potential customers. 'Hope to vend some to-morrow at the Masonic meeting 16 Miles from this,' he wrote in the month of his address to the legislature. Two months later, he noted, 'Tomorrow I set off for Newton to be ready to utter the Masonic Oration— God grant I may sell Bibles etc. etc.' The identification of himself as a Masonic brother on his publications similarly served commercial purposes, underlining his moral authority and encouraging fraternal patronage" (198). Thus Mathew Carey used his Masonic affiliation to aid his business.

In 1822 Mathew Carey retired and turned over the control of his publishing house to his son-in-law Isaac Lea. Carey and Lea seem to have had the respect of the Grand Lodge of Pennsylvania as they donated to the poor committee he headed: "Ten dollars was given to Mr. M. Cary, chairman of the Committee, to give to the Public committee for the relief of the poor." (Bussy 11) In addition, he was also interested and sympathized with the revolt of Spain's Latin American colonies and published several books in Spanish and also a Spanish dictionary (11).

Another reason could have been that the book was published to be sold to the Hispanic community in the United States. Nicolás Kanellos and David Szewczyk, experts on publishing houses in the nineteenth century, argue that the books in Spanish published by Carey were not strictly for export. The Hispanic emigrant population in Philadelphia in the period 1810-1830 was sizeable and a number of the Carey & Lea Spanish language publications would have found a ready audience there. Also, several copies of these publications went directly into the Philadelphia-area libraries and are still there.[6] Thus, these three considerations might be some of the reasons why Carey decided to publish the book.

There is also the possibility that the great number of Latin American intellectuals who were living in Philadelphia at that time asked Carey to publish the *Monitor* in Spanish in order to send it to Latin America to continue the development of Masonic lodges. Mathew Carey received a series of letters that show his Masonic interest. There are eighteen letters at the *Historical Society of Pennsylvania*, sent to Carey by F.W. Robison, who was his agent in Mexico. The letters are from August 18, 1822 until around 1823. On of the letters shows that Robinson upon arriving in Mexico met Don Manuel Reyes, a representative of the Emperor Agustin de Iturbide, the Emperor of thc newly independent country who had come to the throne in May and would be exiled the next year: "I tried him by the Square and Compass but (had) no answer. I then put to him certain interrogations which he answered much to my satisfaction" (Letter August 18, 1822). The content of these letters is extremely valuable, not only for the various Masonic references but because they reveal the smuggling of Masonic books into Mexico. On another letter from, Robinson to Carey and Lea he points out:

> The prohibited books ____ by placing them in the bottom say there lais and thru of the work on cooking on the top place in the bottom of each box 15 copies of the café___ 15 of the ***Monitor*** and 15 of the Library and be careful to place the bound and ______ in separate boxes and also to note how many is bound as follows to safe the trouble of examen in Alvarado Libros pasta is Books bound the same as Derecho, Contrato, Libros Pasta de Carton is barkey bound although in caffo, Libros a la Rustica is those with paper con____ (Letter n/d, emphasis mine)

The *Monitor Masónico* published by Carey and Lea entered Mexico on at least one occasion hidden in a consignment of cook books. This was because at that moment the Inquisition's policies on censorship were followed by Agustin the Iturbide. These letters show the political momentum that Mexico was living at that time. The political and social repression, as well as the political persecutions to some of the most important intellectuals such as Fray Servando Teresa de Mier, as one can see in this letter from Robinson to Carey:

> On the first of this M___ the celebrated Padre Mier, one of the late cong___ whom the Emp. Impressioned made his escape from the convent of St. Domingo, through the agency of a priest, at 4'o clock in the ______, he took me ____ in the house of some lady who has _____ to protect him, but as the Emp. Has done what exasperated that he should have effected his escape dispatched hoops in every direction a pursuit the ladies ______ fearful that some accidents might ______ they gave information to the p_____ authority and the _____ p_____ was renamed with Pr_t___ and annye to the Inquisition which at pur__ is a rendezvous for the soldiers. (Letter n/d)

Another important figure of the time that one of Carey and Lea's agents met was the first U.S. Ambassador in Mexico, Joel Poinsett who was a very active Mason in both countries, in fact, he was pivotal for the development of the York Rite in

Mexico. Robinson mentions that "Mr Poinsett . . . here purchased some[books] and informed me that they ___ him extravagancy." Consequently, there is a possibility that Poinsett requested some copies of the *Monitor*, as well as other books to promote Masonry in Mexico. One can argue that he was probably instrumental in the distribution and even the translation of the *Monitor.* Paul Rich and Guillermo De Los Reyes have argued that even though Poinsett was not the founder of Freemasonry or more specifically, the York Rite in Mexico, he aided Mexican Masons to create more Masonic Lodges and develop the York Rite.

In sum, the agent of Carey and Lea in Mexico keep them informed of the political and economic situation in Mexico. For their business the political and economic stability was important. Thus, they established relationships with the key political players. Robinson, for example, met with many of them. He observed closely what was happening in Mexico to send a report to Philadelphia. The following is another example:

> The revolution which Santana has set in motion with Victoria you no doubts have heard me this reach you by may ___now Orleans, it is important for the wish always ____ to tell what will be the result too many revolutions Ch___ remain on hand who are opposed to the present form of preceding to inform a solid Gov.rs, for form time this revolution moving much evil the hoops who are on what is _____ the republican side on _____ number of _____ and on _____ posture in Vera Cruz and present del Bey, the imperial troops are so few and so seating over this m______ Empire (December 2nd, 1822)

In Search of a Translator

Knowing who was the translator or translators of the *Monitor* can aid us to have a more complete picture of the Masonic publications and/or translations into Spanish during the period. In addition, it can lead us to the recovery of other publications not only searching by the name of the authors, but also the name of the translators.

As I mentioned previously, no reference to the translators appears anywhere in the books. This is a case of an invisible translator, using Venuti's vernacular. No record of the name of the translator(s) appears in the different Masonic bibliographies of the period, not even in Kent Walgen's article "A Bibliography or Pre-1851 Louisiana Scottish Rite Imprints" that describes all of the Masonic books that had significant Scottish Rite content published within the present boundaries of the United States. In this article Walgen presents each bibliographical entry including the author, title, place of publication, publishing house, date of publication, citation of bibliographical reference works, location of copies, subject matter, and usually an annotation. However, he does not provide any reference to the Spanish translators of any of the editions.

In the Philadelphia edition, a note mentions that "el autor de esta nota no es masón, sino un hombre que habla por la evidencia de los sentidos de la razón" (the author of this note is not a Mason. He is a man whose talk follows the evidence of common sense). At the beginning I thought that the note would contain some information about the translator, but it was not the case. The note only has a propagandistic or recruiting purpose. It basically describes how great the Lodges in the United States were at the time. It also mentions that the members of the lodges are the most prominent citizens, "los primeros hombres de la nación cuya moralidad, talentos y carácter les hace ocupar los primeros puestos en la sociedad" (The first men of the nation, whose morality, talents and personality let them have the first places in society) (290). In addition, the translator criticizes people who say that the Masons are responsible for the problems and destabilization of Europe, "these are blasphemies and ignorance" and points out that "the streets where the Masons live are never colored with the blood of the citizens, private property is respected, and men find in these countries the place holding all the social virtues. In these places everything is action, industry, and honesty" (291). It is evident that the translator is using that note to discuss the situation in Mexico and the rest of Latin America during that time; particularly the problem between the Conservatives (following the traditional Spanish model) and the Liberals (following the U.S. model and the French Revolution). It is not difficult to see that this note is a call to become mason 'á la Americana.'

Looking at the books that were published in Philadelphia by Carey and Lea, publications in the *Historical Society of Pennsylvania* and the collection of the *Recovery of the U.S. Hispanic Literary Heritage* at the University of Houston, I found quite a few books translated from English to Spanish by Edward Barry. Among these books are Arlincourt , Ch. V. Prevot, *El solitario o el misterioso del monte*, 1822; *El espíritu del despotismo, in honor to Don Simón Bolivar, President of Colombia*, 1822; *Jachin y Boas, o una llave auténtica para la puerta de Framasonería, especulativa y operativa, como moderna . . . por un caballero de la Logia de Jerusalen*, 1822; *La vida de Jorge Washington, Comandante en Gefe de los Ejércitos de los Estados Unidos de América, en la guerra que estableció su independencia; y su primer presidente*, 1826. These books have the same elements as the *Monitor de los Masones Libres*. They were published and translated in Philadelphia from English to Spanish, in the 1820s, three of them by the same editorial house (the last one was published by Imprenta de R. Desilver), and all of them neatly edited. After looking at the different phone books at the time and lists of translators, I found eight men named Edward Barry, most of them were easy to discard due to their profession or other characteristics, however, two of them could be the possible translator. Motivated by the interest to search for the translator(s) of the *Monitor* I decided to look the evidence more closely and found that one of the Edward Barrys was twelve years old when the *Monitor* was published in Spanish, leaving Edward Barry, the consul of Colombia in Philadelphia, as the most probable translator. Thus, after ample research, I can conclude that Consul Edward Barry was the translator of the Philadelphia edition of the *Masonic Monitor*. Despite the fact that the Carey and Lea publishing house had different translators from English to Spanish, Barry was the one who translated most of the Masonic material during the 1820s. He translated other works form English to Spanish in later years. Paul Rich and Antonio Lara, who have contributed a great deal with the research on this topic, found that Edward Barry had a great connection with Mathew Carey and that during the time the *Monitor* similar number of books were sent to Colombia and Mexico (255).

Corollary

During the 1820s Philadelphia was undoubtedly a center for intellectual life where people from all over the continent traveled to learn about liberty and democracy. Philadelphia, as the political, social and intellectual center of the new nation was an inspiration for Latin American intellectuals who wanted to fight for their independence. In addition, Philadelphia, as Rich and Lara point out, "was a center for the publishing of controversial Spanish books, as the émigré community took advantage of American freedom of the press to advance the cause of independence from Spain"(256).[7] A good example of the publishing industry in Philadelphia is the *Monitor Masónico* that I have discussed in this article.

This single publication has shed light to the study of Freemasonry in Mexico and Latin America, as well as, to the study of intellectual life in Mexico during the early 1820s. The recovery of this book has shown us the secrecy, ritualistic, and political nature of Freemasonry in Mexico. In addition, one can learn about the socio-political situation in Mexico and the control the government had over the materials that were published and distributed in Mexico during the early 1820s.

The two translations of the *Monitor* that I have presented in this article were both published during the same year, the same country but in different cities (Philadelphia and New York) and under a different title. This fact talks about the vibrant interest in Masonic publications in Spanish in the United States and the demand and possible competition among the publishers to publish and translate Masonic materials.

As discussed before, the name of the translators does not appear in any of the books. The model to follow during that period was to keep the translator invisible to the reader, and the Masonic order also sought to preserve the fidelity of the texts. Masonic scholarship is obsessed by originality and ancient tradition. They have a great interest to promote the rituals and preserve them in written form. As an article entitled "Words, Words, Words" points out:

> The study of words, how they acquire meanings, what they do to people who use them and hear them, should interest every Mason. Masonic labors, so far as the ritualistic work and additional instruction are concerned, are almost exclusively verbal. In fact, many a Brother remembers his Masonic experiences as almost wholly verbal experience in which he listened, and then was asked to listen so more [. . .] One of modern Freemasonry's serious problems maybe precisely a problem of semantics— the repetition of words and phrases which evoke warm and appreciative memories of benevolent and noble aspirations, but with are not enriched by new and convincing experiences. The records of lodge service and lodge attendance suggest such a conclusion. (4) [. . .] The ritual is not enough for every initiate. Since words mean to the individual what his own experiences and feelings have taught him, the great affective words by which Freemasonry hopes to make him a wiser and better Builder must be explained to him in terms which he can understand." "Be ye doers of the word" is good semantics. It is also the best technique for Masonic education. Word, words, words— they can be the tools of a builder. (10)

Perhaps it was a personal choice of the translator to keep his/her name secret. In the case of the *Monitor* published in Philadelphia, I have concluded that Edward Barry was the translator (of course there is no full certainty that he was the translator of that edition). The discovery of the name of the translator has lead me to other Masonic publications and Masonic materials of the period. Such discovery has encouraged me and, hopefully, other scholars, as well, to find out who translated the New York edition in order to continue with the recovery of Masonic publications of the nineteenth century. The appearance of Spanish versions of Webb, in two distinct translations, along with a number of other Spanish Masonic titles published in Philadelphia in the following years, raises many questions. Of course, there is no way of knowing who translated these books without going to the archives and bibliographical records. Consequently, it is of utmost important to promote the recovery of texts to learn about the social, cultural, and political context of the time, to understand our present and to anticipate our future. The study of Masonry in Mexico and the rest of Latin

America during the first half of the nineteenth century is of tremendous importance due to the role such organization played in the Mexican independence and the forming of the young Mexican Republic. This publication is only one example of what one can learn about Mexican history through the study of Masonic texts.

Notes

[1]Paul Rich and I were looking at the great number of antiquarian bookshops in downtown Mexico City. I would like to thank Paul Rich and Antonio Lara for sharing their findings with me as well as for the numerous great discussions that had with me about this topic. I also thank Dr. Regina Bendix for her invaluable comments and suggestions.

[2]In Mexico, the York Grand Lodge often confers degrees in English, although all the other state and national lodges work in Spanish. In many countries some expatriates conduct their rituals in their native language. In the case of the United States, one can easily find Mexican Masons practicing their Masonic rituals in Spanish.

[3]See Rich and De Los Reyes 1995 and 2002. See also De Los Reyes 1997.

[4]This problem is a consequence of the way in which the text was translated following the notion of 'fidelity,' which in "translation of individual words can almost never fully reproduce the meaning they have in the original." Benjamin 79.

[5]"Carey published almost 1100 books from 1785 to 1821, an average of 30 per year. He did not hit this stride until 1794 and 1795, the years of Guthrie and Goldsmith. In 1796 to 1801 were lean years, after which there was another period of expansion which continued pretty much uninterrupted until 1821, except for dips during the War of 1821and the Panic of 1819" (Green 22).

[6]This information is based on interviews with Nicolás Kanellos, Brown Foundation Professor of Hispanic Literature at the University of Houston and Director of Arte Público Press, November 18, 2004 and David Szewczyk, Owner of the Philadelphia Rare Books and Manuscripts Company, December 7, 1999.

[7]See Nicolás Kanellos, "The Hispanic Exile Press in the United States," 59-84.

Work Cited

Anderson, Benedict. *Imagined Communities: Reflections on the Origin and Spread of Nationalism.* London: Verso, 1991.

Benjamin, Walter. "The Task of the Translator." Rainer Shulte and John Biguene. *Theories of Translation: An Anthology of Essays from Dryden to Derrida.* Chicago: University of Chicago Press, 1992. 71-82.

Bullock, Steven C. *Revolutionary Brotherhood. Freemasonry and the Transformation of the American Social Order, 1730-1840*. Chapel Hill: University of North Carolina Press, 1996.

Bussy, R. Kenneth. *Two Hundred Years of Publishing: A History of the Oldest Publishing Company in the United States, Lea & Febiger 1785-1985.* Philadelphia: Lea & Febiger, 1985.

De Los Reyes, Guillermo. "Freemasonry and Folklore in Mexican Presidentialism." *Journal of American Culture* 21.2: 61-74.

Green, James. *Mathew Carey Publisher and Patriot*. The Library Company of Philadelphia, Philadelphia, 1985.

Jakobson, Roman."On Linguistic Aspects of Translation." Eds. Rainer Shulte and John Biguene. *Theories of Translation: An Anthology of Essays from Dryden to Derrida.* Chicago: University of Chicago Press, 1992. 144-151.

Kanellos, Nicolás. "The Hispanic Exile Press in the United States." *Indiana Journal of Hispanic Literatures* 12 (Spring,1998): 59-84.

_____. "La expresión cultural de los inmigrantes mexicanos en los Estados Unidos, desde el Porfiriato hasta la Depresión." Unpublished Manuscript.

Leyland, Herbert T. *Thomas Smith Webb: Freemason, Musician, Entrepreneur.* Dayton: The Otterbein Press, 1965.

Linker, Susan. "A Collision of Rationalism and Spiritualism in El hombre de la Rosa of Manuel Rojas: Decoding the Secret Signals." *Hispanic Review* 68 (2000): 21-36.

Nossack, Hans Erich. "Translating and Being Translated." Eds. Rainer Shulte and John Biguene. *Theories of Translation: An Anthology of Essays from Dryden to Derrida.* Chicago: University of Chicago Press, 1992, 228-234.

Pennsylvania Historical Society, Collection No. 227 B, Lea and Febiger, Carey Papers, vol. 1, folder 279, card catalogued under William D. Robinson.

Preston, William. *Illustrations of Masonry*. Foreword by Walter M. Callaway, Jr. A facsmile reprint of the Second edition of 1775. Bloomington: The Masonic Book Club, 1973.

Rich, Paul. "Kim and the Magic House: Freemasonry and Kipling." *Secret Texts: The Literature of Secret Societies.* Ed. Marie M. Roberts and Hugh Ormsby-Lennon. New York: AMS Press, 1995. 322-338.

_____, Guillermo De Los Reyes, and A. Lara. "Smuggling Masonic Books to Mexico." *Freemasonry in Context: History, Ritual, and Controvery.* New York: Lexington Books, 2003. 249-253.

_____, and Antonio Lara. "The Mystery of Mathew Carrey: Continuing Adventures in Masonic Bibliography." *Freemasonry in Context: History, Ritual, and Controvery.* New York: Lexington Books, 2003. 255-258.

Roberts, Marie Mulvey. "Masonics, Metaphor and Misogyny: A Discourse of Marginality?" *Languages and Jargons: Contributions to a Social History of Language.* Cambridge: Polity Press, 1995.

Short Talk Bulletin. The Masonic Service Association of the United States, Washington, D.C August "Some Misconceptions about Freemasonry." August, 1958, XXXVI, No. 8.

_____. "Words, Words, Words." XLI.1 (January 1963).

_____. "Communication." LVI.6 (June 1978).

Stitt, Susan, et al., eds. *Guide to the Manuscript Collections of the Historical Society of Pennsylvania.* Philadelphia: Historical Society of Pennsylvania, 1991.

Venitu, Lawrence. *The Translator's Invisibility: a History of Translation*. New York: Routledge, 1995.

Walgren, Kent. "A Bibliography of Pre-l851 American Scottish Rite Imprints (non-Louisiana)." *Heredom* 3 (1994): 55-120.

_____. "A Bibliography of Pre-Louisiana Scottish Rite Imprints." *Heredom* 4 (1995): 189–206.

Warden, Thomas C. "Whatever Happened to the Written Word?" *Short Talk Bulletin*. The Masonic Service Association of the United States, Washington, D.C August 1978, No. 8.

Webb, Thomas Smith. *The Freemason's Monitor; or, Illustrations of Masonry*. Albany: [by Fry and Southwick?] for Spencer and Webb, Market-Street, 1797.

The Freemason's Monitor; or, Illustrations of Masonry: in two parts. NewYork: Southwick and Crooker, 1802.

_____. Salem: Cushing and Appleton, 1821, c1818, c1816, c1815, c1808, c1805

_____. *El Monitor de los Masones Libres: ó, Illustraciones sobre la Masonería.* Philadelphia: H.C. Corey & I Lea, 1822.

_____. *Monitor ó Guía de los Franc-Mazones, Utílisimo Para la Instruccion de sus Miembros é Información de los que desean imponerse en sus principios.* New York: Joseph Desnoues, 1822.

Part IV
From Canton to the Nation-state and Beyond, Transnational Authors and Activists

La resistencia cultural en la novela de inmigración mexicana a los Estados Unidos

Sergio Reyna

Las novelas sobre la inmigración de los mexicanos al país del norte escritas en español exhiben características entre sí que las hacen diferenciarse de las novelas escritas en inglés sobre el mismo tema. En las primeras, a la vez que se le da más importancia a la situación socioeconómica que se vive en el país de origen —causa principal de que el individuo salga de su patria— se dedica una gran extensión del espacio narrativo para describir el momento del encuentro o de choque que vive el inmigrante mexicano al enfrentarse a la geografía y a la sociedad norteamericana. En estas novelas escritas en español se narra detalladamente y de manera satírica toda una serie de situaciones que vive el inmigrante en su paso por los Estados Unidos, entre éstas sobresale la discriminación, la injusticia y la explotación en el trabajo que experimenta el inmigrante mexicano, por nombrar solo algunas, situaciones que tarde o temprano lo hacen retornar a su querida patria.

Los aspectos anteriores, así como la resistencia cultural del inmigrante ante los embates de la asimilación, se abordan en este trabajo de análisis literario. Para ello se toma como punto de partida el estudio de algunas novelas sobre la inmigración de los mexicanos en el país del norte escritas en español: *El sol de Texas*, de Conrado Espinosa (1926); *La patria perdida,* de Teodoro Torres (1935); *Las aventuras de don Chipote o, Cuando los pericos mamen,* de Daniel Venegas (1928); y *Aventuras de un bracero,* de Jesús Topete (1948), a la luz de los aportes teóricos de algunos especialistas en la materia. El objetivo primordial de este trabajo consiste en explorar de qué manera se manifiestan los elementos de resistencia cultural en respuesta a las situaciones descritas anteriormente, en las novelas escritas en español en el siglo XX que abordan la inmigración de los mexicanos.

La resistencia cultural del inmigrante

Como resultado de la situación de contacto cultural en la que viven los inmigrantes mexicanos con un grupo mayoritario donde el mexicano es el grupo en desventaja y con las mayores posibilidades de ser absorbido culturalmente por el grupo dominante, nace un sistema de autoprotección o resistencia cultural que actúa como una barrera ante los embates de la asimilación. Como Edward Said señala en sus aportaciones sobre la resistencia cultural, uno de los grandes rasgos en la explicación de este fenómeno social consiste en la insistencia en percibir a la comunidad en su conjunto como una entidad con una historia coherente e integral. De acuerdo a Said, el desarrollo de un lenguaje común y la práctica de una cultura comunitaria son aspectos fundamentales e igualmente importantes en este concepto de resistencia cultural:

> The concept of the national language is central, but without the practice of a national culture—from slogans to pamphlets and newspapers, from folktales and heroes to epic poetry, novels, and drama—the language is inert, national culture organizes and sustains communal memory . . . it reinhabits the landscape using restored ways of life, heroes, heroines, and exploiters; it formulates expressions and emotions of pride as well as defiance, which in turn form the backbone of the principal national independence parties. (1993, 215)

Este fenómeno de resistencia cultural que se da en un espacio geográfico compartido por una diversidad de grupos sociales y étnicos que se ven en la situación histórica de compartir un territorio por la necesidad creciente de mejorar las condiciones económicas, sociales y políticas de los inmigrantes, encuentra su explicación en varios conceptos como "nación", "nacionalismo", "nacionalismo cultural" y "México de afuera", los que se relacionan estrechamente —como se verá más adelante— con la filosofía de resistencia cultural que presentan los inmigrantes mexicanos en los Estados Unidos.

Hugh Seton-Watson (5) señala que la "nación" existe cuando un número significativo de personas en una comunidad considera, se imagina o se comporta como si formara parte de una nación. Por su parte, en sus aportaciones sobre "nación", Ernest Renan sostiene que ésta se constituye por la gente, más que por la propia extensión territorial en sí: "Man is everything in the formation of this sacred thing which is called a people. Nothing [purely] material suffices for it. A nation is a spiritual principle, the outcome of the profound complications of history; it is a spiritual family not a group determination by the shape of the earth" (1997, 18-19).

Benedict Anderson por su parte, y desde una perspectiva antropológica, indica que la nación se llega a convertir en una entidad significativa solamente cuando ésta llega a ser imaginada por sus integrantes como una comunidad política limitada y soberana. Anderson explica que es "imaginada" porque aún los miembros de la más pequeña nación nunca llegan a conocer o a oír hablar a sus compatriotas, pero que sin embargo en las mentes de cada uno de ellos vive la imagen de su nación. Anderson señala también que una nación viene a ser "limitada" desde el momento en que hay una extensión geográfica finita que la delimita como nación, y que es "soberana" al constituirse en un estado libre que se rige por sus propias leyes (1983, 15-16).

Anthony D. Smith indica que muchas de las naciones modernas se han construido en las bases de una etnia o nación preexistente. Indica, además, que "many ethnic nationalisms can draw on ethnic sentiments and shared memories, myths, symbols and values" (1996, 446). Es en este sentido que se da la conservación y práctica de los valores y costumbres de los grupos de inmigrantes latinoamericanos agrupados a través de "colonias" o "barrios" en las grandes urbes de los Estados Unidos, situación que se comenta en la novela *El sol de Texas* cuando Federico y su familia llegan a la ciudad de San Antonio, Texas, y se dan cuenta de la existencia de una enorme colonia mexicana que, como se enteran después, constituye un barrio típico mexicano como los que existen en otras ciudades de la Unión Americana.

> Arrancado de la Plaza del Zacate, hacia el sudoeste, se ensanchaba el barrio mexicano de San Antonio. Disforme, inmenso, tiene su avanzada en el mismo corazón de la ciudad y va a perderse en los terrenos montaraces aún; por varios puntos se derrama, tiene derivaciones, y así, hacia todos los vientos de la ciudad, hay apiñamientos de casas mexicanas, muchas veces manzanas enteras, cuadras y cuadras, pero nunca como en ese rumbo del sudoeste, al cual se tiene como el barrio típico de la raza.
>
> Ahí están sus cementerios, las escuelas en que más concurrencia de niños mexicanos hay y en donde más se les comprende, sus templos y hasta sus cantinas y sus lupanares. No pocos estadounidenses del Norte, turistas de esos que van buscando lo exótico, de los que vienen en pos de la ciudad del sol brillante, y del clima insuperable, según rezan los réclames sanantonianos, inquieren luego por el barrio mexicano. Imagínanse encontrar aduares indígenas, tipos vestidos a la azteca, costumbres de otro planeta. (53)

Las tradiciones culturales llegan a formar una parte inalienable de los valores de una población. En el caso de los inmigrantes mexicanos, estas tradiciones resultan de tal vitalidad para el desarrollo de sus vidas que llegan a trasplantarlas en la tierra extranjera donde se internan como inmigrantes. Al darle continuidad y validez a la práctica de estos valores y costumbres, los inmigrantes logran establecer una configuración nacionalista que los identifica como miembros activos de una comunidad que comparte los mismos códigos y las mismas señas culturales. Así, en las novelas analizadas, se pueden detectar algunas tradiciones trasplantadas de la tierra natal tales como el cortejo que se da entre la mujer y el hombre en las plazas de la comunidad, la celebración de los desfiles y las fiestas patrias, las fiestas familiares —quinceañeras, bodas, bautizos— los rituales para lograr el consentimiento de los padres para la celebración del matrimonio, los rituales funerarios, las costumbres y tradiciones para vender los productos y realizar transacciones comerciales, así como muchos otros rasgos culturales, logran identificar a los integrantes del grupo, quienes serán los encargados de practicar, darle sentido, conservar y difundir las tradiciones que los mantendrán culturalmente unidos. La costumbre del pregón y del regateo, convertido en casi un ritual en el comercio mexicano, se menciona en *El sol de Texas:*

> En el día, es la Plaza del Zacate lugar de citas para vendedores y contratistas. A ella llegan los mexicanos o méxico-americanos que han logrado principiar su redención en el cultivo de la tierra. Los carros de legumbres y frutas se alinean junto a las banquetas, los pregones castizos tienen aquí un eco y lo tienen también aquel deporte de las comadres mexicanas: el regateo. (21)

Los miembros de la comunidad tratan de conservar en su esencia sus tradiciones tal y como se practican en los pueblos de la provincia mexicana o de algún otro país latinoamericano aún cuando en los Estados Unidos se efectúe con algunos cambios en la forma, como resultado de la adaptación de las costumbres a las nuevas condiciones de la sociedad en la que ahora se encuentran adscritos. Lo anterior se realiza como una manera de conservar su identidad, aquello que los identifica como parte de un grupo y que los distingue de las demás comunidades.

Como Hunsaker señala en su definición de "nación", a pesar de que existe una gran cantidad de definiciones académicas de este término, la importancia del patrio suelo, la historia y algunos elementos compartidos de identidad (religiosos, lingüísticos o ancestrales) son comunes a todos los miembros de la nación (1999, 2). A este respecto, Smith indica que las siguientes características conforman el "tipo ideal" de nación: 1) el crecimiento de los mitos y memorias de los ancestros comunes, así como la historia de la unidad cultural y de la población; 2) la formación de la cultura pública compartida basada en recursos indígenas —lenguaje, religión, etc.—; 3) la delimitación de un territorio histórico compacto o de una tierra natal; 4) la unificación de unidades económicas locales en unidades socio-económicas únicas basadas en la cultura y la tierra natal; 5) el crecimiento de códigos comunes e instituciones de orden legal únicas, con derechos y obligaciones comunes para todos los miembros (1994, 381).

En referencia al concepto de nación sostenido por Smith, algunas novelas sobre la inmigración de mexicanos a los Estados Unidos plantean estas características en la comunidad de inmigrantes mexicanos, las que por compartir las mismas raíces culturales, el mismo idioma y las mismas creencias religiosas, se llegan a conformar en un tipo de "nación cultural", como una isla enmedio de un gran archipiélago integrado por los diferentes grupos del panorama multicultural que caracteriza a la sociedad norteamericana. Como menciona Hobsbawn, "hoy la típica 'minoría nacional' en la mayoría de los países que reciben inmigración es un archipiélago de islas pequeñas en vez de una coherente masa de tierra (1982, 166)". Esta situación se puede detectar sobre todo en la novela *La patria perdida*, de Teodoro Torres, donde se plantea la creación de una patria ideal; un lugar construido especialmente para los mexicanos, para aquéllos que comparten la misma historia, los mismos códigos culturales y los mismos mitos y memorias de los ancestros comunes. Este lugar de ensueño es Bellavista, una finca creada por el protagonista de la novela a la imagen de las haciendas mexicanas, un espacio donde —a diferencia de estas últimas— no hay capataces crueles y abusivos y donde solamente trabajan personas que comparten los mismos códigos y las mismas señas culturales. Es a este pequeño "paraíso" o "patria ideal" al que se aferran los trabajadores, aquéllos que han aprendido a amar y respetar ese paraíso terrenal como si se tratara de una prolongación de la patria misma:

> Luis Alfaro habría podido tener en su finca todos los trabajadores que quisiera, y lo que lamentaba era verse obligado a rechazar a los que con tanta frecuencia llegaban a pedir acomodo. La fama de Bellavista y de sus bondadosos dueños pronto corrió muy lejos; a veces, "el patrón" recibía cartas ilegibles de gente que solicitaba como un favor ser admitido allí donde no había capataces crueles ni amos irascibles, que a la menor dificultad sacaban el rifle para amedrentar y a veces para matar. . . . [Los trabajadores de Bellavista no querían perder] aquella tierra bondadosa que les daba de comer . . . la prolongación de su propia tierra, de la que quedaba allá abajo; una tierra donde profesaba su misma fe, hablaban su propio idioma y donde la frialdad del oro extraño, que a veces hace sentir su dureza, se atenuaba con la tolerancia amable de quienes lo pagaban y le infundían el calor que da la hermandad de la raza y la paridad de los espíritus. (25-26)

La patria perdida, como la combinación que es de literatura de inmigración y de exilio[1], representa el medio literario para criticar la imposibilidad del gobierno mexicano para proveer a sus ciudadanos un lugar seguro y estable para vivir. La creación literaria de Bellavista como un lugar edénico para los inmigrantes, cumple con la función de lanzar una crítica severa a la política de desarrollo nacional que se practica en México.

En concordancia con los planteamientos de Hobsbawm en cuanto al nacionalismo, los grandes movimientos de gente hacia territorios con notables transformaciones industriales y urbanas, como los Estados Unidos, han traído como consecuencia que se atente contra uno de los supuestos básicos del nacionalismo, "la de un territorio habitado en esencia por una población homogénea desde los puntos de vista étnico, cultural y lingüístico" (1982, 166). La reacción de los habitantes en países como los Estados Unidos ante este traslado masivo de gente hacia su territorio ha consistido históricamente en un racismo exacerbado. Este racismo extremo ha atentado inclusive contra la integridad de los recién llegados haciendo que éstos se concentren en comunidades integradas por compatriotas o por gente que comparte si no todos, al menos algunos rasgos culturales de la comunidad de origen, tales como la lengua, la religión o las costumbres, para contrarrestar los efectos de la asimilación y de los ataques de los que son objeto por parte de los integrantes del grupo mayoritario. Ante esta inminente realidad, y como lo afirma Hobsbawn, "las comunidades y grupos étnicos en las sociedades modernas forzosamente deben coexistir, prescindiendo de la retórica que sueña con que la nación vuelva a verse libre de mezclas" (166).

Estas comunidades en las que se concentran los inmigrantes, llamados "barrios" o "colonias", presentan características físicas peculiares que las hacen identificables a simple vista por los recién llegados. Las fachadas de los establecimientos, los anuncios publicitarios, los nombres de los negocios, el tipo de construcción de las casas, las comidas, los productos alimenticios y muchos otros rasgos y elementos distintivos conforman el panorama de estas comunidades hispanas insertadas en el macro contexto estadounidense. En novelas como *El sol de Texas* y *La patria perdida* se le considera a San Antonio como la gran metrópoli del exiliado político mexicano durante la época de la Revolución Mexicana. En *Aventuras de un bracero* de Jesús Topete, por su parte, se menciona a Stockton como un lugar donde abundan las comunidades mexicanas con negocios de esparcimiento donde se aglutinan los inmigrantes mexicanos:

> Stockton es, propiamente, una ciudad de importancia en esa zona del Estado de California y, como todos los pueblos, tiene su barrio mexicano donde abundan cantinas, cafés, billares, etc., con letreros en español y en pocho. Así pueden verse: "El Faro", "La Estrellita", "El California", etc., lugares que se convertían en nuestros centros de reunión y diversión cuando íbamos. . . . En las cantinas del barrio mexicano se veía a muchos pochos

lagrimear porque en esos días se los llevaban a dar servicio al ejército por lo que hacían unas despedidas dignas de ser las últimas. (67-68)

En el ejemplo anterior también se puede observar la diferenciación que se da a la gente que visita los lugares del barrio mexicano. Se detecta que inclusive dentro del mismo grupo de mexicanos se da una ultra diferenciación entre los mexicanos de origen y los "pochos" o "agringados"[2]. Esta situación de ultra diferenciación al interior de las comunidades, la etnicidad o "la raza", como lo indica Hobsbawn, no es ajena al nacionalismo moderno, pues "las diferencias . . . son demasiado evidentes para pasarlas por alto y con excesiva frecuencia se han utilizado para señalar o reforzar las distinciones entre 'nosotros' y 'ellos', incluyendo las distinciones nacionales" (1982, 74). Estas distinciones entre los diferentes grupos de inmigrantes hacen que los miembros de una comunidad se sientan más integrados a su grupo cultural desde el cual se habla del "nosotros" o se refiere a los demás, a "ellos".

El problema que enfrenta el inmigrante recién llegado es muy serio si se toma en cuenta que no maneja el idioma nacional del nuevo país, ¿cómo adaptarse y lograr sobrevivir a los grandes retos que se presentan en la nueva realidad? ¿Cómo encarar los nuevos retos si no han sido preparados en su país de origen para ello? Ante esta nueva realidad tan difícil, el encontrar gente que hable el mismo idioma y que haya pasado por las mismas experiencias como inmigrante, representa un gran alivio. Nuevamente Hobsbawn señala que, frente a esta situación de desamparo, los inmigrantes "se ven atraídos de forma natural hacia grupos compuestos por otras gentes de 'la patria' o 'de casa', empujados por la inseguridad y la nostalgia, en busca de ayuda mutua, por la reacción ante la hostilidad exterior a gente como ellos y, no en menor medida, por el poderoso medio organizativo de la política electoral, allí donde exista" (166).

El nacionalismo cultural de la comunidad inmigrante mexicana

En cuanto a los inmigrantes mexicanos en los Estados Unidos, es importante hacer notar que aún cuando no se trata de un nacionalismo geopolítico en el estricto sentido del término, sí se puede hablar de un nacionalismo cultural. Pese a que los mexicanos en los Estados Unidos no están en el país de origen, están conscientes de su pertenencia a una comunidad que comparte los mismos valores culturales, el mismo idioma y la misma religión. El recuerdo de la patria, de los héroes y de las acciones que la libertaron de ataduras colonizadoras está presente en cada uno de los integrantes del grupo.

En estas novelas de inmigración se puede percibir el tono patriótico de algunos de los protagonistas de la novela, sobre todo cuando se celebra alguna fiesta nacional de la patria de origen. En *El sol de Texas*, el autor presenta este rasgo en la celebración de la fiesta nacional mexicana del 16 de septiembre cuando cita un discurso oratorio de uno de los participantes de la festividad en la celebración de la independencia de México:

> —Señores y Señoras:
> ¡Porque semos mexicanos, por eso estamos aquí enfrente de Don Miguel Hidalgo y Costilla, de Don José María Morelos y Pavón, de Don Benito Juárez, de Doña Josefa Ortíz de Domínguez, de Don Ignacio Zaragoza, y de todos esos retratos que son los de nuestros héroes, de nuestros libertadores, de los hombres que dieron su vida por libertar a México de la tiranía española! . . . ¡Viva México, compatriotas! (Muchos vivas de la multitud y grandes aplausos). Aquí en el hospitalario país que nos hospeda, necesitamos estar unidos todos los mexicanos, para demostrarles a estos hombres que también somos civilizados, que también sabemos honrar a nuestra patria. ¡Necesitamos que todos nuestros hijos mamen la santísima leche de la Patria! (85)

Este nacionalismo cultural evidenciado por el mexicano se erige como uno de los principales mecanismos de resistencia que el inmigrante ha desarrollado históricamente para preservar su identidad cultural y contrarrestar los embates de la asimilación de la cultura anglosajona. En *La patria perdida*, por su lado, el autor informa en un tono serio los grandes obstáculos de orden nacionalista que el inmigrante mexicano presenta y que lo hacen ver truncado su proceso de aculturación al nuevo país:

> Pero este amor enfermizo del mexicano que al rememorar a su patria se exaltaba como al recuerdo de una pasión avasalladora, de un gran bien lejano o perdido, no lo entendían, no se lo podían explicar.
> No se lo explicarían nunca, por la simple razón de que el mexicano no había dejado de serlo jamás; porque de todos los emigrantes que vivían sobre suelo americano sólo él seguía conservando íntegra la devoción, el amor, la adhesión a su tierra nativa. Sólo él no se había fundido ni se fundiría en el "melting pot" del que tan ufano estaba el Tío Sam. (125)

La gran adhesión del mexicano a su patria, de acuerdo a los planteamientos que presenta el autor en *La patria perdida,* conforma una fuerte barrera para la integración del mexicano al crisol de las razas que caracteriza a la sociedad norteamericana. Sin embargo, no es sólo la adhesión al recuerdo de esa patria lejana lo que mantiene a los mexicanos unidos en un nacionalismo latente, sino también el hecho de compartir una serie de valores culturales de la patria de origen tales como la honestidad, la honradez, la dignidad, la fortaleza para el trabajo duro, la lealtad a la patria, la superioridad religiosa y la unidad familiar frente a la inmoralidad, la baja ética, el materialismo, la discriminación, el racismo y la explotación de la sociedad norteamericana.

En *Aventuras de un bracero*, el protagonista de la obra despliega una actitud de gran dignidad ante los desplantes de burla y rechazo de los que son blanco los inmigrantes por parte de los que se creen superiores por el hecho de haberse asimilado a la cultura norteamericana. En *Aventuras de un bracero*, se ubica al "renegado cultural" tanto en el lugar de trabajo como en la calle misma, y se le identifica no sólo con el género masculino, sino también con el femenino. En este caso, unas mujeres, con desplantes de superioridad ante el recién llegado, le hacen ver a éste que ellas pertenecen ya a otra categoría social. Jesús Topete, el protagonista de *Aventuras de un bracero*, un día no soporta más esta situación de menosprecio y hace explotar su ira ante la arrogancia de las mujeres que muestran la actitud típica de "los renegados". Su gran dignidad y orgullo por ser mexicano, es más que evidente:

> Todo lo que sentía por tales seres (los pochos), lo descargué en cierta ocasión en que unas muchachas, de las pochas, me encontraron para decirme que qué me creía yo que no les hablaba, que no fuera orgulloso y me fuera a platicar con ellas, a lo cual, más o menos textualmente les dije: —No me gusta que nadie se burle de mí, porque creo que no tengo nada que pueda causar risa y me parece que ya tienen muchos con quien divertirse; por otra parte, no me gusta compartir con ustedes porque todo se les va en presumir y en humillar. A los gringos les presumen de mexicanos, y puede ser que entre ustedes, a veces crean serlo; a cuanto mexicano se encuentran le hablan dizque en inglés presumiéndoles de gringas y, según yo, no son ni una cosa ni la otra. (53)

La resistencia a la asimilación y la consiguiente promoción de una filosofía de tipo nacionalista están siempre presentes en la literatura de inmigración. Los personajes de este tipo de obras literarias exhiben una clara conciencia de que hay que luchar por los valores superiores que identifican a su grupo cultural, que deben preservar sus creencias religiosas, sus costumbres y tradiciones y el idioma de su país de origen. Están convencidos de que al desarrollar esta conciencia de tipo nacionalista y de lealtad a la patria estarán preparados para emprender el regreso al terruño que los vio nacer.

El "México de afuera": la territorialización de una cultura común

De acuerdo a Kanellos (2000, 38), un concepto clave en el nacionalismo cultural relacionado con la literatura de inmigración mexicana en los Estados Unidos es precisamente el concepto del "México de afuera", una ideología militante empleada para preservar la identidad mexicana en los Estados Unidos.

Américo Paredes señala al respecto que este fenómeno de continua y mutua influencia entre el folklore mexicano y el del "México de afuera" resulta atípico entre otros grupos culturales y que entre los mexicanos ocurre más que nada debido a la vecindad de los dos países, lo que hace más fácil la comunicación y la movilidad de los mexicanos en ambas geografías y culturas:

> We also find evidence of a series of exchanges between endemic Mexican folklore and that of the México de Afuera, a continuous mutual influence moving in both directions which is not typical of other regional cultures in the United States. This is the result of a simple geographical fact: The Atlantic Ocean divides Pennsylvania from Germany, and Louisiana from France, but only an imaginary line divides México de Adentro (Mexico as a territorial unit) from México de Afuera. This line is easy to cross, legally or illegally. (1993, 6)

El "México de afuera" se da como un fenómeno social y cultural en los Estados Unidos y su existencia obedece principalmente a dos razones. La primera de ellas consiste en la conformación de comunidades cerradas por parte de los inmigrantes mexicanos, donde se crean ciertos elementos de pertenencia que funcionan como una barrera de resistencia cultural contra la asimilación. La segunda de estas razones obedece a los efectos de la segregación racial que la misma sociedad angloamericana ha desarrollado por medio de la legislatura y de la práctica.

La cercanía del "México de adentro" con el "México de afuera", conformado éste último principalmente por el suroeste de los Estados Unidos, hace de esta área un espacio compartido por los habitantes de ambos lados de la frontera. Se trata de un territorio que aunque dividido por la geografía y política de ambos países, representa un espacio de cultura compartida. Allí el idioma, la religión, las costumbres y otras señas culturales se intentan conservar a través del paso de las generaciones. Ello representa un atributo compartido por las novelas sobre la inmigración del mexicano al país del norte analizadas en este trabajo.

En las comunidades cerradas del grupo mexicano, que se representa en estas novelas sobre la inmigración, se conserva el idioma, la religión, las costumbres, los platillos, las formas de diversión, las fiestas nacionales mexicanas como el cinco de mayo, el 16 de septiembre, el 20 de noviembre, etc. . . . Hay una predilección y un afán por la conservación de los modelos anticuados, por todo aquello que representa la patria que se ha dejado atrás físicamente pero que se lleva adentro para siempre y que se pone de manifiesto una vez que se siente la necesidad de hacerlo. En la ideología del "México de afuera" empleada por los exiliados, el verdadero y auténtico México se ha rescatado en el "afuera", mientras que en el "adentro" ha habido una degeneración causada por los efectos de la Revolución Mexicana. En *La patria perdida*, por ejemplo, el autor cuenta la manera como al menos una vez al año la celebración de las fiestas patrias mexicanas, tanto en su organización como en el festejo en sí, unía a todos los integrantes de la gran colonia de mexicanos. El autor aprovecha este espacio para hablar sobre la solemnidad con la que dichas fiestas eran preparadas y ejecutadas, y para establecer la diferenciación de éstas con las fiestas patrias de los europeos que carecían del fervor patrio y la solemnidad que caracterizaba a las celebraciones mexicanas:

> Allí se iba a formar la comitiva que vendría en solemne procesión hasta la sala donde se alzaba el "altar patrio", el granero que ya todos conocemos. Desde allí se veían los afanes de Vallejo y de Luis para organizar el dichoso desfile. Negreaban los trajes de los colonos más distinguidos, que, ajenos a los ardores de la temperatura, no habían perdonado este detalle de la fúnebre y, para ellos elegante indumentaria. . . . Sus amigos europeos que semejaban ir resueltos a ver cosas extrañas e inevitables, tenían un aire de ávida curiosidad, una sed de exotismos que interiormente hacía sonreír a Luis. En ninguno de sus países se acostumbraba, seguramente, a vestir de traza tan lúgubre en una fiesta patriótica. Los yanquis —y ellos lo eran ya, por nacionalización y por todo— no gustaban de los discursos ni de los homenajes serios y solemnes. . . . En cambio nuestros hombres observaban un recogimiento religioso. Por nada del mundo hubieran roto la pompa ritual con que marchaban de dos en dos en fila, llevando los estandartes con la denominación del gremio al que pertenecían: "Sociedad Benito Juárez", "Orden de Amigos del Pueblo", "Benemérita Asociación Miguel Hidalgo", de Arley, Kansas, "Junta Honorífica de Kansas", "Cruz Azul de Señoritas Mexicanas" y otras más. (116-117)

Existe un marcado orgullo en los personajes de las novelas sobre la inmigración de mexicanos en los Estados Unidos en torno a las celebraciones que se hacen en sus barrios o colonias mexicanas, a tal grado de que se ufanan de realizar las celebraciones mexicanas con mayor patriotismo de las que se efectúan en el "México de adentro".

Al colectivizarse las memorias o recuerdos de la patria entre los miembros de la colonia y al darse su conexión con lugares específicos y territorios definidos que todos puedan reconocer como símbolos nacionales, se da lo que Smith denomina "la territorialización de las memorias", lo cual es reconocido como un elemento vital en la construcción de la nación y el entendimiento del nacionalismo por cada uno de los miembros que conforman la nación (1996, 453-454). En el caso específico de los integrantes del "México de afuera", los ancianos fungen como fuertes transmisores de los elementos que mantienen vivo el nacionalismo entre la colectividad. Estos agentes culturales actúan de manera efectiva ante las nuevas generaciones del grupo cultural al trasmitirles los recuerdos de las hazañas y de los lugares considerados como símbolos nacionales de la patria de origen. Así, se rescata la existencia de un territorio común que, aunque lejano físicamente, se encuentra tan cercano como el vivo recuerdo de la patria, esa patria que es recordada con veneración y gran nostalgia, como se indica en *La patria perdida*:

> ¡La patria! Esa palabra vibraba en todos los labios y se apoderaba de todos los pensamientos. Un fuerte amor, enconado como un dolor, surgía de pronto en todas las conciencias, donde estuviera aletargado mucho tiempo: se alzaba avasallador, como una epifanía y como una revelación a un tiempo mismo. Porque para muchos de aquellos pobres campesinos que solo conocieron de su país la miseria y la tiranía, la explotación de los "patrones" y la voracidad de los políticos, la patria se les revelaba allá afuera, como una madre a la que nunca conocieran, a la que nunca vieran y que así, a la distancia, se precisaba con los contornos vagos y dulces de una deidad prometedora. Cuando ellos volvieran sería otra cosa. Ya habían aprendido a verla. Ya sabían amarla. (119-120)

En las obras literarias sobre la inmigración de mexicanos a los Estados Unidos existe la tendencia a presentar al mexicano del "México de afuera" con una fuerte conciencia nacionalista que se ha acrecentado fuera del terruño. No obstante todos los problemas vividos en el país de origen caracterizados por la miseria económica y por la destrucción causada por los movimientos armados de la Revolución Mexicana, los personajes están conscientes de que hay que demostrar un fuerte sentimiento de lealtad a la patria que se debe concretizar en la lucha por conservar el idioma, la religión y los valores morales y culturales que peculiarizan al grupo del que se forma parte. En estas obras, la pertenencia a la patria mexicana no es experimentada solamente por los mexicanos que han emigrado al país del norte, sino también por sus vástagos, quienes pese al hecho de haber nacido en tierra extranjera y de no haber estado nunca en la tierra de sus padres, muestran un derecho inalienable a ser parte de ese México por el que tanto suspiran sus padres, tal y como se evidencia en *La patria perdida*:

> [El pueblo mexicano] era un pueblo esencialmente amoroso, enamorado de su país, dispuesto a todos los sacrificios, propenso a todas las exaltaciones, cuando le hablan de su nombre. Estos muchachos que habían nacido en tierra extraña no consideraban haber perdido sus derechos para querer a México por más que supieran que tenían obligaciones con su nueva patria. (81)

Así, el nacionalismo cultural manifestado por los mexicanos del "México de afuera" que se ve acrecentado sólidamente en el exterior, representa un fuerte elemento de resistencia contra la aculturación del mexicano. Las comunidades conformadas por quienes practican esta filosofía representan un lugar donde el inmigrante puede desarrollar su vida y practicar las costumbres de su tierra natal sin el temor de ser criticado o discriminado.

El papel de la prensa y los cronistas en la formación del nacionalismo cultural

Bruce-Novoa, Kanellos y Park, abordan el tema del nacionalismo cultural formado por la colectividad de los hispanos en los Estados Unidos y coinciden en que la imprenta ha contribuido enormemente en cuanto a la formación de una conciencia nacionalista en la comunidad hispana. Esta conciencia nacionalista llega a fungir como una barrera de resistencia cultural ante los embates de la asimilación y la consiguiente pérdida del idioma, la religión y otros valores y tradiciones que caracterizan al grupo hispano.

El papel de la imprenta en la formación de las "comunidades imaginadas" ha sido ya considerado de fundamental importancia por Anderson cuando señala que el periódico y la novela han sido dos formas de imaginación que florecieron primero en Europa en el siglo XVII. "For these forms provided the technical means for 're-presenting' the *kind* of imagined community that is the nation" (30). A juicio de Anderson, nada precipitó más esta búsqueda del nacionalismo cultural, de pertenencia a una colectividad, que la prensa, pues ésta hizo posible a un mayor número de personas pensar acerca de sí mismas y relacionarse con las demás en nuevas y profundas maneras (40). Esto era posible debido a la gran capacidad —dentro de los límites que impone la gramática y la sintaxis— del lenguaje impreso que era reproducido mecánicamente en cantidades nunca antes imaginadas y que además era capaz de ser diseminado a través del mercado (47).

En sus estudios sobre el papel de la prensa de inmigración en los Estados Unidos, Robert Park señala que en general, ésta tiende a mostrar un carácter profundamente nacionalista al pretender alejar al inmigrante de todo aquello que atente contra los valores culturales de la patria de origen, tales como el idioma, la religión y las costumbres:

> The nationalistic tendencies of the immigrants find their natural expression and strongest stimulus in the national societies, the Church, and the foreign-language press—the institution most closely connected with the preservation of the racial languages. In these, the immigrant feels the home ties more strongly; they keep him in touch with the political struggle at home and even give him opportunities to take part in it. (1922, 50-51)

La prensa constituía en sí un elemento de vital importancia para diseminar las noticias de toda índole entre la población de inmigrantes mexicanos en los Estados Unidos. Mantenerlos informados y unidos parecía ser el principal objetivo de esta empresa. Su importancia era tan evidente que no se puede obviar su presencia en algunas de las novelas sobre la inmigración de mexicanos al país del norte. En *La patria perdida*, por ejemplo, el protagonista cita dos entidades de gran importancia para el inmigrante: el consulado y el periódico.

> En el remolino que hacía la emigración mexicana en San Antonio, lo mismo al entrar a los Estados Unidos que al volver a México, forzosamente giraba de dos puntos, de dos casas; se detenía un momento en esos lugares, antes de seguir la corriente que lo desparramaba después con destinos varios.
>
> Esas casas eran el Consulado —la representación mexicana— y el periódico de la colonia [*La Prensa*], un gran diario que había alcanzado singular prestigio a causa de su nacionalismo, de sus campañas generosas, de su espíritu de protección para la raza, a la que auxiliaba con una mano, fundando clínicas, escuelas, asociaciones, y le pedía con la otra para mandar auxilios a México en momentos de angustia a fin de fundar, igualmente, escuelas o reconstruir pueblos abatidos por ciclones o temblores. (150-151)

La prensa representaba, como lo indica el protagonista de *La patria perdida*, todo un esfuerzo supremo del pueblo hispano por conservar sus valores culturales dentro de una sociedad diferente. De acuerdo a Kanellos (2001, 19-20), desde sus inicios la literatura de inmigración presentó como tendencia general la de aislar a la comunidad hispana de la influencia cultural anglo americana y de la religión protestante. De manera particular, y a través de la creación y promoción de la idea del "México de afuera", los escritores y editores mexicanos en el suroeste de los Estados Unidos se encargaron de luchar por la preservación del idioma español, la conservación de la fe católica y de la protección de los hijos en contra de lo que los líderes de la comunidad percibían como bajos estándares de vida practicados por los integrantes del grupo angloamericano. Kanellos (20) indica que esta ideología fue creada y diseminada por escritores inmigrantes y exiliados durante la época de la Revolución Mexicana. Estas personas pertenecían en su mayoría a las clases pudientes de la sociedad mexicana y desarrollaron un importante papel en el liderazgo social, político y cultural de la "colonia" mexicana, solidificando una base cultural fuerte y conservadora para la comunidad méxico-americana. Entre los líderes de esta tendencia ideológica del "México de afuera" creada y diseminada a través de los rotativos, Kanellos cita a Ignacio E. Lozano como una de las figuras más prominentes en el sur de los Estados Unidos:

> Among the most powerful of the political, business and intellectual figures in the Mexican immigrant community was Ignacio E. Lozano, founder and operator of the two most powerful and well distributed daily newspapers: San Antonio's *La Prensa*, founded in 1913, and Los Angeles's *La Opinión*, founded in 1926 and still publishing today. (2000, 38-39)

Tanta era la importancia y la interrelación entre la prensa y la literatura sobre la inmigración de los mexicanos en los Estados Unidos, que tres de los autores de las novelas analizadas en este trabajo eran periodistas, además de escritores de obras literarias: Daniel Venegas, Teodoro Torres y Conrado Espinosa. Por su parte, Ignacio E. Lozano, además de ser el fundador de *La Prensa* de San Antonio y de *La Opinión* de Los Ángeles, fungió como el editor de la novela *La patria perdida* de Teodoro Torres, uno de los editorialistas del periódico *La Prensa*. La conexión entre estos personajes de la vida periodística e intelectual es evidente. Se trataba de un grupo cerrado de empresarios e intelectuales pertenecientes a la clase pudiente de la sociedad mexicana quienes se encargaban de propagar la filosofía de tipo nacionalista entre sus compatriotas exiliados en los Estados Unidos. Lo anterior, como una manera de mostrar su compromiso político con los exiliados de su tierra natal, en un principio, para convertirse posteriormente en escritores de una prensa más dirigida a la comunidad de inmigrantes, a la que servían como una especie de puente en su proceso de acomodación a la vida norteamericana[3].

Este tipo de periódicos, como *La Prensa* y *La* Opinión, además de prestar sus servicios en el idioma que buscaban preservar y de mantener informados a sus destinatarios con las noticias de lo que ocurría en el país de origen, de promocionar festividades, campañas y artículos comerciales, presentaban una sección muy interesante y muy esperada por la comunidad mexicana en los Estados Unidos: la redactada por el cronista de la comunidad de inmigrantes. El trabajo de estos cronistas consistía por lo general en acrecentar el nacionalismo y reforzar la filosofía del "México de afuera". Lo anterior se hacía de una manera indirecta, llena de picardía y humor. El cronista de este tipo de periódicos se encargaba de recordarles a cada momento y a través de las voraces críticas dirigidas a los "agringados" —a aquellos que rechazaban la cultura de origen con tal de asimilarse a la cultura anglosajona— que el deber de todo mexicano en tierra extranjera consistía precisamente en preservar los valores y costumbres culturales de la patria de origen para transmitírselos libres de corrupción a las nuevas generaciones.

Lo carnavalesco como una filosofía de vida

Dentro de las actitudes de resistencia cultural que se observan entre los personajes de las novelas de inmigración mexicana a los Estados Unidos se puede citar una filosofía de vida de tipo carnavalesca[4]. El inmigrante en estas novelas presenta una actitud de vida muy peculiar para sobrellevar las penalidades y miserias que ocasiona estar en un país extraño donde no se habla el mismo idioma y no se practican las mismas costumbres. Su manera de enfrentar lo duro de la realidad es precisamente a través del humor (los chistes, los doble sentidos, los albures, los temas jocosos, etc.), a través de la risa, de la carcajada; de esa actitud que hace que se perciba la realidad como si se estuviera siempre en un carnaval. De esta manera, no resulta nada raro que se hable del humor de los mexicanos en dichas novelas con cierta admiración, ya que se considera éste como una característica muy especial del inmigrante mexicano aún en tiempos de tribulación y cansancio, tal y como se señala en *Las aventuras de don Chipote*:

> La chicanada, que váyale bien o mal, muy rara vez pierde su buen humor, aunque cansados y con hambre, pues no les habían dado martillo desde la mañana, empezaron a vacilar, tomando como tema el cazo de los frijoles que, según todas las posibilidades iban a ser para ellos. (53)

La novela sobre la inmigración en español está caracterizada por esta filosofía de vida llena de risa del mexicano, por esa manera tan peculiar de enfrentar su realidad, sus miserias, su diario vivir lleno de zozobra y de duras batallas. En este tipo de obras el lector se encuentra con una visión y recreación de la vida en una comunidad que siempre está sufriendo pero que enfrenta su destino con risas y carcajadas.

La oportunidad de poner "al mundo de cabeza", de invertir lo oficial, lo establecido, de presentar lo opuesto al orden, se logra a través del grotesco en la literatura, de la máscara, la parodia, la burla, lo escatológico (Bajtín 1981, 236). En *Don Chipote*, por ejemplo, todavía en la frontera mexicana y después de que el protagonista de la historia en compañía de su perro Sufrelambre va a dar a la cárcel municipal acusado de estar borracho en la vía pública, se presenta esta oportunidad de "poner al mundo de cabeza" a través de la expresión escatológica de sus actos. Don Chipote y su perro, antes de disponerse a limpiar las calles de la ciudad como acostumbrado castigo a los borrachos que son aprehendidos, vacían su contenido intestinal sobre esta institución gubernamental mejor conocida como el "Hotel Municipal" por los moradores del lugar. Por medio de lo escatológico se carnavaliza la situación oficial establecida sobre los mecanismos represivos del estado para mantener el orden entre la ciudadanía.

Es una manera de combatir, a través de los más bajos procesos biológicos del cuerpo humano, lo oficial, lo establecido institucionalmente por el mismo hombre.

> Como a las ocho terminaron la tarea y los volvieron al Hotel Municipal a esperar la calificación y sentencia, pero antes, como una gracia especial permitieron a los crudos que se curaran la cruda en la fuente para que de este modo calmaran sus angustias estomacales. Enseguida los pusieron a lavar los excusados, no sin antes haber depositado lo que habían comido el día anterior, y como dicen que de ver dan ganas, Sufrelambre no tuvo inconveniente en arrojar las tripas ya digeridas que se había comido la noche anterior en compañía de su amo. (30)

En la novela *Aventuras de un bracero*, por su parte, hay una insistencia a lo largo de la narrativa por presentar a los indocumentados de una manera grotesca llevando a cabo sus funciones vitales para sobrevivir[5]. A través de estas escenas se presenta un panorama carnavalesco donde los participantes del festín dan rienda suelta a su gran voracidad, a sus más bajos instintos por saciar los vacíos estómagos:

> . . . en unas largas mesas estaba preparada la cena que desde hacía tanto tiempo reclamaban nuestros estómagos. Se veían charolas colmadas de patas de puerco cocidas y calientitas invitando al ataque.
>
> Éste no se hizo esperar, nadie se escapó de lavarse las manos y previo algún tumulto, en pocos minutos no había bracero recién llegado que no diera enérgico ejercicio a las quijadas.
>
> Muchos no sabían manejar los cubiertos, se empeñaban en comer con herramienta las patas de puerco y a cada momento los huesos saltaban del plato para estrellarse en las caras de los vecinos de enfrente de la mesa; lo anterior era festejado por unos gringos que se reían a más no poder. Pero la risa se les transformó en asombro cuando empezaron a caer los huesos debajo de las mesas y como el piso era de madera se oía un ruido como de tormenta. (27-28)

En *El sol de Texas* hay una tendencia por mostrar las secreciones naturales de la piel, como el sudor, para presentar al inmigrante en su estado cotidiano: sudoroso, sucio, maloliente, agotado por las duras, dolorosas y casi inhumanas jornadas de trabajo en el campo agrícola:

> Chorreando sudor pegajoso y sucio, arrastrándose jadeante, casi a punto de caer sobre el surco, sigue la "pizca". . . Y arrastrándose, jadeante, chorreando un sudor pegajoso y sucio, sigue por el surco jalando un saco enorme, más pesado mientras más se avanza, avasallador . . . (7)

En la novela *Aventuras de un bracero*, y siguiendo la misma tendencia de presentar al protagonista de una manera grotesca en su imagen diaria de inmigrante proletario, se proyecta la figura de un aguerrido trabajador inmigrante que paulatinamente se va deshaciendo en el sudor de su cuerpo hasta convertirse en un guiñapo, en una imagen grotesca que deja su energía e ilusiones en cada gota de sudor que rueda por los surcos:

> Poco a poco se fue volviendo caluroso el tiempo y con el ejercicio que hacíamos todo el día cargando sacos de papas nos deshacíamos en sudor; por las tardes ya no teníamos fuerzas para cargarlos, se nos resbalaban dejándonos las manos ardiendo, y por las noches, el rato de sueño era para ver sacos de papas por todos lados pues los costales se habían convertido en nuestra pesadilla. (40)

En *Don Chipote*, por su parte, hay una insistencia a lo largo de la narrativa por representar las funciones básicas del cuerpo humano como tomar y beber, pero también por presentar las denominadas por Bajtín como funciones "bajas" del organismo (1984, 256) tales como el vómito, la mierda y los gases, como una respuesta psicosomática del cuerpo humano del inmigrante por rechazar la tierra extranjera. Al presentar una serie de situaciones escatológicas donde se presenta el cuerpo humano de una manera grotesca, se carnavaliza la situación de desesperación, desaliento y desesperanza. A través de esta actividad de grotesca expulsión del cuerpo humano de todo aquello que le estorba, se rechaza también lo que los Estados Unidos representa: lo superior, lo inalcanzable, la ambición por alcanzar el "Sueño Americano". Hay una inmersión de los valores, una necesidad de "ensuciar" con las secreciones y expulsiones corporales todo lo sagradamente superior que representa la "Tierra Prometida"; se da de esta manera un tratamiento carnavalesco a la experiencia del inmigrante y al mismo tiempo una regeneración de la vida. En un análisis sobre la novela *Las aventuras de Don Chipote*, Gonzales-Berry indica que podría afirmarse de hecho que esta novela "constituye un cómico y alegre himno a lo que Bajtín identifica con el espíritu carnavalesco del pueblo. . . . La persistente irrupción de esas funciones corporales mantiene una comicidad . . . que es eficaz burla crítica de la 'aventura estadounidense' de sus compatriotas, que tanto lamentaba" (1996, 115). Y esta permanente irrupción no se hace esperar a lo largo de toda la novela, la cual está permeada por un informe exhaustivo al lector de la ocurrencia de estas funciones elementales del cuerpo humano[6]:

> La noche la pasaron sin novedad y sobre todo feliz, pues toda la noche estuvieron soñando en quesadillas de queso, tal vez debido a que los zapatos les quedaron muy cerca de la cabeza. De todos modos, como decimos, la noche la pasaron sin novedad, pues aunque la atmósfera estaba cargada, no había

> más que puros truenos, pero nada de agua, o lo que es lo mismo: en el cuarto había habido revolución de truenos y gases asfixiantes, pero sin haber heridos. (Venegas, 92)

Así, con toda esta presencia de elementos de tipo escatológico en tierra norteamericana, don Chipote, fiel representante de los inmigrantes de extracción humilde, se burla del Sueño Americano, impregna con sus emanaciones corporales el gran mito del país de las "grandes oportunidades" mostrando con sus acciones un significado nacionalista, un espíritu de resistencia cultural y de profundo rechazo a la sociedad norteamericana y a todo lo que ésta representa.

En términos generales, si bien no se puede afirmar categóricamente que todos los elementos que menciona Bajtín en su análisis sobre lo carnavalesco en la literatura aparecen en todas las novelas de inmigración mexicana en español como una constante generalizada[7], sí se puede decir que lo carnavalesco en su esencia, como una filosofía de vida, forma parte intrínseca de estas narrativas. En ellas se detecta el humor cotidiano como una manera de enfrentar las vicisitudes que la vida le presenta al inmigrante en la sociedad norteamericana. Se observa el absurdo y la manera juguetona y un tanto atrevida del inmigrante para enfrentar los problemas sin medir las consecuencias futuras, sin ver las herramientas de lucha con las que se cuenta para enfrentar la vida en un territorio extraño. En estas novelas se ve a un protagonista con ese humor que caracteriza al mexicano de ver la vida de una manera muy peculiar, con un sentido del humor que lo hace cambiar o invertir las perspectivas de las cosas, donde a través del poder curativo de la risa y del valor regenerador de los más bajos procesos biológicos vitales lo serio y oficial se vuelve chusco, carnavalesco, como un mecanismo de resistencia que le permite al individuo sobrevivir y sobreponerse a su amarga aventura como inmigrante.

Notes

[1]Más información sobre este tipo de literaturas sobre los hispanos en los Estados Unidos se puede consultar en: Nicolás Kanellos, *En otra voz. Antología de la literatura hispana en los Estados Unidos* (Houston: Arte Público Press, 2002).

[2]De acuerdo a las investigaciones de José Limón sobre el folklore de los méxicoamericanos del sur de Texas, el término "agringado" ha surgido como una manera despectiva de nombrar a aquéllos que han renegado de sus raíces culturales para asimilarse a los patrones de la cultura norteamericana: "In a context of social conflict the Texas-Mexican community has developed terms referring to those group members who fail to maintain in group boundaries,

either as a result of social pressure or as a matter of choice. . . one of these terms—*inglesado* (anglicized) marks those middle and upper class individuals in south Texas who demonstrate a high level of acculturation by emulating perceived Anglo-American customs, language, values and socio-economic status, while implicitly or explicitly denying their own culture and society. *Inglesado*, like the related term *americanizado*, are mild in comparison to others developed from the ethnic slur terms for Anglos, namely *gabachos* and *gringos*. Those who appear to betray the group socio-culturally may therefore be referred to as *engavachados* or *agringados*, and like their ethnic slur roots, these terms have a particularly negative tone (1988, 35).

[3]Más información sobre el desarrollo de la prensa mexicana de exilio en los Estados Unidos puede ser consultada en: Nicolás Kanellos, *En otra voz. Antología de la literatura hispana en los Estados Unidos* (Houston: Arte Público Press, 2002).

[4]El concepto de una filosofía de tipo carnavalesca es tomado del concepto de carnaval en la literatura que realiza Bajtín. Bajtín enfatiza la existencia de una compleja interacción entre el mundo "oficial" y el mundo de la liberación carnavalesca. "'Ambivalence' and 'joyful relativity' are favorite terms. Carnival or festive license does not simply consist of an inversion of everyday norms, a strict opposition to official culture. It expresses instead the inevitability and at the same time the creative power of the shift-and-renewal, the joyful relativity of all structure and order" (1984, 124).

[5]Con respecto a las series de la comida y la bebida, Bajtín señala el alto significado de éstas en la cultura: "As with the body series, we have in these [the eating and drinking series], along with grotesque exaggeration, Rabelais´ basically affirmative view of the significance, the culture of eating and drinking. Rabelais by no means advocates crude gluttony and drunkenness. But he does affirm the lofty importance of eating and drinking in human life, and strives to justify them ideologically, to make them respectable, to erect a culture of them. The transcendental ascetic world view had deprived them of any affirmative value, had taken them as nothing more than a sad necessity of the sinful flesh, such a world view knew only one formula for making such processes respectable, and that was the fast —a negative form, hostile to their nature, dictated not only by love but enmity" (1981, 185).

[6]Erlinda Gonzales-Berry y Alfredo Rodríguez, en su artículo "*Las aventuras de don Chipote*: de lo quijotesco a lo carnavalesco" realizan un análisis sobre la novela a la luz de la teoría de Bajtín y al tratar el tema de lo escatológico o las bajas funciones del cuerpo humano que se hace alusión en la obra, informan que "la breve novela contiene sobre ciento cincuenta distintas y explícitas referencias a esas funciones" (114-115).

[7]Se hace referencia aquí más que nada a que algunas características de lo carnavalesco, tales como el elemento escatológico, no aparecen en algunas novelas sobre la inmigración mexicana en español, al menos no como un elemento preponderante. Mayormente se hace alusión a lo escatológico en dos de ellas: *Don Chipote* y *Aventuras de un bracero*, en ese orden en cuanto a la persistencia de ese elemento. El resto de las novelas analizadas presentan bastante discreción en cuanto a la expresión de lo escatológico.

Obras citadas

Anderson, Benedict. *Imagined Communities: Reflections on the Origin and Spread of Nationalism.* London: New Left, 1983.

Bajtín, M.M. *The Dialogic Imagination: Four Essays*. Ed. Michael Holquist. Trad. Caryl Emerson and Michael Holquist. Austin: University of Texas Press, 1981.

_____. *Rabelais and His World.* Trans. H. Iswolsky. Bloogmington: Indiana University Press, 1984.

_____. *Teoría y estética de la novela*. Trad. Helena S. Kriúkova y Vicente Cascarra. Barcelona: Santillana, 1991.

Espinosa, Conrado. *El sol de Texas*. San Antonio: Viola Novelty, 1926.

Gonzales-Berry Erlinda y Alfredo R. "*Las aventuras de don Chipote*: de lo quijiotesco a lo carnavalesco". *Cuadernos Americanos* 55 (1996): 110-117.

Hobsbawn, E. J. *Naciones y nacionalismo desde 1980*. Barcelona: Crítica, 1982.

Hunsacker, Steven V. *Autobiography and National Identities in the Americas*. Charlottesville: University Press of Virginia, 1999.

Kanellos, Nicolás, ed. *Herencia. The Antologhy of Hispanic Literature of the United States*. New York: Oxford University Press, 2001.

_____, and Helvetia Martell. *Hispanic Periodicals in the United States: A Brief History and Comprehensive Bibliography*. Houston: Arte Público Press, 2000.

_____. "*Las aventuras de don Chipote*, obra precursora de la novela chicana". *Hispania* 67.3 (1984): 358-363.

Limón, José. "*Agringado* Joking in Texas Mexican Society." *Perspectives in Mexican American Studies* 1 (1988): 109-128.

Paredes, Américo. *Folklore and Culture on the Texas-Mexican Border*. Austin: University of Texas Press, 1993.

Park, Robert E. *The Immigrant Press and Its Control*. Nueva York: Harper and Brothers, 1922.

Renan, Ernest. "What is a Nation?" *Nation and Narration*. Ed. Homi K. Bhabha. New York: Routledge, 1990. 8-22.

Said, Edward W. *Culture and Imperialism*. New York: Vinatage Books, 1993.

Seton-Watson, Hugh. *Nations and States. An Inquiry into the Origins of Nations and the Politics of Nationalism*. Boulder: Westview Press, 1977.

Smith, Anthony D. "Culture, Community and Territory: The Politics of Ethnicity and Nationalism." *International Affairs* 72.3 (1996): 445-458.

_____. "The Problem of National Identity: Ancient, Medieval and Modern?" *Ethnic and Racial Studies* 17.3 (1994): 375-399.

Topete, Jesús. *Aventuras de un bracero*. México: Gráfica Moderna, 1948.

Torres, Teodoro. *La patria perdida*. México: Ediciones Botas, 1935.

Venegas, Daniel. *Las aventuras de don Chipote o, Cuando los pericos mamen*. Houston: Arte Público Press, 1999.

Sara Estela Ramírez and Andrea Villarreal González: Revolutionary Voices?

Pilar Melero
University of Wisconsin

Las mexicanas . . . no han visto la necesidad de gozar de privilegios políticos. Esto se debe a que . . . el único y exclusivo modelo que deben de seguir no es el de la estadista reina Elizabeth sino el de María, la Virgen Madre, con su hijo, el Redentor, en brazos.

Antonieta Rivas Mercado,
"Ideales de las mujeres. Maternidad vs. igualdad de derechos" *(1928)*

The contributions of male figures to the Mexican Revolution have been widely represented and discussed through literature, history, film, and music; turning revolutionaries like Francisco "Pancho" Villa, Emiliano Zapata, and Francisco I. Madero, as well as intellectuals such as José Vasconcelos, into symbols of Mexican nationalism or messianic figures immortalized in the collective Mexican psyche as supermen.[1] Other male insurgents, such as the Flores Magón brothers, Enrique and Ricardo, have not fared as well but occupy, nonetheless, a respectable place in the recorded history of the period. Still missing, however, from the pages on the Revolution are the names and deeds of most female participants, aside from romanticized figures such as la Adelita.[2] Elizabeth Salas contends that "male-constructed renditions of the *soldaderas* in Mexican popular culture distorted the women's activities in battle and recast them as prostitutes, self-abnegating patriots, or Amazons subdued by male romantic prowess" (93). Though there has been a surge in interest in the study of women's involvement in the Revolution, a comprehensive body of the critical assessment of the literature, journalism, epistolary material, and other writing by women during the period of 1900 to 1940 is still missing. Clara Lomas points out that the texts of the activists have disappeared or been condemned to oblivion because, among other reasons, they are "[w]ithered by time, ignored and silenced by ethnocentrism, destroyed by the flames of arsonists, [and] lost to unscrupulous publishers" (Introduction vii).

In this article, after a brief introduction into the small but significant number of existing studies examining the work of the female activists of the Mexican Revolution, I analyze texts by Sara Estela Ramírez and Andrea Villarreal González. I focus on the cultural space of motherhood as the site from where they launch their contestatory discourse on the emancipation of women. I examine how, accepting motherhood as an extension of womanhood, both Ramírez and Villarreal González utilize it as a heterotopian discursive space to redefine the role of women in the cultural landscape that they inhabit, and that—equally important—inhabits them.

Mapping Voices: Recovering and Analyzing the *Activistas's Texts*

Nelly Campobello and Leonor Villegas de Magnón have recorded the active participation of women in the Mexican Revolution before, during, and after the armed phase of the uprising through their literary work.[3] In addition, the textual presence of women in the contestatory discursive space of the Mexican Revolution has begun to be mapped through the reproduction of their texts in Ana Lau and Carmen Ramos's pivotal volume *Mujeres y revolución, 1900-1917,* and in the compilations of Ángeles Mendieta Alatorre, author of *Juana Belén Gutiérrez de Mendoza (1875-1942) Extraordinaria precursora de la Revolución Mexicana* and *La mujer en la revolución mexicana*. The works of Mendieta Alatorre, Lau, and Ramos have begun to unearth the wealth of letters, essays, and newspaper articles, written by the *activistas*, and still preserved in archives in Mexico and in the United States.[4] Indeed, Emilio Zamora, Inés Hernández Tovar, Elizabeth Salas, Ana Macías, Emma M. Pérez, and Clara Lomas have begun to examine the role of women in the Revolution as well as their textual contributions. Zamora's article explores Ramírez's activism and writing.[5] Tovar has added extensively to our knowledge of Ramírez's life calling attention to her work as a teacher, journalist, labor organizer, political activist, feminist, and poet.[6] Salas documents and challenges the misrepresentation and romanticizing of women's participation in the Revolution, both by official and popular discourse. She contends that although women participated as soldiers, their participation was ignored (and even denied) when it was time to share the arguable gains of the armed conflict and that female soldiers were not recognized as veterans and were denied pensions. Further, Salas explains that when a woman's presence in the battlefield is noted, it is not the woman's presence that is acknowledged, but its romanticized shadow, such as la Adelita of the *corrido*. Macías has identified fundamental reasons why Mexican women faced overwhelming odds when attempting to assume agency, as outlined by Lomas in her introduction to *The Rebel*:

> the problem of machismo which compelled women to begin by educating "Mexican men to view women as persons and not as symbols or objects;" (2) the enormous influence of the church whose hierarchy "discouraged even the most moderate brand of feminism, refusing to countenance the establishment of any feminine organizations not controlled by the hierarchy;" (3) the disagreement among feminist factions on issues, tactics and programs as well as the high incidence of "burn out" among leaders; (4) "little support and encouragement from government leaders, especially between 1900-34," who were "suspicious of all women because of prevailing male attitudes" and who felt that they were "politically unreliable due to their attachment to the church;" (5) "little support but much ridicule from the press;" and (6) most active political Mexican women "came from the middle class and had to work for a living. Most of them were elementary school teachers," (xiii).[5]

Pérez studied the rhetoric of the Magón brothers and other leaders of the Partido Liberal Mexicano (PLM). She concluded that, though *magonista* rhetoric committed the Party to women's social equality, the *magonistas*, bound to traditional ideology of gender, "were trapped between a rhetoric that declared their (women's) freedom and the reality that ignored it"(468).

Some of the most significant work on the texts of the *activistas*, both at the recovery and analytical levels, has been conducted by Lomas herself. She researched and published *The Rebel* (1994) and has written several articles analyzing the texts of the *activistas*. Lomas traces how several newspapers published by women called attention to gender issues.[6] In addition, she also examines Sara Estela Ramírez's essay "Surge," proposing that Ramírez "explores and questions the established beliefs in deities and their effects on women's lives" and that Ramírez calls attention to traditional myths employed "to keep women in an inactive role within society" as woman/goddess. Lomas concludes that Ramírez "lifts women to a higher level of consciousness not only to question their own role in society but that of gods and rulers" ("Mexican Precursors . . ." 26-28). Though I concur with Lomas's main argument that Ramírez questions traditional models of womanhood, my analysis examines the manner in which Ramírez and Villarreal González (re)articulate femininity from within established models of womanhood, using motherhood as a dissident discursive space. Motherhood, both as an institution and an ideological construct, is an integral element in Mexican women's construction of self. Therefore, unable and/or unwilling to abandon motherhood as a locus of discourse, Ramírez and Villarreal González utilize it as a heterotopian site of resistance. They use it as a space that both reproduces and challenges hegemonic positions; in their case, orthodox renditions of femininity.

Writing from the Borrowed Space of Motherhood

Ángel Rama explains how the construction of the Latin American imaginary is a function of the *letrados*.[7] The *letrados* are men in charge of defining the Latin American city since colonial times and of assigning a role to its inhabitants. Women are generally kept out of this society, which Rama describes as on the peak of the hierarchical order by which Latin American societies function. Politics and political discourse are located within *la ciudad letrada*, and if women are not part of *la ciudad letrada*, then they are also left out of politics and political discourse. The case of Antonieta Rivas Mercado, the wealthy, educated, intellectual friend of Vasconcelos who funded several cultural endeavors in the 1920s, such as the work of *los contemporáneos*, illustrates that gender, in addition to race, were constructs that limited a woman's access to meaningful political involvement. Deeply interested in the political destiny of her country, even Rivas Mercado understood that she could only participate on a secondary role, as unofficial adviser to the Vasconcelos's presidential campaign of 1928-1929.[8] She could not, as a woman, be a candidate for office. She could not vote. She could not even speak about politics and be taken seriously. If Rivas Mercado has no personal access to the political arena, we can only imagine the obstacles faced by the *activistas*, with less monetary and cultural capital then Rivas Mercado. Not only must they overcome gender barriers, but also class and economic hurdles. Macías has already pointed out that most of the *activistas* had to work for a living. Thus, the female activists, having no political capital of their own, and having to cross culturally constructed gender and class barriers that they themselves may have internalized, must find a way to approach political discourse without alienating the political leaders whose actions they were trying to influence. Thus, even if, and perhaps *especially if*, they write with the intention of undermining the laws and cultural mores that keep them grounded to tradition, the *activistas* must write from a mediated cultural space that will help them spread their message without alienating their intended listener. They write from the space of motherhood.

For Mexican women, as the writing of the activists illustrates, speaking from the space of motherhood has little to do with maternity, or with being mothers of biological children. Documents detailing the life of Villarreal

González and Ramírez do not give any indication that either had any biological children. Villarreal González is often described as a teacher and activist, and as the Mexican Joan of Arc. Ramírez, also an activist, is referred to as a teacher and poet. Yet in the cultural context that they inhabited, whether they were or were not biological mothers is almost irrelevant, since the role of motherhood is a fundamental component in their definition of womanhood. Both Ramírez and Villarreal González, born in Mexico, lived and worked in the Texas/Mexico border in the early 1900s. Lomas notes that in the early 1900s "the social position of women in the borderlands was still dictated by traditional nineteenth-century Mexican social mores" ("Transborder Discourse" 51) that favored the patriarchal family. And the family, Pérez contends, "ideologically binds women to their roles as wives, mothers and nurturers" (462).

Indeed, if one looks into the dominant Mexican cultural models of femininity, one finds that motherhood is an integral part of the traditional definition of womanhood. Motherhood, embodied in the figure of the Virgin of Guadalupe, la Malinche, and la Llorona, forms the basis of the traditional female paradigm in Mexican culture. The Virgin of Guadalupe is the pillar of conventional Mexican female identity while la Malinche and la Llorona, both representations of the Terrible Mother archetype, are important components of the Mexican mythology of motherhood in the modern Mexican collective psyche. The Virgin embodies all the positive traits of traditional femininity—she is the self-denying mother. La Malinche is the traitor, *la Chingada*, "the Indigenous woman who betrays her children by aiding her lover in their demise, the conquest."[9] La Llorona represents female hysteria: she becomes mentally unstable when she finds out that her lover betrays her by marrying someone else. She, like La Malinche, loving her lover more than she loves her children, drowns them in a river. Culture condemns her to wander eternally in a desperate weeping search to recover her lost (betrayed) children and cleanse her soul. All three mothers are hegemonic renditions of motherhood in its two extreme forms—Mary (Guadalupe) and Eve/Magdalene (la Malinche and la Llorona)—that dominate traditional Mexican thought about womanhood. Therefore, it is logical that Mexican women appeal precisely to motherhood to formulate their demands, even when such demands denounce the traditional ideas of femininity. Motherhood is a space Mexican women—and men—know and value as a female space.

Speaking precisely on why Mexican women appeal to motherhood to construct their political discourse, even when the discourse they seek to articulate is dissident, Antonieta Rivas Mercado acknowledges that Mexican women in search of a definition of self can only follow the model of the Virgin Mary, with her son, the Redeemer in her arms. She argues that this cultural perspective differs from the Anglo tradition of femininity, which is and has been equality with men (324). Yet it is not that Mexican women do not aspire to some type of equality with men, Rivas Mercado and other Latin American female intellectuals of the early 1900s, such as Gabriela Mistral, point out.[10] Rather, their definition of equality differs from traditional feminist definitions that do not allow for gender difference. Equality for them is based not so much on men and women being equal, but in having equal rights, while not losing sight of—and indeed valuing—the gender difference. Part of that difference implies the acceptance and even full embrace of motherhood; though in their case not of motherhood as traditionally defined as a passive construct, but as an active being defined by the women themselves. Rivas Mercado summarizes that position as follows: "la mujer es distinta del varón y debe afirmar su diferencia, en vez de aspirar a igualársele" (313). Victoria Ocampo contends that Latin American feminism, rooted under the cultural auspices of the Catholic Church, seeks equality for women—equal access to education, jobs and equal pay, as well as respect for women's freedom just as much as men's freedom is respected (21). Yet, it allows for motherhood as an essential, important expression of femininity. Motherhood, or child rearing, she wrote: "es una obra que exige, en las que tienen conciencia de ello, infinitamente más preocupaciones, escrúpulos, atención sostenida, rectificaciones delicadas, respeto inteligente y puro amor que el que exige la creación de un poema inmortal" (15).

If the thinking of Mistral, Ocampo, and Rivas Mercado, three of the leading female minds of the early twentieth century, is any indication of how Latin American women understood motherhood, then it makes sense that the *activistas* position themselves precisely in the space of motherhood to construct their discourse on behalf of women and humanity in general. Motherhood is a space they value. Equally important, motherhood is a space valued by their interlocutor, the body politic that they are attempting to reach. Motherhood functions as an interstitial space or a cultural bridge women use to construct themselves as political subjects, both from within and without tradition.

Writing precisely from what appears to be paradoxical positions, or from heterotopian sites, such as the position of motherhood championed by the activists studied here, is one way in which the subaltern subject can articulate his or her message without alienating his or her interlocutor. Michel Foucault defines *utopia* as a site lacking a real place that presents society in its ideal or perfect form, and *heterotopia*, or counter-site, a type of effectively enacted utopia in which the real sites, all the other real sites that can be found within a culture are simultaneously represented, contested, and inverted (24). Understanding the difference between the two terms is fundamental to our understanding of the different layers of discourse of the Ramírez and Villarreal

González texts. Formulated from the heart of hegemonic models, the discourse of the activists is not one that reflects an ideal or utopian feminine subjective space, but an in-between space, a space between patriarchy and feminism that can be traditional and modern at the same time. Gayatry Spivak defines the mediated discursive site of female subjectivity as follows:

> Between patriarchy and imperialism, subject constitution and object formation, the figure of the woman disappears, not into a pristine nothingness, but into a violent shuttling which is the displaced figuration of the "third-world woman" caught between tradition and modernization. (307)

Likewise, Lucía Guerra-Cunningham, a critic who has engaged in the dissemination of non-canonical texts, explains that women as subaltern subjects must seek refuge in the shadows of male discourse to formulate contestatory discourse in an effective manner. She explains that from the shadow, woman "se permite trasgresiones momentáneas de espacio que desfiguran y subvierten lo tangible dominante" (129). Similarly, the concept of interpellation of discourse examined by Paul Smith in *Discerning the Subject* postulates that women's writing, from the shadows, implies the necessity of a strategic appropriation of masculine models or legitimized object which may be deconstructed in an apparently inoffensive manner because, in its subordinate position, female experience must hide its dissident zones (130).

It is from the cultural and theoretical frame just outlined that I analyze the texts by Ramírez and Villarreal González. Summarizing, Mexican women of the early twentieth century understand motherhood as a heterotopian space that they value as part of their femininity and understand as a space that allows them to speak to the powers that be without alienating them. Moreover, as subaltern subjects, they have no recourse but to deconstruct discourse in an apparently inoffensive manner, from the shadows of male definitions of womanhood, to articulate their dissident view of self, or of femininity: they use motherhood as a space of discursive resistance.

Ramírez and the (Re)articulation of Femininity

Sara Estela Ramírez, was born in Villa de Progreso, Coahuila, in 1881. She moved to Laredo, Texas, in 1898, where she wrote poems, essays, literary articles, editorials, and a play. She published in *La Crónica, El Demócrata Fronterizo,* and in literary journals.[11] She was a member of the *Partido Liberal Mexicano* headed by the Flores Magón brothers. Although she wrote political pieces, germane is her poetic essay "Surge," which analyzes the space that woman must occupy on the table of humanity. "Surge" was first published in *La*

Crónica on April 9, 1910. Zamora re-printed the essay in 1980 as part of a triad of Ramírez's texts that he considered representative of her total collected works. In 1989, Lomas reprinted part of the essay in "Mexican Precursors of Chicana Feminist Writing." The essay is also partially cited in Lau and Ramos's *Mujeres y Revolución. 1900-1917* (1993). Lacking access to *La Crónica*, unless otherwise noted, references to the essay will come from Zamora's reproduction of the essay. I will begin the analysis by highlighting Ramírez's awareness of her position as a gendered subject, and continue with the examination of "Surge."

Ramírez is highly aware of the discursive position of women and men, as is implicit in a letter to Ricardo Flores Magón: "Entre las muchas cosas que quiero aprender de mi hermanito es saber administrar un periódico. ¿Me enseñará Ud.? Soy mala discípula y torpe, pero me esmeraré en aprender, para no dar malos ratos a mi bondadoso maestro (Lau and Ramos, 185). The suppliant tone of the letter denotes the subject position of Ramírez in relationship to Ricardo. Ramírez, in her beseeching tone, reveals the marginality of her position as a subject, referring to Ricardo with the words "bondadoso maestro." This position reveals her as the (passive) pupil waiting to receive instruction from the benevolent teacher. The benevolent teacher can also be seen as the benevolent patriarch, or the *letrado* who has the power to share, or deny, access to his students to *la ciudad letrada*, or the power structure, which he controls. The letter to Ricardo is interesting in several other levels. Because of the friendship the two activists share, the letter is written in a familiar tone, although she still uses the formal "usted" to address him.[12] She opens the letter with "Mi querido hermanito." This phrase contains the most salient discursive element of the entire letter: the use of the diminutive. The letter is basically a cry for Ricardo to answer her letters, while at the same time acknowledging that *la situación* (the Revolution) might be a factor in his lack of response. Moreover, Ramírez as a subject further stresses her marginality through her repetitive use of the diminutive (in italics): "una línea que me escriba mi *hermanito* . . . bastará para que yo esté contenta;" "*Juanita* mejora su salud;" "he recibido carta de nuestras *hermanitas*;" "Fue para Ud. un *atadito* de recuerdos el *tomito* de poesías?" "las *hermanitas* presas;" "Mis *amiguitos* y yo somos los de la nueva empresa periodística;" "Qué le parece a mi *hermanito* todo eso?" "Le adjunto una para nuestras *hermanitas*;" y "Adiós, mi *hermanito*." Though the use of the diminutive "hermanito" gives the letter a familiar, informal, and caring tone, which could arguably signal the position of both subjects in a discursive space as equals, the repetitive use of the diminutive might project this document as an example of the inferior discursive position a woman occupies in reference to a man in the traditional cultural context Ramírez inhabits.

Despite the tone of the letter, a different voice emerges in "Surge," which, as Lomas has already noted, encourages women to abandon traditional roles and "rise" to life, to shine with their own light as active women.

"Surge" is non-traditional from beginning to end. The essay opens with "¡Surge! Surge a la vida, a la actividad," and the thought is repeated at the end of the essay, where life is defined as action: "Sólo la acción es vida." With these words, Ramírez challenges traditional paradigms of femininity. If the main virtue of Mexican women resides in her passivity, in her not being as proposed by Rivas Mercado, this poem suggests opposing virtues: activism, that is, "hacer" (to do) instead of *no ser* (not being).[13] It adds, "surge radiante y poderosa." Again, passivity is not a way of being or of doing. Woman must be "fuerte de energías." And by "being," by "doing," woman can write her own definition of self, away from the passive model constructed for her. Woman must define woman. She must break away from the image in the patriarchal mirror and look at her own reflection of self.

The rest of the essay outlines the elements of traditional and redefined femininity: woman has been constructed as queen and as "Diosa de la adoración universal." But Ramírez insists that those are passive roles that women must abandon: "no te encierres así en tu templo de Diosa, ni en tu camarín de cortesana triunfadora." The temple and the dressing room, both hegemonic constructions, are passive spaces, prisons that limit movement, freedom to act and therefore to be. As noted by Lomas, the goddess and queen roles are restrictive, and woman must discard them: "No te embriagues en el incienso en el altar, ni en el aplauso en el escenario, hay algo más grande que todo eso." The prescribed roles of goddess or queen confine a woman, "inebriating" her in false praise (incense, applause), denying her, in her inebriated state, full use of mental faculties, or the capacity to think. Furthermore, in her passive role, the goddess and queen are at the mercy of their devotees, who in their agent role, may toss them from the altar or throne: "Los dioses son arrojados de sus templos; los reyes son arrojados de sus tronos . . . Los Dioses viven hasta que sus creyentes quieren, los reyes viven mientras no son destronados." In the inactive roles of goddess and queen, it is the one who has placed women in these roles who has the power to dethrone them, to erase them. She lacks agency. She is a character in a novel and the author may eliminate her anytime he pleases. She must author herself in order to escape passivity. She must define herself by (re)articulating her own role, by doing, by taking action. She must *hacer para ser*. Only action is life.

The call to abandon prescribed roles continues throughout the essay: "Surge, pues, a la belleza de la vida: pero surge así, bella de cualidades, esplendente de virtudes, fuerte de energías." Again, the text calls for emancipation from defined roles, which describe women as "el sexo débil."

Despite the progressive tone of the text analyzed so far, the essay includes a statement that appears to reaffirm tradition: "antes que ser Diosa y Reina, sé madre, sé mujer." This statement becomes significant once we place it in the context of Mexican mythology of motherhood. First, by equating motherhood to womanhood, the voice in "Surge" implies that she considers motherhood a part of being female. A Mexican woman cannot choose to escape the model of the mother. Motherhood is part of her social construct of female identity. But more importantly, motherhood allows woman to create a mediated discursive space from which to speak, and in Ramírez's case, (re)articulate her role in the world as woman/woman, and no longer woman/myth (goddess/queen). The essay states that a true woman, or an authentic woman, "una mujer que lo es verdaderamente," is self-defined, self-created. She is not a myth. Thus, this apparently traditional comment equating motherhood to womanhood becomes subversive because it liberates the mother/woman from her traditionally assigned (re)productive role as mother/myth. This revised motherhood advocates for woman to create herself, instead of reproducing a role someone else has created. In Foucoultian terms, Ramírez has constructed a heterotopian discursive space, a discursive counter-site, in which the real sites that can be found within a culture, such as motherhood and the female's position as discursive Other, are simultaneously represented but are also contested and inverted. Ramírez inverts and subverts by (re)defining femininity in general, and motherhood in particular, as *activity* and *being*: *hacer* and *ser*. Ramírez's subject is a mediated subject, a subaltern subject who writes from the shadows without abandoning the hegemonic paradigm because this is the only way that her voice will appear nonthreatening, because she must not reveal her dissident zones. She must write from the shadows, from where she can allow herself momentary transgressions of space that disfigure and subvert dominant models. Ramírez executes a momentary transgression when she invites women to abandon traditional roles. She asks women to expand their denifition of self from pasivity to activity, but urges them to keep their identity as mothers. Ramírez, with her foot firm on motherhood, her only culturally stable discursive position, urges women to redefine themselves and abandon the submissive role assigned to them by society.

Villarreal González. A Woman's Job: "Hacer Rebeldes"

La mujer moderna tiene, más allá de los viejos límites marcados, por el capricho masculino, una misión nobilísima que cumplir. La de hacer rebeldes.

Andrea Villarreal González
La Mujer Moderna

Like Ramírez, Villarreal González also had an active role in the Mexican Revolution in support of the PLM. She was famous for being a talented speaker, and the *San Antonio Light Gazette*, often called her the Mexican Joan of Arc.[14]

This article analyzes one text by Villarreal González, a newspaper article which deals directly with issues of gender and the role of men and women in the Revolution. The article first appeared in *La Mujer Moderna* in San Antonio, Texas, in December 1909. All references in this article come from a reproduction of the article in *Mujeres y revolución*, titled "A qué venimos" (192-3).

Andrea Villarreal González, founder of *La Mujer Moderna*, (1909) "un periódico dedicado por entero a la propaganda de ideas que faciliten la evolución de la mujer," in her article proposes the same seemingly paradoxical discourse apparent in Ramírez's texts. Even as she advocates for female emancipation, Villarreal González constructs her discourse from within the traditional discursive space of motherhood.

"A qué venimos" makes clear the mission of the newspaper: to propagate ideas that facilitate the evolution of women. The article explains that some Mexican and Texan newspapers sometimes publish "este o aquel artículo a la mujer," but that this type of sporadic article is insufficient to consider these publications "devotos al desenvolvimiento y emancipación de la personalidad femenina, todavía hoy postergada a preocupaciones añejas, 'parasitadas' al corazón de las sociedades." The article criticizes society as a parasite that nurtures itself from the very life of women, exposing then the idea of women's liberation. This liberation, Villarreal González explains, must refuse "[los] egoísmos de ciertos hombres que prefieren la sierva humilde, ignara y sometida, a la compañera digna, inteligente y libre." The article delivers a dissident message in that it advocates for women's place in society as an intelligent partner of men, rather than as an ignorant servant. But while dissident, Villarreal González, like Ramírez, also seems unwilling or unable to abandon prescribed female modes. Though she advocates for women's education, she still speaks of women as partner (*compañera*) of men, albeit an educated partner. Like Ramírez's, Villarreal González's feminism also reflects the idea of feminism as an ideology that seeks equal opportunity for women, at the same time it accepts and values gender difference.

More revealing, though, of the seemingly paradoxical position Villarreal González occupies, is her assertion, that to fight for the rights of women is a dignified labor of all women but that women cannot and must not seek to improve their social conditions for their own sake alone: "Pero no solamente por nosotras venimos a combatir, tarea más grande acometemos." What constitutes that task? The answer fits well within the conventional model: "La de hacer rebeldes," to make rebels. This article, again, summarizes the paradox discussed before: Villarreal González, a Mexican woman who only advocates for her own rights from her position as mother. She embraces the idea of women as mother. Symbolically, in even more traditional terms than Ramírez, Villarreal González advocates for motherhood in her role of the Virgin Mary, holding Jesus, the Messiah who will save humanity. It is not women who will save Mexico from the Díaz dictatorship, but men. A woman's role is to be the mother of the Messiah: *Hacer rebeldes*. Ramírez's discursive space is clearly interstitial or heterotopian. At once, it places women in the role of mothers, but deconstructs traditional paradigms of motherhood away from passivity.

For Villarreal González, passivity is negative for women and men. In fact, she denounces, in the same article, that she condemns the passivity of men who have allowed the Porfirio Díaz dictatorship, and reminds them of their culturally assigned space:

> Tanto como al oído de la mujer hablaremos al de los hombres, desgangrenaremos en su alma la gama doliente de las inmensas amarguras patrias, junta con la rebelde nota despertadora de heroísmos.
> Gritaremos si es preciso para que los hombres recuerden *lo que deben ser*. *Sientan vergüenza* de su infamia actual, y despedacen sus yugos. Si es necesario, *nuestras manos serán rudas para sacudir los desmayados brazos de los tímidos*.

Villarreal González advocates the liberation of women, but that liberation must happen so that men are liberated in the process, and, with them, humanity. Here is the heterotopian subject. Villarreal González advocates for woman's education and emancipation, and even funds a newspaper specifically to advocate for those rights, but she undertakes this task still from a prescribed space: motherhood.

Villarreal González's subject is contestatory in the sense that it challenges women to abandon their culturally assigned passive role, yet hers continues being a traditional discourse, espousing even stronger traditional values than those expressed by Ramírez. The quote stresses that woman must remind man of his social role: "lo que deben ser." This means that, in their passive role, men have become effeminate. Women have the duty to point this out to them, "para que sientan vergüenza," so they feel ashamed of their lack of virility, so that they defend their country. Villarreal González further expresses that women's hands "will be rough," if necessary, to awake the sleeping men. This indicates her rejection of the hegemonic female model as passive, with "soft" hands, hands that don't undertake physical activity, hands that don't do, *que no hacen*. Like Ramírez, Villarreal González values femininity but (re)defines it away from its passive state. Villarreal González writes from the shadows of patriarchy, grounds herself on patriarchy's most sacred space, motherhood, and constructs a discursive space to formulate demands for her gender: education and emancipation.

Both Ramírez and Villarreal González wrote on behalf of their gender. But they did so aware of their gendered voice. Writing from a mediated space, between modernity and tradition, they undertook the task of participating in the gender and political discussions of their country. However, conscious of their limitations as female subjects, and perhaps unable and/or unwilling to escape prescribed roles, they discarded utopia and settled for heterotopia: they repeated male discourse, at times intercepted it and subverted it from the shadows, all the while recognizing the effects of such discourse in their lives as well as in the fate of their country. Unable to speak freely in their subaltern state, unable to abandon the cloak of the mother that defined their very identity, yet unwilling to settle quietly under its confining cover, they dedicated their lives to the emission of a mediated discourse on behalf of women's rights forged with the grounds of the cultural coffee served to them at the patriarchal table. That is why they spoke from the space of motherhood, challenging it, expanding it, (re)defining it, and reclaiming it as they advocated for freedom to do and, therefore, be. Are the voices of Ramírez and Villarreal González strong enough to constitute feminist discourse? Not in a feminist utopia. However, they are strong enough to form echoing ripples in the vast sea of male discourse, which women are, to this day, attempting to navigate.

Notes

[1]Please see Jean Franco, *Plotting Women. Gender & Representation in Mexico* (New York: Columbia University Press, 1989).

[2]In popular culture, as portrayed in song, the Adelita is generally the lover of the male revolutionary, as in the *corrido* of the same name.

[3]Campobello writes about women and men of northern Mexico during the Mexican Revolution in *Cartucho* (1931) and *Las manos de mamá* (1937). Villegas de Magnón records her own participation, and that of other women such as the sisters Teresa and Andrea Villarreal in the revolutionary movement before, during, and after 1910 in *The Rebel* (1994) and *La Rebelde* (2004).

[4]Newspaper and epistolary activity of the period in question (specifically 1900-1917) reveals a wealth of texts. The collection at the Centro de Estudios de Historia de México (CEHM), in Chimalistac, Mexico, for example, contains thousands of letters written by activists during and after the Mexican Revolution, such as those contained in the Carrancista archive, one of several collections on

the Revolution in Mexico City. The Carrancista archive holds, for example, letters from Juana Belén Gutiérrez de Mendoza and Dolores Jiménez y Muro. This epistolary collection also includes letters written to Venustiano Carranza, Francisco I. Madero and other leaders of the armed movement. A review of the Magonista files, also in Mexico City, at the Archivo Histórico de la Secretaría de Relaciones Exteriores (AHSRE), further reveals a number of texts written by women before and during the Mexican Revolution, specifically newspaper contributions to *Regeneración,* a newspaper published by the Flores Magón brothers. Archives in San Antonio, Texas, and Albuquerque, New Mexico, also contain Spanish-language newspapers with articles written by the *activistas*, many in support of the Revolution, and others expressing strong opinions about women's rights, or the rights of those in the lower social stratum. Many of these activists either published their own newspapers or contributed to established publications in support of the issues listed above. Among the newspapers that circulated during this period are *La Mujer Mexicana* (Morelia, Mich., 1901), a monthly newspaper; *Vésper,* a daily published by Gutiérrez de Mendoza that circulated, with interruptions brought on by tribulations such as the seizure of the newspaper printer by Díaz officials from 1901 to 1931.

[5]Quoted in Lomas's introduction to *The Rebel.*

[6]Among the alternative press newspapers published in the early 1900s Lomas identifies *El Obrero*, published by Teresa Villarreal; *La Voz de la Mujer* (1909), by Isidra T. Cárdenas and María Sánchez; *Pluma Roja* by Blanca De Moncaleano (1914, 1915); and *La Crónica* (1911) by the Idar family.

[7]Ángel Rama *La ciudad letrada* (Hanover: Ediciones del Norte, 1984).

[8]Antonieta Rivas Mercado was the daughter of Porfirian architect Antonio Rivas Mercado. She was multilingual and had a higher level of education than most men of her time. She inherited her father's money and funded the literary group *Los contemporáneos*, who accepted her because of her monetary contributions and because she knew as much about literature and the arts in general as any of them if not more. She is also credited with the creation of modern theater and the National Symphony Orchestra in Mexico. She also contributed articles to newspapers and wrote essays and short stories on gender in general and on issues such as divorce and the identity of women. In the late 1920s, she became an unofficial advisor to the Vasconcelos presidential campaign and, in 1930, she wrote a series of articles on the campaign ("La campaña de Vasconcelos") denouncing the electoral fraud that she believed kept Vasconcelos from the presidency as well as denouncing limitations she faced as a woman interested in the political destiny of her country. See Fabienne de Bradu *Antonieta, 1900-1931* (Mexico: Fondo de Cultura Económica, 1991).

[9]See Octavio Paz *El laberinto de la soledad* (Mexico: Fondo de Cultura Económica, 1959).

[10]See Gabriela Mistral *Lecturas para mujeres* (Mexico: Secretaria de Educación Pública, 1923).

[11]She published *La Corregidora*, a daily newspaper in Mexico City, Laredo and San Antonio, and *Aurora,* in Laredo between 1904 and 1910. She wrote for *La Crónica* and *El Demócrata* between 1898 and 1910. See Lau and Ramos, 34.

[12]The use of the formal "usted" with friends is common in northern Mexico, where Ramírez is raised.

[13]Rivas Mercado writes that there is no such thing as "the Mexican woman" (la mujer mexicana). There are, instead, Mexican women. Yet, Mexican women share one cultural element "su ineficiencia, su nulidad." And as a group, she writes, the Mexican woman "sigue siendo, casi siempre, una mujer colonial, en la que se exaltan las virtudes pasivas, si es posible que la pasividad sea virtud." See *Obras completas*.

[14]*San Antonio Light Gazette*. AHSRE, L-E-947, issue XXX, file 331. Aug. 18 1909.

References

Campobello, Nellie. *Cartucho. Relatos de la lucha en el norte de México*. (1931) Mexico: Factoría Ediciones, 2000.

_____. *Las manos de mamá. Tres Poemas. Mis libros*. (1937) Mexico: Factoría Ediciones, 1999.

Franco, Jean. *Plotting Women, Gender and Representation in México*. New York: Colombia University Press, 1989.

Foucault, Michel. "Of Other Spaces." *Diacritics* 16.1 (1986). 22-27.

Guerra Cunningham, Lucía. "Las sombras de escritura: hacia una teoría de la producción literaria de la mujer latinoamericana." *Cultural and Historical Grounding for Hispanic and Luso-Brazilian Literary Criticism*. Ed. Hernán Vidal. Minneapolis: Institute for the Study of Ideologies and Literature, 1989. 129.

Hernández Tovar, Inés. "Sara Estela Ramírez: The Early Twentieth Century Texas-Mexican Poet." Diss. U of Houston, 1984.

Lau, Ana and Carmen Ramos, eds. *Mujeres y revolución, 1900-1917*. Mexico: Instituto Nacional de Estudios Históricos de la Revolución Mexicana, 1993.

Lomas, Clara. "Revolutionary Women and the Alternative Press in the Borderlands." Introduction. Villegas de Magnón xi-lvi.

_____. "Mexican Precursors of Chicana Feminist Writing." *Multiethnic Literature of the United States. Critical Introductions and Classroom Resources.* Ed. Cordelia Candelaria. Boulder: University of Colorado at Boulder, 1989. 21–33.

_____. "Transborder Discourse: An Articulation of Gender in the Borderlands in the Early Twentieth Century." *Frontiers: A Journal of Women Studies*. 24. 2-3 (2003): 54-74. Special Issue: *Gender on the Borderlands,* Guest Ed. Antonia Castañeda.

Mistral, Ana. *Against All Odds: The Feminist Movement in Mexico to 1940.* Connecticut: Greenwood Press, 1982.

Macías, Gabriela. *Lecturas para mujeres.* Mexico: Secretaría de Educación, 1923.

Mendieta Alatorre, Ángeles. *Juana Belén Gutiérrez de Mendoza (1875-1942). Extraordinaria Precursora de la Revolución Mexicana.* Mexico: Impresores de Morelos, 1983.

_____. *La mujer en la Revolución Mexicana.* Mexico: Instituto Nacional de Estudios de Historia de la Revolución, 1961.

Ocampo, Victoria. *La mujer y su expresión*. Buenos Aires: Sur, 1936. 15.

Paz, Octavio. *El laberinto de la soledad*. Mexico: Fondo de Cultura Económica, 1959.

Pérez, Emma M. "'A la mujer': A Critique of the Partido Liberal Mexicano's Gender Ideology on Women." *Between Borders: Essays on Mexicana/Chicana History*. Encino: Floricanto Press, 1990. 459–82.

Pratt, Mary Louise. "'Don't Interrupt Me' The Gender Essay as Conversation and Countercannon." *Reinterpreting The Spanish American Essay. Women Writers of the Nineteenth and Twentieth Centuries.* Ed. Doris Meyer. Austin: University of Texas Press, 1995. 10–26.

Ramírez, Sara Estela. "Surge." *Mexican Women in the United States: Struggles Past and Present*. Eds. Magdalena Mora and Adelaida Castillo. Los Angeles: University of California, 1980. 163–9.

Rivas Mercado, Antonieta. *Obras completas de María Antonieta Rivas Mercado.* (1981). Mexico: Secretaría de la Educación Pública, 1987.

Salas, Elizabeth. "The Soldadera in the Mexican Revolution: War and men's Illusions." *Women of the Mexican Countryside, 1850-1990*. Eds. Heather Fowler-Salamini and Mary Kay Vaughan. Tucson: University of Arizona Press, 1994. 93–105.

Smith, Paul. *Discerning the Subject.* Minneapolis: University of Minnesota Press, 1988. 271–317.

Spivak, Gayatry. "Can the Subaltern Speak?" *Marxism and the Interpretation of Culture*. Eds. Cary Nelson and Lawrence Grossberg. Urbana: University of Illinois Press, 1988. 271–317.

Villarreal González, Andrea. "A qué venimos." Lau and Ramos 192–193.

Villegas de Magnón, Leonor. *La rebelde*. Houston, Arte Público Press, 2004.

_____. *The Rebel*. Houston: Arte Público Press, 1994.

Zamora, Emilio. "Sara Estela Ramírez: Una rosa roja en el movimiento." *Mexican Women in the United Status: Struggles Past and Present*. Eds. Magdalena Mora and Adelaida Castillo. Los Angeles: University of California, 1980. 163–170.

Deism and the Authorship of *Jicoténcal*

Marissa L. Garland
Columbia University

Since its publication in 1826 by Philadelphia's William Stavely Press, the authorship of *Jicoténcal*, a historical novel centered on the defeat by Cortés of a Tlaxcalan military hero, has continued to intrigue and elude scholars. To discern the identity of the author, scholars have evaluated the historical context in which the work was written, along with the linguistic features and ideological positions present in the novel. While many scholars have offered hypotheses as to the nationality of the author, no one had provided convincing evidence attributing authorship to an individual until 1960 when Luis Leal proposed that the novel was the work of the Cuban priest, Félix Varela. Despite the convincing linguistic and ideological evidence offered in Leal's study, the deism-Catholicism debate presented in the novel appears problematic when considering the Cuban priest's authorship. More specifically, the ostensibly positive portrayal of deism and the censure of Catholicism seem to be inconsistent with the religious views presented in Varela's other writings. Through a comparative analysis of the novel and Varela's other works, this study concludes that the novel's discussion of deism and Catholicism not only is consistent with the Cuban priest's views but offers additional evidence for Félix Varela's authorship of *Jicoténcal*.

Initial commentary regarding the novel's anonymity focused on the nationality of the author. Published in Puebla, Mexico in 1829, José María Mangino's play "Xicoténcatl: Comedia Heróica en Cuatro Actos" contains one of the earliest references to the anonymous work. In an author's postscript, Mangino acknowledges that his play contains historical inaccuracies and errors in Mexican topography, but takes no responsibility for the misinformation, claiming that his work is simply an interpretation of the source text, *Jicoténcal.* According to Mangino, the numerous mistakes regarding Mexican history and geography found throughout *Jicoténcal* suggest that the novel's author was not Mexican. Although there are other contemporary references to *Jicoténcal*, scholars did not seriously begin to address the question of the novel's authorship until the mid-twentieth century.[1] In *Las Corrientes Literarias en la América Hispánica,* Pedro Henríquez Ureña concludes that the author of *Jicoténcal* was Spanish-American, and most likely Mexican, due to the strong Mexican patriotism and the equally fervent anti-Spanish sentiment expressed throughout the novel (128, 243). Enrique Anderson Imbert, while not opposed to the possibility that the author was Mexican, asserts that the politically liberal ideas on which Henríquez Ureña bases his assessment were shared by Spaniards and Spanish-Americans alike, making it equally plausible for the author to have been from either the peninsula or the colonies (5). He further conjectures that the use of phrases such as "nuestros antepasados" and "país remoto" to refer to Spaniards and to Mexico, respectively, implies that the author was probably Spanish and not Spanish-American (22).[2] Rojas Garcidueñas, however, disagrees with Anderson Imbert's hypothesis by arguing that there was a distinction between European and Spanish-American liberals. Although both groups sought increased political freedom for the colonies, Spanish-American liberals distinguished themselves from their European counterparts by advocating colonial independence (Rojas Garcidueñas, 73). *Jicoténcal,* a novel which explicitly condemns the oppressive nature of Spanish rule in the Americas in favor of independence, does not espouse European liberalism as suggested by Anderson Imbert, but rather the more radical political liberalism found in the Americas. Consequently, it is unlikely that the author of the novel was Spanish.

While many scholars have offered hypotheses as to the nationality of the author, no one provided convincing evidence attributing authorship to an individual until 1960 when Luis Leal proposed that the novel was the work of the Cuban priest, Félix Varela. In his research, Leal considers all Spanish-Americans and Spaniards living in either New York or Philadelphia at the time of publication.[3] To determine the likelihood of an individual's authorship of the novel, he examines circumstantial information. In the case of Félix Varela there are two pieces of circumstantial evidence that support his authorship of the novel.

Shortly after moving to Philadelphia from New York in 1824, Varela published the first issue of his political newspaper, *El Habanero*, and the second edition of his *Lecciones de filosofía.* Both of these works were published by the William Stavely Press; the same publishing house that printed *Jicoténcal.* That Varela conducted business with the William Stavely Press does not prove he wrote the novel, but it does increase the likelihood that he did. Similarly,

Varela's relationship with the owner of the copyright of *Jicoténcal,* Frederick Huttner, also increases the probability that it was he, Varela, that authored the novel. As Leal explains, Dr. Frederick Huttner lived at 239 Spruce Street in Philadelphia, not far from Félix Varela, who lived at 244 on the same street. Although there is no evidence to prove that Varela agreed to have Dr. Huttner acquire proprietorship of the novel, the physical proximity of the two men does allow for the possibility of such an arrangement.[4]

While the circumstantial information reinforces the link between Varela and *Jicoténcal,* it is Leal's assessment of the lexicon and ideology that creates a more definitive connection. Leal assembles an extensive list of words employed in the novel and in Varela's other works. Furthermore, he notes that the author of *Jicoténcal,* like Varela, uses the article "la" when referring to geographic locations that normally do not require the article, such as "la América" and "la España." Similarly both authors refer to themselves as "el filósofo." Lastly, Leal compares the philosophical and religious sentiments in *Jicoténcal* with those found in Varela's other writings and concludes:

> Ambos autores tienen una inalterable noción de lo justo y, con frecuencia, expresan sus ideas de la misma manera. Mas es en la ideología, sin embargo, donde encontramos mayor semejanza. En *Jicoténcal* no hay ninguna idea—moral, religiosa o filosófica—que no pudiera ser atribuída al P. Varela. Al mismo tiempo, en las obras del filósofo cubano no hemos hallado ideas que contradigan las de la novela. (Leal and Cortina, xxx)

If Félix Varela is indeed the author of *Jicoténcal*, the inclusion of Enlightenment thought is not at all surprising. Varela, a lifelong scholar, was familiar with Enlightenment ideology.[5] He developed and implemented his own philosophical beliefs in which aspects of Enlightenment thought were revered. His eclectic philosophy urged the combination of both reason and experience, warning not to rely too heavily on one as opposed to the other (García-Menocal, 92). Yet, despite his acceptance of Enlightenment principles, Félix Varela was not a proponent of the deism that developed during the Age of Reason. Although it did not negate the existence of a supreme being, deism did denounce many Christian beliefs and the Church. Varela's writings and his devotion to the Church suggest that the priest in no way condoned deistic thought. He wrote his *Cartas a Elpidio,* for example, in response to the more radical movement of liberal thought in the early nineteenth century that saw religion and the Enlightenment as irreconcilable. In these fictional letters Varela seeks to convince his audience of the importance of religion in scientific and intellectual pursuits, and addresses the three impediments he believes to be most harmful to human progress and happiness: irreligiosity, superstition, and fanaticism. In fact, he goes on to define several types of irreligiosity, one of which corresponds to "those who admitting to the existence of a Supreme Being want to subject Him to their ideas" (33). This definition may be applied to deists who acknowledge a divine being, yet believe that this supreme entity conformed to the same rational and immutable laws of the universe He created. If Varela's views against deism are made clear in his *Cartas*, written in 1835, his depiction of deism in *Jicoténcal,* which was written ten years earlier, while not as explicit and unambiguous, is certainly not inconsistent with his previous views.

Throughout the novel the Tlaxcalans are characterized as representatives of Enlightenment thought. It is not incongruous, therefore, that they should also be proponents of deism. In his dialogue with Fray Bartolomé de Olmedo, Jicoténcal the Elder explains his people's religious beliefs as follows:

> Yo sé que hay un Dios, esto es, un Ser muy poderoso que ha ordenado todo el universo con una inteligencia tan grande, que cada cosa corresponde a un gran fin con una admirable precisión. Dentro de mí mismo lo siento, en las cosas más abstractas lo mismo que en las más materiales. Hasta aquí llegan mis conocimientos; pero pues que tú los tienes mayores, según dices, dame a conocer este Dios, que yo creo muy poderoso y muy sabio, pero del que no tengo más idea de la que me dan sus obras. (83)

The Elder's comment reflects the Newtonian philosophy that was later adapted as the central tenet of deism (Walters, 27). Newton proposed that the elements within the universe and within nature were the creation of one superior entity. He also claimed that these elements existed in relationship with one another and were guided by natural laws, hence creating a universe based on "precision." The Elder's comment that he "feels" the existence of God suggests his conviction of the existence of a God whose power is infinite. Yet he acknowledges his finite ability to comprehend this superior being. This finite/infinite dichotomy of man/God is characteristic of deistic thought, particularly of that found in the American colonies during the middle to late eighteenth century. While deists primarily relied on perceived reality and reason to assess their world, they also incorporated abstract thought, concluding that "humans were imbued with a spark of the divine reason and so were privy to a limited knowledge of the divine. Ultimately, however, awareness of God's essence was beyond the race's ken" (Walters 32). Thus, deists were able to reconcile a speculative belief in God, based on an inherent "feeling," within their predominantly rationalist ideology.

Accepting that his comprehension of God is limited, Jicoténcal is intrigued by Fray Bartolomé's claim to have complete understanding of this divine being. He then challenges the priest to explain Catholic doctrine and his understanding of God. To Jicoténcal's disappointment, the priest is unable to fully explain the articles of his religion, claiming that they are a matter of faith. Fray Bartolomé, like Jicoténcal, acknowledges that there are elements of religion that escape human comprehension. But it is the balance of faith and reason that most clearly differentiates these two ideologies. More specifically, Jicoténcal espouses deism, a religion based primarily on reason with only one article of faith: the existence of a supreme being. Catholicism, conversely, incorporates many articles of faith, such as the concept of miracles, thus inverting this balance of faith and reason. Jicoténcal rejects the faith-based Catholic doctrine, underscoring the lack of reason as its primary flaw:

> ¿Y tú quieres hacerme creer que ese Ser tan sabio, ha comunicado unas cosas que repugnan a mi razón? ¿Qué fin podría haberse propuesto en una conducta semejante? . . . ¿Y que necesidad hay para eso de unos misterios contradictorios y absurdos cuando tengo mi juicio . . . mis deberes están bien claros, y, cuando la miseria de mi naturaleza intenta extraviarme de su senda, tengo en mí un instinto, una cosa que me los recuerda y que tú llamas razón. (84)

The discussion ends with the defeat of Fray Bartolomé, and consequently the Catholic doctrine. But the debate between Catholicism and deism is not a peripheral discussion within the novel. Rather, there are a number of conversations throughout the book which posit the two against one another, such as the discussion between Fray Bartolomé and Don Diego de Ordaz.

One would suppose that this dialogue between the Catholic priest and his Spanish brethren would be harmonious, as opposed to confrontational, since both characters are Spaniards. Although the nationality of protagonists does not necessarily imply that the characters bear any resemblance to one another, in this novel nationality is closely linked with set characteristics. As a result, each character, while assuming individual and external traits (i.e., age, social role, gender, etc.), is also representative of the collective and internal attributes (i.e., religion, political ideology, etc.) of the national group to which he or she pertains. The character of Don Diego, however, disrupts this pattern. Despite forming part of Cortés's retinue, Don Diego is more closely related in character and principle to the Tlaxcalans than to his compatriots. In his conversation with Fray Bartolomé, Don Diego, like his Tlaxcalan counterparts, rejects orthodox religion in favor of deistic principles.

The conversation begins with Fray Bartolomé's attack on reason. Given the overwhelming number of Tlaxcalan warriors and the relatively small contingent of Spanish conquistadores, Fray Bartolomé deduces that the Spaniards should have succumbed to the natives. To Fray Bartolomé the recent success of the

Spaniards defies rational thought and can only be attributed to divine intervention. Don Diego openly contests this conclusion:

> Yo reconozco ahora, y siempre he reconocido, la providencia sabia y benéfica que ha ordenado al universo con leyes inmutables y a las que se sujetan sin excepción todos los fenómenos que vemos, lo mismo que los que se nos ocultan. Pero no puedo reducirme a creer que el ser que preside a la Naturaleza se ocupe particularmente en unos detalles tan minuciosos, de una manera tan arbitraria, y algunas veces tan incompatible con su bondad. (45)

Don Diego's initial statement about an ordered universe with immutable laws is strikingly similar to Jicoténcal's comment about the "precision" of nature mentioned earlier. This comment can likewise be attributed to Newton's conclusion that physical reality, and hence nature, was not an abstract conglomeration of entities, but an ordered mechanism of intricate and fail-safe accuracy (Walters 8). Again, while the concept of an orderly universe was not a commentary on religious doctrine in and of itself, it was later incorporated into deistic thought. However, Don Diego's next comment about God and His relation to man make this conversation particularly relevant to deism. Specifically, his portrayal of a God that "presides over nature," is removed from man's reality, and does not directly intervene in worldly affairs is in accordance with eighteenth-century deistic thought. According to deism, nature is the only and greatest manifestation of God. A miracle or divine intervention as the antithesis of nature was, therefore, refuted by deists.

In this conversation we see, again, the questioning of authority. Don Diego, upset by Cortés's decision to keep Teutila prisoner, exhibits the same sentiment of distrust of authority characteristic of the Enlightenment. However, the conversation turns specifically to the question of religion when Don Diego remarks that authoritative figures if left unchecked may corrupt religious belief. He proposes that instead of blindly following authority, one should comply with God's commands first which, "nos manda defender la inocencia oprimida, no ser jamás los instrumentos de la injusticia; en una palabra: llenar los deberes de la moral que sanciona la religión" (46). The emphasis placed on individual responsibility and morality, which Don Diego points out, are also central to deism.

The conversation between the priest and Don Diego ends much like the conversation between Fray Bartolomé and Jicoténcal the Elder. The priest charged with defending and disseminating Catholic doctrine fails to convince his opponent and either retires unable to meet the challenge or is interrupted by some other event, never to continue the debate. The priest's inability to respond to the attacks made against his religion implies that deistic views are superior to his own Catholic beliefs. In both conversations the deists appear to be victorious.

In order to evaluate the role of deism in *Jicoténcal*, it is important to consider how this ideology functions within the multiple dimensions of this historical novel.[6] In the case of *Jicoténcal,* the author's decision to ascribe deistic principles to the Tlaxcalan people allows for the coexistence of the historical and contemporary. The earliest chronicles from the conquest and subsequent studies indicate that the Tlaxcalans practiced polytheism. Varela's decision to characterize the indigenous people as deists, therefore, is inconsistent with accepted historical findings. Yet, the presentation of the Tlaxcalans as deists does not seem entirely incongruent either. Similarities can be drawn between deism and our understanding of the natives of Tlaxcala. The prominent role of nature and the absence of Christian references are common to both deistic thought and native polytheistic ideologies. And while these similarities are rather general, they do allow for a superimposition of the Enlightenment ideology onto the indigenous people.

One of the ways in which Varela creates a distinction between the historical and contemporary is his treatment of religious beliefs. Ascribing a Christian religion to the natives, for example, would have been inconsistent with historical findings. Varela's decision to include deism in the novel, therefore, can most easily been seen as the author's desire to comment on contemporary issues. But we can also evaluate the religious debate solely within the historical dimension of the novel since Varela, while associating the natives with deistic principles, never explicitly labels their belief system as such.

The Tlaxcalans are not labeled as followers of any particular religion, but instead simply portrayed as highly moral individuals. Just prior to his death, Jicoténcal the Elder reiterates the principles of his native belief system to his kin, "hablándoles de la justicia, primero y principal deber de los hombres; de la beneficencia, gran virtud y consuelo de la humanidad; del conocimiento de un ser supremo, gobernador del universo y juez remunerador y vengador de las acciones humanas" (114). Despite the conflicting views between the Tlaxcalans and Spaniards with regard to religion (among other ideologies), these moral teachings are celebrated by both parties. The following conversation between Fray Bartolomé and the Elder reveals the commonality between the two groups:

> Fr. Bartolomé: Obcecado anciano: mi divina religión prescribe unas reglas de moral que te aseguran, si las observas, la felicidad en este mundo y te quitan los temores para el otro. He aquí su resumen: "Ama a Dios sobre todas las cosas y al prójimo como a ti mismo." Dime ahora que no es divina la religión que te ordena esta conducta.

> The Elder: Sin duda, mi amigo, esas reglas vienen de Dios; ellas están aquí en mi pecho y me las ha dado el mismo a quien debo estas manos, esta lengua con que te hablo y los pensamientos que te expresa. Sí, yo siento, de la misma manera que siento el hambre y la sed, que es menester ser justo y benéfico . . . Tú eres más blanco que nosotros, tienes barbas y otras diferencias que, al parecer, te hacen un hombre de otra especie que la nuestra; y, no obstante, tu moral es la misma que la mía. Luego ésta viene de Dios. (85)

Evaluating the Tlaxcalan beliefs presented here, one could conclude that unbeknownst to him, Jicoténcal the Elder professes the basic tenets of Catholicism. In *The Protestant's Abridger and Annotator*, written in 1830 in response to the Protestant attack on the Catholic Church, Varela argues that an individual is considered a member of the Catholic Church, and therefore worthy of salvation, if he or she abides by two basic stipulations: he or she 1) must be baptized and; 2) abide by Catholic doctrine. Of particular import is his address regarding individuals who may not be aware of Catholicism. He asserts that an individual's association with the Church is based foremost on one's actions. If one is not familiar with Catholic doctrine and acts in accordance to the law of nature, he or she may be saved by God, and "united to the only Church of Jesus Christ, to that church, whose head on earth is the Bishop of Rome, although he should not have any idea of such a Bishop nor of that city" (*The Protestant's Abridger* 11). Individuals unaware of Catholic doctrine may, therefore, become baptized *implicitly* through the value of their actions. With respect to adherence to Catholic doctrine, one cannot be condemned for violating Catholic dogma if he is unaware of it. Although Varela states that it would be extraordinary for an individual who is neither explicitly baptized nor familiar with Catholic doctrine to be considered part of the Catholic Church and redeemed, it is nevertheless possible.

The emphasis on one's actions as the primary determinant of one's religious state, noted in Varela's *Protestant's Abridger*, is also echoed in the novel when Jicoténcal the Elder recognizes the overlap in native and Catholic doctrine. He uses the following analogy, in which domestic animals attempt to please their masters, to stress the correlation between behavior and religion: "Observa los animales domésticos cuando nos halagan: cada uno lo hace a su modo, y nosotros no nos cuidamos de la manera con que se explican y atendemos solo a lo que manifiestan sus señales. Así el Autor de la Naturaleza no atenderá sin duda más que a nuestra intención" (86). The Elder effectively argues that God will evaluate individuals primarily based on *what they show or how they act*. In light of Varela's discourse on the determinants of one's religious state and the

Tlaxcalan view of morality, the natives could be considered members of the Catholic Church, worthy of salvation.

An argument can be made in favor of this interpretation prior to the natives' encounter with the Spaniards, when the Tlaxcalans were unfamiliar with Catholicism. Since the natives act in accordance with Catholic doctrine yet have no knowledge of its principles, they may be baptized implicitly and therefore incorporated into the Church. The interpretation of the natives as potential members of the Catholic Church establishes a parallel between the natives and the Spaniards due to their common moral beliefs. Yet, this interpretation is based on the natives' existence before their encounter with the Spaniards, and therefore prior to the introduction of Catholicism. Considering the overlap in native and Catholic doctrine, one might expect the Tlaxcalans to convert to Catholicism upon meeting with Fray Bartolomé. In fact, Jicoténcal the Elder entertains the possibility of converting and informs Fray Bartolomé that "Os creeremos cuantos misterios nos querráis proponer, por absurdos que sean, porque entonces el sacrificio de nuestra luz natural sería recompensado con la felicidad del género humano" (86). Yet he ultimately rejects conversion because, "predicar una doctrina semejante con la guerra, el libertinaje y los vicios más escandalosos! ¡Que contradicción! ¡Dios mío estos sucesos ponen a prueba mi creencia de tu sabiduría!" (86). In this conversation, the Elder poignantly notes the disparate nature between the Catholic doctrine which Fray Bartolomé preaches and the actions of his Spanish compatriots. The Elder's decision to resist conversion, therefore, should not be interpreted as an objection to Catholic doctrine, but rather the Spaniards' failure to act in accordance with their religious beliefs. Although the Elder recognizes the shared moral principles of his people and the Spaniards, his conversation with Fray Bartolomé does not yield him any convincing information about Catholic doctrine and its practices. As a result, even after their meeting with the Catholic Spaniards, the natives can still be viewed as potential members of the Catholic Church through the virtousness of their actions and despite the priest's failure to indoctrinate them.

It is doubtful that Varela wanted to overtly portray the natives as Catholics, since this would have undermined his novel's historicity. Yet, deism and Catholicism are highlighted for their commonalities. Since the set of values is established as consistent, the focus of the debate shifts to the individual's interpretation or manifestation of those values. That both parties profess the same principles would seem to indicate that they are members of one religion. But time and again the natives note the Spaniards' hypocrisy with respect to doctrine and action: "Me sorprendes, extranjero, con unas máximas tan conformes con las que existen en mi corazón, cuando vuestras acciones son tan contrarias a estas mismas máximas" (83); or, "La doctrina se predica con el ejemplo" (109). The vastly different behavior of the natives and the Spaniards make it impossible for these two groups to be followers of the same religion. The emphasis, therefore, is again on the discrepancy between word and deed, which results in the Tlaxcalan's questioning of the Spaniard's role as spiritual savior and their religious justification for political domination.

The criticism of the manipulation of religion to achieve political goals presented in the novel appears in Varela's other works, such as *The Protestant's Abridger and Annotator* and *El Habanero*. In volume one of *El Habanero,* Varela specifically challenges Spain's justification for imperial domination and contends: "Defensores *del trono y del altar*: quitaros la mascara. Vosotros podréis servir de apoyo al primero, mas la sagrada víctima que se sacrifica en el segundo abomina vuestra hipocresía, y detesta vuestra impiedad. Ya que sois déspotas, no seáis sacrílegos. La fuerza es el apoyo de la tiranía, y la religión no puede servirla de pretexto" (68).

This condemnation of Spain's imperial policy, which oppressed people under the guise of religion, transcends both the historical and contemporary dimensions of *Jicoténcal*. Thus far, we have only considered the religious debate within the historical context. The religious discussion evaluated from this perspective suggests that the debate is not focused on contending ideologies, but rather on the interpretation of a singular and Catholic doctrine. As such, it does not present any concepts that would contradict or challenge Varela's views. If we assess the religious debate from the contemporary, rather than historical, perspective we must consider the deism-Catholicism discussion within the framework of the Enlightenment. Deism, then, takes on a broader connotation than that which is presented in the novel. The deistic movement during the nineteenth century went beyond the basic premises presented in the novel and actively attacked Catholic doctrine. Considering deism within this larger context, its inclusion within the novel could discredit Varela's authorship, or alternatively perhaps explain the novel's anonymity.

We may understand the religious discussion as portrayed in the novel, however, as exemplary of Varela's method of argument and his personal beliefs. Varela strongly denounced the use of military means to resolve conflict, preferring open, verbal debate as a means of reconciliation. Only when all peaceable means had been exhausted did Varela favor armed conflict in order to achieve a resolution; and even this he did begrudgingly. Much like his *Protestant's Abridger, Jicoténcal* can be viewed as Varela's participation in the ideological debate of his time.

As Varela notes at the beginning of *The Protestant's Abridger,* the work was not composed with the intent to alienate or insult the Protestant community, but rather to openly discuss and contest some of the Protestant's harsh criticisms of the Catholic Church. Varela, in effect, attempts to assuage the growing animosity between the Catholic and Protestant groups during the early nineteenth century in New York. In his response, Varela is careful not to make sweeping conclusions. Instead he evaluates individual facets of Protestantism and discredits the argument against Catholicism presented in the weekly paper, the *Protestant*. He addresses a variety of the Protestants' censures, such as the claim that Peter, founder of the Catholic Church, never visited Rome, and allegations regarding the clergy's abuse of power (39). Furthermore, he acknowledges the existence of sects as the chief defect of Protestantism. According to Varela, "the name of Christian is nothing, if we keep not the true doctrine of Christ" (40). Since Protestant sects are founded upon differing interpretations of Christ's teachings, Varela views them as personal, and therefore, illegitimate religions: "Personal religion is personal caprice, and therefore Protestants do not understand themselves, and there are in fact, as many religions among them as there are men" (39). The detail with which he examines the Protestants' arguments lends validity to his defense of the Catholic Church since he is able to demonstrate their errors on all accounts.

In view of Varela's approach as expressed in *The Protestant's Abridger,* we may read his treatment of deism in *Jicoténcal* as an example of his method of evaluation, in which he identifies and assesses all ideological components. Undoubtedly, although Varela would have refuted the deists' attacks on Catholic doctrine, his novel does not address those aspects of deism. Therefore, it may be unjust to suppose that Varela is endorsing deism as a whole. Instead, it is more accurate to conclude that Varela validates only those deistic beliefs *presented within the novel* that are in accordance with Catholic doctrine. Just as he closely examines and evaluates certain elements of Protestant doctrine in *The Protestant's Abridger,* so too does Varela assess specific elements of deism in *Jicoténcal*. By including foils such as Ordaz, the Spaniard that embraces Tlaxcalan ideals, and Magiscatzin, the native who betrays his own people in favor of Cortés, he recognizes the complexity of the doctrines he evaluates and avoids general assessments.

The study of Varela's other works may also reveal the author's motivation for the inclusion of deism and its positive portrayal in the novel. In 1826, the same year in which *Jicoténcal* was published, Varela translated and annotated Thomas Jefferson's *Manual of Parliamentary Practice*. Despite the amendments Varela makes to the document, he believes Jefferson's work to be a model for the establishment of democratic practices in Cuba.[7] Varela's praise of Jefferson, however, may not be limited to this translation. Indeed, Varela's inclusion of deism in *Jicoténcal* may be another means by which the author expresses his esteem for Jefferson.

The question of Jefferson's religious affiliation was always a topic of debate, especially when he became a Presidential candidate in the 1800 and 1804 elections. Despite his regular attendance at religious services and continued financial donations to Episcopalian, Presbyterian, and Baptist organizations, Jefferson continued to be labeled as an "atheist, deist or devil" (Sanford 6). Jefferson's opponents published hundreds of pamphlets and newspaper articles attesting to his immoral character. Sermons were also delivered warning the people that his election would lead to the moral corruption of the Nation and the demise of religion. Despite the numerous and harsh allegations against Jefferson's personal and religious character, he made very few public statements to refute them. Because he believed that religion was a deeply private matter, his statements were brief and often vague. As a consequence, the ambiguity of such statements as "We are accountable to God alone for our religious views" (Wilder Foote 50), or, "It is in our lives, and not from our words that our religion must be read" (Sanford 13), served to provoke further criticism rather than discredit false allegations. Considering Varela's praise for Jefferson and the public denunciations of the politician's deistic practices, it is possible that Varela's inclusion and portrayal of the deistic Tlaxcalans was influenced by his reverence for Jefferson.

Through *Jicoténcal* Varela attempts to garner support for some of the prevailing Enlightenment ideologies of his time. Already disenchanted by the Spanish system of government and dedicated to liberating his homeland, Varela presents his argument in favor of political and social beliefs of the Age of Reason, which espouse personal freedom, morality and efforts made for the collective good. Drawing on the thoughts of Enlightenment thinkers, Varela parcels together his vision of an exemplary society while denouncing the antiquated and imperialistic impulses of the Spanish Crown. While at first glance the positive portrayal of deism seems to contradict Varela's fervent support of Catholicism, it should instead be viewed as a testament to his ability to engage in the ideological debate of his time and formulate a vision for the future of his country, such that it is no longer isolated by imperial rule but becomes a member of a larger and more modern global society. The treatment of religion in *Jicoténcal* is specifically used to underscore Catholic principles and distinguish among its various components—doctrine, institution, and individual—and how these interact with each other. That both the Tlaxcalans and the Spaniards advocate the same moral teachings establishes the novel's pro-Catholic sentiment and serves to criticize the individual who strays from these principles. The religious questions raised in the novel and the vantage point from which they are discussed do not at all contradict Félix Varela's beliefs. In fact, they are echoed in his other writings. This provides further evidence that, as Luis Leal first suggested: Varela is indeed the author of *Jicoténcal.*

Notes

[1]A book review of *Jicoténcal,* written by William Cullen Bryant, appeared in the February 1826 edition of the U.S. Review and Literary Gazette. Although the article does not address the issue of authorship, it does provide a synopsis of the novel, and a historical-political analysis of the work.

[2]In *Liberales y Románticos: una emigración española en Inglaterra (1823-1834),* Vicente Lloréns Castillo supports Anderson Imbert's conclusion that *Jicoténcal's* author was Spanish (212). Ironically, José Rojas Garcidueñas utilizes Lloréns Castillo's comparative analysis of Spanish and Spanish American liberalism to bolster Henríquez Ureña's hypothesis that the novel's author was not Spanish, but rather Spanish-American and probably Mexican (74). Also see Lloréns Castillo (19, 134-135, 212, 249).

[3]For a full listing of the individuals see Leal's study, "Estudios: Jicoténcal, primera novela histórica en castellano." The list of potential authors is arranged by nationality, and includes individuals from Cuba, Mexico, Colombia, Venezuela, Argentina, Peru, Ecuador and Spain.

[4]The policy of the United States during the early nineteenth century required that proprietorship of all published materials be documented. In the case of *Jicoténcal,* proprietor information can be found on the reverse side of the cover page of the original edition, and reads as follows: "Eastern District of Pennsylvania, to wit: Be it remembered, that on the eighteenth day of August, in the fifty-first year of the Independence of the United States of America, A.D. 1826, Frederick Huttner, of the said District, hath deposited in this office the Title of a book, the right whereof he claims as Proprietor, in the words following, to wit: "JICOTENCAL." In conformity to the act of the congress of the United States, intituled, "an act for the encouragement of learning, by securing the copies of maps, charts and books, to the Authors and Proprietors of such copies, during the times therein mentioned"—and also to the act, entitled, "an act for the encouragement of learning, by securing the copies of maps, charts and books, to the Authors and Proprietors of such copies, during the times therein mentioned," and extending the benefits thereof to the arts of designing, engraving, and etching historical and other prints. D. Caldwell, Clerk of the Eastern District of Pennsylvania."

[5]For information regarding Varela's intellectual formation see Carlos Manuel de Céspedes García-Menocal's *Pasión por Cuba y por la Iglesia.* At the San Car-

los y San Ambrosio Seminary and the Real y Pontifica Universidad San Gerónimo, Varela received instruction in ideas associated with Enlightenment philosophy. Given José Agustín Caballero's knowledge of Bacon, Descartes, Locke, Voltaire, and Rousseau, it is not surprising that his protégé, Félix Varlea, would later incorporate Enlightenment principles in his own philosophical scholarship (49-54). Hernández Travieso concludes that Varela's work does bear the imprint of the Enlightenment thinkers such as Locke, Condillac, and Newton (65-66, 120). Likewise, the Cuban priest's criticism of Rousseau demonstrates his familiarity with this other *encyclopedist* (112).

[6]In the first chapter of *El enigma de Jicoténcal* Gonzalez Acosta discusses the historical novel and its influence on Spanish and Spanish American literature. Although the appearance of Scott's historical model strongly influenced the Latin American novelistic tradition of the early decades of the nineteenth century Gonzalez Acosta notes that *Jicoténcal* is not part of this of literary trend, but rather precedes it (33).

[7]For further discussion of Varela's annotations to the *Manual of Parliamentary Practices* see Antonio Hernandez Travieso's *El padre Varela: biografía del forjador de la conciencia cubana,* (343-345).

Works Cited

Anderson Imbert, Enrique. "Notas sobre la novela histórica en el siglo XIX." *La novela iberoamericana.* Ed. Arturo Torres Ríoseco. Albuquerque: University of New Mexico, 1957: 1-24.

Bryant, William Cullen. Rev. of "*Jicoténcal.*" *U.S. Literary Review and Gazette* 1 February 1826: 336-346.

García-Menocal, Carlos Manuel de Céspedes. *Pasión por Cuba y por la iglesia: Aproximación biográfica al Padre Félix Varela.* Madrid: Biblioteca de Autores Cristianos, 1998.

González-Acosta, Alejandro. *El enigma de Jicoténcal*: *Estudios de dos novelas sobre el héroe de Tlaxcala.* Mexico: Universidad Autónoma de México, 1997.

Henríquez Ureña, Pedro. *Las Corrientes Literarias en la América Hispánica.* Mexico: Fondo de Cultura Económica, 1949.

Leal, Luis. "*Jicoténcal*, Primera Novela Histórica en Castellano." *Revista Iberoamericana* 25 (1960): 9-31.

Lloréns Castillo, Vicente. *Liberales y románticos, una emigración española a Inglaterra (1823-1843).* Mexico: Colegio de México, 1954.

Mangino, José María. *Xicoténcatl: Comedia Heróica en Cuatro Actos"* Puebla: Pedro de la Rosa, 1829.

Rojas Garcidueñas, José. "*Jicoténcal*, una novela histórica hispanoamericana precedente al romanticismo español." *Anales del Instituto de Investigaciones Estéticas* 24 (1956): 53-76.

Varela, Félix. *Frases de sabiduría.* Ed. Abislaimán, Rafael B. Miami: Ediciones Universal, 2000.

_____. *El Habanero: Papel Político, Científico y Literario.* Miami: Ediciones Universal, 1997.

_____. *Jicoténcal.* Ed. Luis Leal and Rodolfo J. Cortina. Houston: Arte Público Press, 1995.

_____. *Letters to Elpidio*. Trans. Felipe J. Estévez. New York: Paulist Press, 1989.

_____. *The Protestant's Abridger and Annotator*. New York: G.F. Bunce, 1830.

Walters, Kerry S. *The American Deists: Voices of Reason and Dissent in the Early Republic.* Lawrence: University of Kansas, 1992.

Contributors

Juan José Alonzo is Assistant Professor of English at Texas A&M University. His research and teaching interests include American literature, Chicano/a and Latino/a literature, and the representation of race and ethnicity in film.

Antonia I. Castañeda is Associate Professor of History at St. Mary's University, San Antonio, Texas. Recent works include guest editor of Gender on the Borderlands, a double issue of *Frontiers: A Journal of Women Studies* (2004). She is currently working on a comparative study of gender on the multiracial borderland frontiers of Islamic Spain and colonial Mexico.

Marissa L. Garland is a doctoral candidate at Columbia University who specializes in 19th Century Spanish American literature. Her interests include orality, journalism, and U.S.-Spanish American hemispheric relations. Her current research involves the impact of the Enlightenment in Spanish America.

Erlinda Gonzales-Berry is Chair of the Department of Ethnic Studies at Oregon State University, where she teaches Chicano/a and Latino/a studies. She has published extensively on Chicano/a culture and literature and has been a member of the Recovery Project since its initiation in 1991.

Melissa Marie González is a graduate student in the Department of Spanish and Portuguese at Columbia University. She works on Latin American and U.S. Latino literature with a focus on Cuban and Cuban-American narrative. Her research interests include: issues of gender and sexuality, translation, and the politics of bilingualism.

Patricia Gubitosi is currently finishing her dissertation in Spanish linguistics at the University of Houston. She obtained her BA from Universidad de Buenos

Aires, where she taught linguistics courses for ten years. She has published several articles on linguistic topics and participated in conferences in Argentina, Chile, Spain, and the United States.

Donna M. Kabalen de Bichara is Associate Professor of Humanities Studies at the Tecnológico de Monterrey in Monterrey, Mexico. She is a member of the Research Chair, "Memoria, Literatura y Discurso." Her work focuses on the border autobiographies of Mexican-American women.

Manuel M. Martín-Rodríguez is Professor of Literature and a founding faculty member at the University of California, Merced. His publications include *Life in Search of Readers: Reading (in) Chicano/a Literature* (2003), *Rolando Hinojosa y su "cronicón" chicano: Una novela del lector* (1993), *La voz urgente: Antología de literatura chicana en español* (1995, and 1999), as well as numerous articles in journals and edited volumes.

A. Gabriel Meléndez is Professor and Chair of American Studies at the University of New Mexico. His books include *Spanish-language Newspapers in New Mexico, 1834-1958* (Arizona, 2005), *The Biography of Casimiro Barela* (New Mexico, 2003), and *The Southwest: A Multicultural Reader* (Arizona, 2001). He is currently working on a book on Hispanic-themed films shot in New Mexico.

Pilar Melero teaches Spanish and Chicano/a literature at the University of Wisconsin-Whitewater. Her research focuses on the discursive strategies of subaltern subjects. She has presented her research and creative work in the United States, Mexico, Cuba, and Peru.

Edwin Karli Padilla Aponte is Associate Professor at the University of Houston-Downtown. Born in Bayamón, Puerto Rico, Padilla Aponte came to the United States after graduating from the University of Puerto Rico with a degree in Comparative Literature. He received an MA from the University of Texas at El Paso in Latin-American Literature and a Ph.D. in Hispanic Literature in the United States from the University of Houston.

Guillermo de los Reyes Heredia is an Assistant Professor of Latin American Literature and Culture at the University of Houston. His areas of research and teaching include gender, colonial literature and history, and Latin American cultural studies. He is currently working on a book on Freemasonry and Political Culture in Mexico. He has published several articles on Secret Societies, Voluntary Organizations, and Democracy in Mexico.

Sergio Reyna is from Tamaulipas, Mexico. He has been working in public education for the past eleven years. Currently, he works as a full time school teacher in the bilingual program of Alief ISD. There, he teaches first graders and is a presenter of workshops to school teachers on literacy and traditional literature. Moreover, he works as an adjunct professor at the University of Houston-Downtown where he has taught children's literature and lower Spanish-division courses since 2002.

Melina Vizcaíno-Alemán is a Ph.D. candidate in the American Studies Department at the University of New Mexico. She teaches courses in Southwest and Chicana Studies and is currently working on her dissertation, "The Writings of Fray Angélico Chávez, 1939-1974."

Recovering the U.S. Hispanic Literary Heritage Series

Volume I
Edited, with an Introduction,
by Ramón Gutiérrez and Genaro Padilla
1993, 318 Pages
Clothbound, ISBN 1-55885-063-5, $34.95
Trade Paperback, ISBN 1-55885-058-9, $17.95

Volume II
Edited, with an Introduction,
by Erlinda Gonzales-Berry and
Chuck Tatum
1996, 296 Pages, Clothbound
ISBN 1-55885-139-9, $34.95

Volume III
Edited, with an Introduction,
by María Herrera-Sobek
and Virginia Sánchez Korrol
1998, 320 pages, Clothbound
ISBN 1-55885-251-4, $39.95

Volume IV
Edited, with an Introduction by
José Aranda, Jr. and Silvio Torres-Saillant
2002, 304 pages, Clothbound
ISBN 1-55885-361-8, $27.95

Volume V
Edited, with an Introduction by
Kenya Dworkin y Méndez and Agnes Lugo-Ortiz
2006, 240 pages, Clothbound
ISBN 1-55885-371-5, $39.95

Hispanic Periodicals in the United States, Origins to 1960: A Brief History and Comprehensive Bibliography
Nicolás Kanellos with Helvetia Martell
2000, 368 pages, Clothbound
ISBN 1-55885-253-0, $69.95

A Nation of Women: An Early Feminist Speaks Out / Mi opinión sobre las libertades, derechos y deberes de la mujer
Luisa Capetillo
English translation by Alan West-Durán
Introduction by Félix V. Matos Rodríguez
2004, 224 pages, Trade Paperback
ISBN 1-55885-427-4, $16.95

Cantares: Canticles and Poems of Youth
Fray Angélico Chávez
Introduction by Nasario García
2000, 134 pages, Trade Paperback
ISBN 1-55885-311-1, $12.95

Lo que el pueblo me dice
Jesús Colón
Edited, with an Introduction by Edwin Karli Padilla Aponte
2001, 272 pages, Trade Paperback
ISBN 1-55885-330-8, $12.95

Jicoténcal
Félix Varela; Edited by Luis Leal and Rodolfo J. Cortina
1995, 164 Pages, Trade Paperback
ISBN 1-55885-132-1, $10.95

The Collected Stories of María Cristina Mena
María Cristina Mena; Edited by Amy Doherty
1997, 208 pages, Trade Paperback
ISBN 1-55885-211-5, $12.95

Las aventuras de Don Chipote, o, cuando los pericos mamen
Daniel Venegas
Edited, with an Introduction, by Nicolás Kanellos
1998, 176 pages, Trade Paperback
ISBN 1-55885-252-2, $12.95

Dew on the Thorn
Adina de Zavala; Edited by José Limón
1997, 181 Pages, Trade Paperback
ISBN 1-55885-175-5, $12.95